2013

For my dear friends Tom & Karen
who walk the talk of human service
and community values 'reaching
around the world'

Strong Roots

Sandy Allтом

Strong Roots

A Group Memoir of George Williams College

by Sandra Alcorn

George Williams College Press
Williams Bay, Wisconsin

George Williams College Press
Williams Bay, Wisconsin 53191-0210
Visit us at: www.aurora.edu/gwc
To order copies, or for more information: 630-844-5486

The photographs in the gallery following page 112 are from the George Williams College Archives, Williams Bay, Wisconsin; the Aurora University Archives, Aurora, Illinois; the YMCA of the USA and the Kautz Family YMCA Archives, University of Minnesota Libraries; and the private collections of Jean Bilstrom and Martin Msseemmaa.

The photographs on the front cover and on pages 35 and 85 are from the George Williams College Archives, Williams Bay, Wisconsin. All photographs from the George Williams College Archives are used with permission.

The photographs on the back cover and on page 243 are from the Aurora University Archives, Aurora, Illinois. All photographs from the Aurora University Archives are used with permission.

The photographs on pages 5, 151, and 199 are from the YMCA of the USA and the Kautz Family YMCA Archives, University of Minnesota Libraries.

ISBN-13: 978-0-9790413-0-3
ISBN-10: 0-9790413-0-9

to *Charlie,*
my husband and best friend

Contents

Photographs follow page 112.

Preface

When I first heard of George Williams College, it was known to me as "the group work school." I was a graduate student in social work at a large eastern university, majoring in group work because I had been advised that it would be the best preparation for a career working with urban youth. I learned that the college was named for Sir George Williams, the Englishman who founded the YMCA in London in 1844, and that the college had begun as a training center for YMCA workers. I learned that the YMCA had pioneered in group work services and organizations and that the college occasionally sponsored conferences on camping, recreation, and advances in group work theory.

That was all I knew about George Williams College until 1970, when I found myself interviewing for, and then accepting, a faculty position in the social work department. The setting seemed strangely disconnected from the college's reputation for urban youth work. Its spanking-new, modern-looking buildings were nestled in woodlands, marshes, and expansive lawns in a developing suburb of Chicago. I gave no further thought to the history of the college, as I took on the task of preparing students for a career in the human services of today and tomorrow.

I soon found the learning environment to be out of keeping with any past experience I had in higher education. Faculty members dressed casually. Sometimes students sat on the floor during classes, sometimes on chairs, but always they sat in a circle. They addressed their teachers by their first name, not by "Doctor" or "Professor." Classes were a mix of animated discussions, in large and small groups, and experiential exercises. Though student interactions with their teachers and peers were quite affable, it quickly became clear to me that students were purposeful and resolute about the learning process. I felt disoriented, but at the same time I felt I'd come home. I remained on the faculty for fifteen years.

Then it happened. It was Friday the 13th, in December of 1985. In the middle of the academic year, the Board of Trustees announced that the college had severe financial troubles and would have to close its doors immediately. There would be no winter term. Faculty were released, and students were counseled to enroll elsewhere. The news was astonishing, and triggered a series of responses from students and faculty that were even more astonishing. These uncharacteristic responses were not what one would expect under such conditions. It reminded me of my first observations of the students and faculty: so congruent, spontaneous, natural . . . and different. Most important, their responses were effective. My tale has a fairly happy ending, leading to the survival of at least a remnant of the college; a remnant that actually thrived, when all seemed to be lost.

This became my story. In the years since, I have often reflected on my experience, and shared with new students my story. It shows them what kind of tradition they've become part of, and how the principles that George Williams College stood for actually work in real life. This book, which grew from my teaching and reflections, is an effort to join my story with others who have passed through the college as students and faculty, and who have found deep personal meaning in the values the college held and practiced. I have interviewed students and faculty who give voice to their experience with the college. College publications and historical documents record generations of additional voices who experienced George Williams College, and they are included in this group memoir.

The five chapters are devoted to themes repeatedly noted by those who speak about the essence of George Williams College. The themes are:

Serving others;
Developing body with mind and spirit;
Building community inside and out;
Learning-by-doing; and
Reaching around the world

Each chapter traces a theme chronologically through the college's history, with particular attention paid to the impact on its four principal locations: Williams Bay on Geneva Lake in Wisconsin; the city of Chicago; the western Chicago suburb of Downers Grove; and the city of Aurora, Illinois.

The narrators represent many generations. They tell their stories in the language of their time, in their own ways, but the common vision and shared values of the college are evident in each and every voice. I hope these stories will inspire not only readers who are familiar with George Williams College, but all who recognize and affirm values of service; community; lifelong learning from experience; the unity of body, mind, spirit, and social relations in our healthy development; and attunement to the global community for learning and service.

Acknowledgments

The personal memoirs recorded in this history of George Williams College are a work created from love and personal meaning. There are many who contributed to the preservation of the college, so that this story is not all just history. There is Dr. Alan Stone, the president of Aurora University who once was a professor at George Williams College and knew what the college stood for. He brought the social work program and the recreation program to Aurora University when the Downers Grove campus of George Williams College closed in 1985 and pledged that we could "be George Williams College" in our new environment. There is Dr. Tom Zarle, the next president of Aurora University who was a graduate of Springfield College, the "sister college" of George Williams College. Tom had an affinity and sensitivity to the George Williams plight and for twelve years worked to keep George Williams College alive by bringing it into the Aurora University fold. He provided leadership through a ten-year affiliation agreement, building trust between GWC and AU, and in the final act of his presidential legacy witnessed the legal merger of George Williams College with Aurora University in 2000. The next president of Aurora University is Dr. Rebecca Sherrick. She has treated the merger like a marriage that enables two parties to reach full stature by their union. She is an historian by profession, working from an understanding of history as a strong foundation for creating a viable future. The historic campus on Geneva Lake, its educational programs built on experiential learning, the new buildings congruent with the past architecture, the special events like Music by the Lake come out of her sensitivity to the history of George Williams College. Becky commissioned me to write this book and funded the three-year project leading to publication. I am grateful to her for her constant personal encouragement and her sensitivity to those who grieved over the losses and find hope in signs of restoration and future development of George Williams College at Aurora University so it will continue to be what it stood for. Thanks to Phil Harper, GWC board member and last president of GWC, who thoroughly researched the right "home" for the college legacy after it closed and as a result saw that it came to Aurora University. Thanks to board members and faculty of Aurora University who graciously received us, though we came unexpectedly, like a bull in a china closet; yet they supported and strengthened our presence. Thanks to GWC-related board members who bridged the past with the future at Aurora University: Florence Hart, Mickey Resnick, Rich Bailey, Del Arsenault.

There are many who have encouraged me and supported me in over thirty-five years of experience with George Williams College, bringing me to this point. I thank my husband, Charlie, and two sons, Chad and Andy; our family grew up knowing that Mom always had this commitment to George Williams College that often took time from them, but complaints were few. Thanks to Del Arsenault, alum and former director of Chicago Youth Centers, for his personal encouragement through those dark days of trying to find a way to survive after the college closed in Downers Grove and for his work as a board member of Aurora University to support the college transition to Aurora University. Thanks to AU presidential assistant Maggie Sharrer, who was always there for me, doing whatever it takes to provide support. Thanks to the "Minnesota Archives Diggers," Lyle and Corky Johnson, Whitey Luehrs, the late Jim Gilbert (we will miss him), and Clelia Giles, all faculty or alumni who helped me uncover gems from the Kautz Family YMCA Archives, and for the helpful direction of archivist Dagmar Getz. Thanks to Dianna Woss and her archive group of volunteers in Williams Bay who found pictures and significant historical documents for this book. Thanks to Diane Blanton, GWC alum and AU staff person who recalls with head, heart, and her trusty files, generations of people who passed through the college. Thanks to Amy Schlumpf

Manion for her project guidance and editorial assistance, and to Mark Rospenda, graphic designer at Aurora University. Thanks to those who contributed material from their own personal archives: Del Arsenault, the family of Walter Steffen, Howard Winebrenner, Bill and Mary Glenn, and many others.

Finally thanks to all the students and faculty who traveled through the college at some point in history, created the legend that it is, and continue to tell the story. Only some of the stories are captured in this group memoir, but every one is deserving as a contribution to one grand story of George Williams College.

Introduction

*T*his book is a collection of memoirs, not a record of historical facts about George Williams College. However, there is much to understand about the historic context of these stories, or the reader will be lost right away.

For instance, the locations of the college have changed several times, and most of the stories allude to the environment of the college, because the college's educational purpose was so tied to human service in community. The college saw its beginnings as summer institutes on the quiet shores of Geneva Lake in Wisconsin, a place for retreat, reflection, visioning, and planning. Land was purchased in 1886 for a permanent site in Williams Bay on Geneva Lake. The purpose of the weeklong institutes was to train men going into YMCA work. There were special institutes for physical educators, run by Luther Gulick from the only sister institution dedicated to the purpose of training YMCA workers, Springfield College in Massachusetts. There were also very popular student conferences, where college students who were tied to the YMCA (or YWCA) on their campuses would come for a week. Then, in 1890, when full-time YMCA work was becoming professional, requiring more intensive training, a year-round "Training School" was established under the same leadership in Chicago, Illinois. The college was greatly influenced in its human service mission by the social and educational changes going on in that dynamic city. At the same time, it maintained the Williams Bay campus in the Lake Geneva area, which was used for its educational purposes as well as for outside groups. In the late 1960s the college moved to a western suburb of Chicago, Downers Grove. The radically different environment influenced the culture of the college, as you will hear from the stories in this book.

George Williams College, as an independent college in Downers Grove, closed in 1985 for financial reasons. For many, this was seen as the end of a legacy. However, at least a remnant, two of its programs, moved to Aurora University in Aurora, Illinois. Those programs were social work and recreation, both strongly tied to the human service mission of the college. The city of Aurora is changing from a rustbelt industrial town to a dynamic, growing city, the second-largest city in Illinois, after Chicago. It has all the human service challenges of Chicago, only on a slightly smaller scale. Aurora University acknowledged and nurtured the mission and traditions of George Williams College, and in 1992 a formal affiliation agreement was established between the two, so the name and legacy of George Williams College could continue on and alumni would have a "home." It was not until 2000 that George Williams College fully merged the programs at both the Aurora campus and the historic Williams Bay campus with Aurora University. In an effort to continue not only the name but also the purpose of George Williams College, educational programs have returned to Williams Bay.

The changing names of the college can be confusing. It was first called the Western Secretarial Institute. The term *secretary* is used in the YMCA to refer to its leaders, or, as it became a more complex organization, its CEOs or managers. The college was called "Western" because it was established to train YMCA workers in the western sectors of the United States and Canada. Robert Weidensall was the visionary who advocated for and established the institute. He was one of the first full-time YMCA secretaries, and his charge was to develop "the work of the association" out West, since most of the work started on the East Coast of the U.S. Being a railroad man of the Union Pacific from Nebraska, the charge to "Go west" must have been appealing. By 1913 the word *secretarial* was dropped, and the college became the YMCA College. In 1933 it was changed again to George Williams College to honor the English man who founded the YMCA in 1844. The name George Williams College has remained, even as it was incorporated within Aurora University.

Though the location of the Wisconsin site remains unchanged, references to its name have changed. The name of the lake, though often referred to as "Lake Geneva," is technically "Geneva Lake." The historic site of the college on the lake has been called "Lake Geneva," "College Camp," the "Lake Geneva campus," and now the "Williams Bay campus." (The location on the lake is in Williams Bay, Wisconsin.) A chart of the changing names and locations of the college follows, to track those contexts, as people share their stories.

The Changing Names and Locations of George Williams College

Western Secretarial Institute	1884–1890 Williams Bay, Wisconsin
Training School of the YMCA	1890–1896 Chicago, Illinois
Secretarial Institute and Training School (SITS)	1896–1903 Chicago, Illinois and Williams Bay, Wisconsin
Institute and Training School of the YMCA (ITS)	1903–1913 Chicago, Illinois and Williams Bay, Wisconsin
YMCA College (Association College)	1913–1933 Chicago, Illinois; 1915–1933 Hyde Park of Chicago, Illinois
George Williams College (GWC)	1933–1966 Hyde Park of Chicago, Illinois; 1966–1985 Downers Grove, Illinois
George Williams College of Aurora University	1992 Aurora, Illinois (affiliation); 2000 Aurora, Illinois (merger); 2000–present Williams Bay, Wisconsin

Chapter 1
Serving Others

*"We are born
not for
ourselves alone,
but for
the whole world."

(Motto, class of 1913)*

$\mathcal{G}$eorge Williams College was established in 1884 to train young men for service in the YMCA. This was some forty years after the YMCA "movement" took hold in England and then spread to the United States and other countries. The college was conceived as a summer retreat and training institute for Y workers, located on the quiet, remote shores of Geneva Lake in Wisconsin. It sprung from Robert Weidensall's vision. Weidensall was a YMCA leader commissioned to develop the

work in the western sector of the United States. He pressed hard for the idea of a permanent training institute for several years before it came into being. Weidensall described his vision of what the training institute could become: "What a law school is to a young man who aims to enter the profession of law or what a medical school is to such a one as desires to practice medicine," he envisioned a permanent, professional school to train for the work of the YMCA.[1]

In 1890 the summer institutes became a year-round training school, and the location was changed to the rapidly growing, industrial city of Chicago. It was called the Western Secretarial Institute. When the summer institutes merged with the year-round training school, it became the Institute and Training School of the YMCA (ITS). Evangelism and "Christian work" was clearly at the heart of both the YMCA and the training school, but "the work of the association" was never dissociated from a social service purpose. The service mission was one of sensitivity to

problematic social situations young men faced as they migrated from rural families and communities to an urban industrial environment: things like falling into poverty, labor exploitation, and social isolation. Sir George Williams, the founder of the YMCA in London, saw the mission of Christian service to be not only Bible study and prayer for young men, but also advocating for change in their work conditions where necessary and uniting young men in fellowship in their new environment.[2]

Today most of us are familiar with the YMCA and its services in some way, and we may have noticed their symbol of purpose, the "YMCA triangle." We may have some understanding that the three points of the triangle represent three dimensions: the body, mind, and spirit. However, when I browsed through old yearbooks of the college, and old student and college pictures from the late nineteenth and early twentieth centuries, I noticed something I hadn't seen before. Students wore symbols on their T-shirts and clothes that looked like a cross. That same cross was stamped on the articles of incorporation of the college when it was first founded.[3] I noticed the cross again on the ceiling of the gym floor of the first building the college inhabited in Chicago. What was that cross about? Students in early times referred to "the foursquare man" or "fourfold purpose" of their service. I learned that before the YMCA triangle was used to

YMCA's holistic purpose—the development of the "body" or physical dimension of the whole person. However visually captivating the YMCA triangle was, representing holistic development, one dimension was obviously eliminated in this shift from a cross to a triangle: the social dimension. Based on the triangle symbol, one could envision a self-contained, physically fit, and holistically developed

"The work of the association was never dissociated from a social service purpose."

symbolize the purpose, the YMCA held to what was called a "fourfold purpose": the development of body, mind, spirit—and one more dimension—the social dimensions of the life of young men. The social dimension was conceived to be "beyond recreative social intercourse to embrace also the individual's responsibility to shape society around him."[4] Four years after George Williams College was born, the YMCA triangle was promoted in the East, at Springfield College, Massachusetts, a newly established sister college, also conceived as a YMCA training institute. The Y triangle became the symbolic representation that replaced the four-dimensional cross to highlight a newer emphasis of the

individual as the purpose of this YMCA international movement. By 1945, Tracy Strong, an international YMCA worker, regretted the elimination of the social dimension in the YMCA's newer symbol, and offered the following comment: "unfortunately no symbol has yet been devised which includes the 'social' aspect with the other three."[5]

Photograph, page 5: A George Williams College student engages young girls in a "group work" activity in a Chicago youth center. Activities are directed toward individual development and cooperative living. (ca. 1960s)

Early Voices: Chicago in the Progressive Era

George Williams College always maintained that social and humanitarian service was at the core of its educational purpose. From its earliest history, students spoke of the spirit of service driving their vocation.

Student voices on service

Robert Forbes, student, ('13)

"We are born not for ourselves, but for the whole world." (Motto of Class of 1913)[6]

Raymond P. Dougherty, student, ('14)

He who thinks of self alone,
And seeks no welfare but his own
Will never know the pleasure rare
Of sharing human grief and care
Yet that is happiness indeed
Which springs from helping those in need.[7]

F. W. Landefeld, student, ('16)

Here we are, standing on the threshold of a new epoch in our lives. . . . We are moved with higher ideals, filled with zeal and possess a real Christian passion to work with men and boys. We are convinced that the YMCA, with its novel and adaptable **four-fold scheme** of work, is surpassed by no other movement which touches the lives of men and boys. But we are just starting. We hold before us two very definite ideals. We want to make good and we want to grow. We will make good if we go out from the college with the same purpose and attitude which was in the mind of Christ—to assume leadership and have our influence go out touching the community life. . . . Then we want to "grow in the grace and knowledge of the Lord"; grow with the association, which is a great, big, growing movement; grow up with a growing community and a growing society. Perish the thought that we should ever remain little and narrow, for we want to grow, grow grow![8]

Vincent Way Allin, student, ('16)

We always have been and always will be loyal to the college which has done so much to prepare us for greater service. Former members of our class are now in association work in this country and abroad; others are in playgrounds, schools, and similar organizations. Many of our class, now in college, have had a prominent place in the work of the YMCA, churches, schools, colleges, playgrounds, social settlements, and other similar agencies in the city.[9]

Dr. Henry Kallenberg, dean of the School of Physical Education, speaks to us of the purpose of the college related to physical education. In chapter 2, "Developing Body with Mind and Spirit," we will hear more of Kallenberg. At Springfield College, he and James Naismith helped dream up the "hanging peach basket" sport that became basketball.

"Physical activities are means to greater ends"

Henry Kallenberg, professor and dean, 1913

While physical education in general is recognized as a profession of great importance, there is no field that offers greater opportunity for service than the physical directorship of the YMCA. The demand is more and more for Christian leaders with high ideals who see in all the various forms of physical activities, the means for the development of Christian and efficient citizenship. . . .

Playgrounds, gymnasiums, and athletic fields are of inestimable value as the laboratories of general education in which the most important factor of human efficiency is developed, namely, character. . . . Physical activities conducted in the gymnasium or on the playground are not ends in themselves, but means to greater ends. . . .

The world is rapidly appreciating the fact that the body and the mind play and react upon each other reciprocally—that anything which interferes with the development of the physical life, interferes with mental and moral efficiency. . . . The attempt to prohibit child labor, to establish the eight-hour workday, to prevent the adulteration of foods, and the efforts to decrease the spread of disease indicate concern for the conservation of the physical life of man.[10]

In 1914 Kallenberg led the physical education department in drafting a statement on what they called "The Spirit of Efficiency." Their purpose included the development of the "foursquare man." Community service and personal development were more important than gyms, equipment, and even physical skills.

Even more gratifying than the expansion of the college as indicated by the new equipment, however pleasing that may be, is the fact that there is a growth in the life of the men themselves, which is keeping pace with this material progress. The evidence of this growth is found in the spirit of a meeting held by the School of Physical Education during the fall term of 1914. . . . The purpose of the discussion was to bring more clearly to mind the essential qualities of a man who desires to serve to the best advantage any community. Christian character and leadership, executive ability, and a thorough technical training were shown to be even more important than skill in gymnastics or athletics. A most striking thought [that] developed was that there is more need for personal efficiency than for more modern gymnasiums, more elaborate equipment, more luxurious swimming pools, or even more expert gymnasts. In fact, little was said about these external things. By this term "efficiency" is meant the incorporation of the qualities mentioned in the everyday life of the man so that he is able to "put things across." Too often fine buildings and elaborate programs of activity produce results by no means commensurate to the time and money expended, simply because of the lack of this efficient personality.

To meet this need in the realm of physical education, the college has designed its courses. They do not train for specialized branches of athletics. They lay the thorough foundation for true physical education, which develops the four-square man. It is no longer thought possible to touch man's need through any one phase of life alone; the spiritual, mental, social, and physical are so inextricably bound together. Therefore, there are, besides courses in anatomy, physiology, hygiene, and gymnastic and athletic work, courses in Bible study, psychology, and sociology combined, to make the physical director an expert and a safe leader in his community. The loyalty of the alumni, the increasing enrollment of students, and the number of positions offered to its graduates is ample proof that this end is being realized. Let our slogan ever be Efficiency First.[11]

Two early influences shaped the strong service mission of the college. One was what was going on in American Protestant Christianity; the other was the location of the college in Chicago.

The Social Gospel

In the Progressive Era years of 1890 to about 1920, social and religious institutions were reacting to poor social conditions that grew out of the Industrial Era. A shift took place in some Protestant Christian circles to the Social Gospel, which espoused that the purpose of the Christian gospel was not so much personal salvation and mission evangelism as it was for social service, locally and worldwide. The Social Gospel movement saw America's young people, largely college students, preparing for life in social service as the purpose and expression of their Christian faith. At this time the Williams Bay campus of the training institute (George Williams College) was hosting hundreds of college students, mostly from colleges in the Midwest and West, in what were called "student conferences." The student conferences were initially modeled after Dwight L. Moody's Northfield conferences, and they focused on Bible study, prayer, and launching students into worldwide evangelism as "volunteers." The student conferences at Lake Geneva took on their own character under the leadership of John R. Mott, with a strong emphasis on "world service," a kind of service that extended beyond evangelism to include the entire social situation of people, domestically and globally.[12] The college students, for the most part, had strong ties to the YMCA. The college was strongly influenced by the flow of ideas and inspirational speakers who were guests of the student conferences at Lake Geneva, and espoused this Social Gospel. Sherwood Eddy was one dynamic leader and guest speaker, who volunteered for world service in Asia. He speaks of his "two conversions." The first was a personal transformation from the message of the gospel in his adolescence; the second was a commitment to social activism, stemming from his beliefs in the Social Gospel.

My "second conversion"

Sherwood Eddy, guest speaker, Lake Geneva student conferences, post–World War I

I saw [World War I] as only a symptom of the striving world beneath. I saw the world rent and divided in industrial, racial, and international strife; a world of sordid materialism, autocratic exploitation, and organized militarism, over-preparing for further war. . . . Now there broke upon me the first gleams of a Social Gospel that would not only save the individual for the future, but here and now in this world of bitter need, to Christianize the whole of life and all its relationships—industrial, social, racial, international. Religion was not primarily something to be believed or felt; it was something to be done, a life to be lived, a principle and a program to be incarnated in character and built in to a social order. . . . I saw [Christ] now hungry and athirst, naked, sick, and in prison, in the blighted lives of our social order both at home and abroad.[13]

In the Progressive Era, the college was not without some conflict in its ranks about wholly substituting a social service mission for its "spirit" purpose. Two faculty members between the years 1918 and 1920 had opposing views on the meaning and influence of the Social Gospel in the college: Earl Eubanks and Eduard Lindeman.

Conflict in the college on the Social Gospel

Earl Eubanks, professor and dean, 1917

> Let it be said that there is no thought of training association men for social service as an end in itself. In the enthusiasm for social service that is sweeping the country, there is a tendency in some quarters to substitute this contact with men for contact with God, and to preach a "social religion." A department of this college must not fall into that tendency. The YMCA is something far more than a mere agency for social betterment; it must continue to be a great religious force. It cannot rest content merely with assisting men in their temporal necessities; it must transform their inner lives. This department [sociology] must seek not only to develop men for more efficient service along social lines, but to spiritualize that service. Its existence can be justified only as it fulfills this larger purpose.[14]

Eduard Lindeman, professor, 1918

In 1918 Eduard Lindeman came to teach at the YMCA College. Lindeman became a renowned leader and pioneer thinker in social work education. He is sometimes recognized as the "Father of Adult Education." He eventually spent over twenty-five years on the faculty of the New York School of Social Work at Columbia University, always stimulating thinking on the concepts, principles, and philosophic foundations of social work.

However, he did not last long at the YMCA College. After less than one year (1918–1919), students wrote in their yearbook, *The Crucible,* that he was asked to leave, much to the regret of students who were in the county work specialization, where he taught. They said, "He made an impression upon this college that will last for all time to come. We will all watch the career of our fearless young teacher, as he makes his personality felt on the great battlefields of life."[15] Gisela Konopka, another renowned social group worker, wrote a biography of Lindeman stating, "Lindeman started teaching at the YMCA College (later called George Williams College) in Chicago. He stayed there for only a short time—not quite a year. He was dissatisfied with the conservatism in the college and felt he 'could not take it.'" During this time he met Jane Addams of Hull House and was a member of one of the first groups of social workers to take a short course at Hull House. According to Konopka, Lindeman's concern for community action was great. He wanted to understand better how one could help communities determine their own fate, and how experts and citizens could work together.[16] Lindeman developed a strong collegial relationship with John Dewey, and they shared the same pragmatic philosophy that expressed itself in community dialogue and "learning-by-doing" approaches that were to become the foundation of the field of adult education. It was also an enduring learning approach at George Williams College. Lindeman truly "made an impression upon this college that will last for all time to come," as his students predicted.

Besides the Social Gospel movement in Protestant Christianity, nothing could be more influential in the development of the college's strong social service mission than the move from its summer-resort environment of the Lake Geneva area to the city of Chicago. The city was flooded with immigrants who experienced poor social conditions springing from rapid urban industrial growth. George Williams College had its infancy in Chicago during the Progressive Era, which was roughly from 1890 to 1920. In this time the worldwide spotlight was on Chicago, not just for its immigrant populations and the stressors of the Industrial Era but for models as to how social service to these peoples could be addressed. One year before George Williams College began in Chicago, Jane Addams founded Hull House, a settlement house not far away from the college. Hull House was the seminal model for social service that guided the settlement house movement. The settlement house movement focused on building community, developing the whole person, celebrating cultural strengths of specific immigrant groups, and addressing problematic social situations facing immigrants. The social service purpose was congruent with the college's YMCA-related purpose. There were as many George Williams College students working in Chicago's settlement houses as there were students working in YMCAs, as students "learned by doing" in these service fields. Jane Addams lends her voice on the influence of the George Williams College students in her memoirs of Hull House. She spoke at the college, and for years her staff included its students.[17]

Thoughts on the "Association College" student

**Jane Addams, Nobel Peace Prize winner
and director of Hull House Settlement, circa 1910**

On the Social Gospel

There is a certain renaissance going forward in Christianity. The impulse to share the lives of the poor, the desire to make social service . . . express the spirit of Christ is as old as Christianity itself. . . . What Jesus said must be put into terms of action; that action is the only medium man has for receiving and appropriating truth. Man's action is found in his social relationship in the way in which he connects with his fellows. His motives for action are the zeal and affection with which he regards his fellows. I believe there is a distinct turning among many young men and women toward this simple acceptance of Christ's message. They resent the assumption that

Christianity is a set of ideas. . . . It cannot be proclaimed and instituted apart from the social life of the community. . . . This renaissance . . . is going on in Chicago, without leaders who philosophize, without much speaking, but with a bent to express in social service and in terms of action the spirit of Christ. . . . This spiritual force must be evoked and must be called into play before the success of any settlement is assured. The settlement house movement must be grounded in a philosophy whose foundations are the solidarity of the human race.

On group work

The value of social clubs broadens out in one's mind to be an instrument of companionship through which many may be led from a sense of isolation to one of civic responsibility, even as another club provides recreational facilities for those who have had only meaningless excitements, or as a third type, opens new and interesting vistas of life to those who are ambitious.

On recreation

Out of the fifteen hundred members of the Hull House boys' club, hundreds seem to respond only to the opportunities for recreation. . . . Our gymnasium has been filled with large and enthusiastic classes for eighteen years. . . . The settlement strives for that which presupposes the curbing of impulse, as well as for those athletic contests in which the mind of the contestant must be vigilant to keep the body closely to the rules of the game. . . . Young people who work long hours at sedentary occupations in factories and offices need perhaps more than anything else the freedom and ease to be acquired from a symmetrical muscular development and are quick to respond to that fellowship which athletics apparently affords more easily than anything else.

On military drills

Nobel Peace Prize recipient Addams also did not mince words to the boys who attended the gymnastics classes about the glamour of militarism that infused physical education in the era of "muscular Christianity." Her early recollection of the boys' club, probably around 1893, had to do with a military drill the boys did as a part of the "Columbia Guards," a group preparing to demonstrate at the World's Columbian Exposition, also called the Chicago World's Fair.

As the cleaning of the filthy streets and alleys was the ostensible purpose of the Columbian guards, I suggested to the boys that we work out a drill with sewer spades, which, with their long, narrow blades and shortened handles, were not so unlike bayonet guns in size, weight, and general appearance, but that much of the usual military drill could be readapted. I myself was present at the gymnasium to explain that it was nobler to drill in imitation of removing disease-breeding filth than to drill in simulation of warfare.

Her proposal failed to be adopted by the boys, but years later, when she found one of those sewer spades in the Hull House storeroom, she mused, "I can only look at it in the forlorn hope that it may foreshadow that piping time when the weapons of warfare shall be turned into the implements of civic salvation."[18]

From Hull House to Gandhi's tent

Wallace Kirkland, student, ('23)

Wallace Kirkland was a student of George Williams College (then called "YMCA College") in the 1920s who lived in Hull House and worked for Jane Addams as director of the boys' clubs.

Wallace Kirkland came to America from Jamaica in the British West Indies, the son of British subjects. He first worked in a Boys Club in Passaic, New Jersey, and from there moved into YMCA work as an outpost secretary in Texas. His YMCA connection brought him to the YMCA College (George Williams College) in Hyde Park, majoring in county work, a specialization of YMCA work that would be a forerunner of the community organizer: one who works for collaboration of existing social institutions to meet needs of youth and families.

While at the YMCA College, he and his wife, Ethel, became one of about sixty-five people who took up residence at Hull House under the leadership of Jane Addams. They were excited about joining other residents who wanted to share their talents in music, the arts, education, and recreation to build community among immigrant neighbors. At that time there were about nine thousand who came weekly to Hull House activities.

Upon graduation from YMCA College, Kirkland was offered a position as director of the Hull House boys' and mens' clubs, and Jane Addams asked his wife, Ethel, to be a social worker for them. Kirkland was able to get local street gangs involved in the social activities at Hull House by building on the group dynamics of the social organization that the boys had in the gang. Sometimes the gang adopted a new name and became one of the settlement house groups.

When Eastman Kodak gave a well-equipped photo studio to the boys' club, Kirkland became fascinated with photography and began to establish a collection of photos of Hull House activities. In 1934 he resigned from Hull House and took on a position with *Life* magazine as a photographer.

In 1940, on special assignment to India, he approached Gandhi, requesting five minutes of his time to photograph India's leader. Gandhi at first rejected the request because he did not want to be associated with what he said was a capitalistic magazine. However, when Kirkland mentioned he worked with Jane Addams at Hull House, Gandhi was fascinated, wanted to know more, and invited Kirkland into his tent, allowing Kirkland to stay for five days to document Gandhi's life in photographs.

Kirkland passed away in Oak Park, Illinois, at the age of 88, shortly after a Hull House exhibition of his work in 1979. This story of Kirkland and his photographs of Hull House are documented in the photographic journal, *The Many Faces of Hull-House,* a memorial document released for Hull House's centennial celebration in 1989.[19] Kirkland also exhibited his photographs at the Art Institute in Chicago.[20] His photographs are compelling because they capture the spirit of group work in settlements in the lively interactions and joyful expression of group solidarity among its participants.

Kirkland left a legacy not only with many residents of Hull House but also with his own children. One of Kirkland's three children, Wallace Kirkland Jr., became a doctor in Oak Park, and when he died in 2003, his obituary was a reoccurring tribute to his father. Kirkland Jr. shared his father's values and became a persistent advocate for integrated housing in Oak Park. Kirkland Jr. regarded being raised in Hull House one of the greatest influences of his life. Another story about his father was his spirit of adventure and high challenge in outdoor activity. When his son graduated from Princeton University, Kirkland Sr. biked across the country to attend his graduation. Kirkland is a good example of the "four-square man" who enjoyed the challenge of "the strenuous life" to be lived out in physical fitness as well as in social service.[21]

The local, urban, social service mission of the college was interrupted twice through two World Wars. The college played a major role in shifting its focus, curriculum, and programs to serve the needs of the military, which fit the pragmatic service mission of the YMCA student to "do whatever it takes" to meet the concrete needs of the whole person in their situation. During World War I the college set up "war training schools" on both the Chicago and Williams Bay sites, providing training for YMCA workers enlisted in the service. In World War I the YMCA provided "those social, recreational, educational, and religious activities that are lacking in the routine of army and navy life"; in that war, more relief aid came from the YMCA than from the Red Cross.[22] In World War II the college trained in physical fitness for the Civil Defense Corps; trained "recreation and morale officers" in the military; and provided housing, messing, and a junior college curriculum for V-12 Navy enlistees.[23]

Pioneers of Group Work

Between the two World Wars, during and after the Great Depression in the early 1930s, the college found its niche again on the local community level, as a leader in the professional development of a kind of social service that became known as "group work." Group work was a way of working with groups of people to develop the whole person in body, mind, and spirit; building a sense of fellowship or community through the use of activities; and taking social action when necessary to change unsupportive social situations. Social services that shared this common purpose were developing rapidly in Chicago and across the country. The service purpose extended beyond the YMCA or settlements to include Boy/Girl Scouts, Campfire Girls, Boys/Girls Clubs, park district programs, camping programs, and many other church and community-based youth service programs. They defined this "common meaning" or purpose as "group education" or "group work."

"Group education is coming of age"

Hedley Dimock, Charles Hendry, and Karl Zerfoss, professors, 1930s

In 1947 a booklet was published by Association Press, called *A Professional Outlook on Group Education*. It was a compilation of professional articles printed in the George Williams College newspaper, *The Bulletin*. The preface reads,

> The swift tempo of developments in the field of informal and group education in recent years has uncovered many issues, around some of which there is as yet no consensus of opinion. Since 1935 several of the GWC *Bulletins* have been devoted to a discussion of some of these issues. . . . The continuing demand for these *Bulletins* has made reprinting necessary. Although each article in it was written separately, the series represents an essential unity and a common point of view.[24]

In this publication several faculty comment on the emergence of group work as a form of professional human service.

> In spite of traditional differences, certain basic principles, resources, techniques, and criteria are coming to be identified, and the terms "group work" and "group education'" are acquiring the sanction of usage as symbols of this new body of common meanings. Group education is coming of age.[25]

"The Marks of a Profession"

Hedley Dimock, professor, 1930s

A profession . . . rests upon a social function that is distinct, . . . possesses a specialized body of knowledge and skill, . . . demands specialized preparation, . . . is characterized by guilds or societies, . . . formulates and applies standards that govern the practice, . . . is motivated by a special spirit and purpose, . . . [and] implies a personal standard of workmanship characterized by sincerity and intellectual integrity. . . . Much talk is now current about the possibility of a profession developing around the function of informal and group education as carried out by leisure-time agencies in the community. Probably only the most prophetic mind would dare to predict with complete confidence that such a development will take place but [if it does] will it be part of social work, or of education, or of some other existing profession, or will it be a new and independent profession?[26]

Now that the college had established a distinct niche in the community for providing professional human service in the form of "group work" (or "group education" or "informal education," as it was also commonly called), students felt confident of the value of their education at George Williams College; their knowledge and skills were in high demand.

"Needed in the world"

Chicago Daily News, 1940

These students at George Williams College are learning more than how to coach basketball and swimming. They are getting the idea that what people do in their spare time is terribly important, and that if a small group can play and work and learn together and think things out together, perhaps cities, states, and nations can do it, too. . . . [The students] are just a little surer of themselves—without being one bit cocky or uppish—than most of the young men and women you meet in the course of the day's work. And they are just a little less cynical—without being one bit priggish or preachy.

I've spent quite a bit of time wondering why they seem more sure and less cynical. Is it the result of the practical idealism taught at George Williams? Is it because they are working, right while they are studying, at something they believe in? Or does the fact that this college has been unable to turn out graduates fast enough to fill half the positions offered them since 1932 have something to do with it? . . . Wouldn't we all be surer of ourselves and less cynical if we felt that we were needed in the world?[27]

At the same time that group work was becoming a profession, other forms of human service were going through stages of professionalization. Social work was just beginning to develop as a profession. Recreation was becoming professional. Influenced by John Dewey, the teaching profession incorporated "progressive education" ideas, expanding into continuing education and adult education fields that share the same group-work philosophy. Physical education was becoming a professional entity. At George Williams College, group work faced a challenge: Should the group-work curriculum and educational programs separate themselves from these professions whose very roots were the same, or should they incorporate themselves into one or all of these emerging professions? The college chose to incorporate group work into the developing professions of social work and recreation, while attempting to hold on to the holistic service mission of "developing the whole person" in all its programs, including physical education. For years the college had essentially two majors: group work, which included social work and recreation, and physical education, which was strongly focused on physical education for community service.

Unfortunately for the college, these developing professions were taking on other purposes that were not in keeping with the group-work purpose. For example, the developing social work profession was drawn to a "casework" model, based on a clinical professional procedure of "study, diagnosis, and treatment" of an individual's particular problem. This "medical model" was not holistic, not focused on inherent strengths of people, and not about building community; it led to a contractual view of serving others by entering into a focused helping relationship, solving a "diagnosed" problem, and "terminating" when the problem is solved. Even before social work became a profession, Jane Addams noted that this "medical model" was not what group workers or settlement workers were all about. She said, "[They say] goodbye, good fellow! I hope never to see you again. You are now out of my reach [when the problem is solved]. That is exactly what the settlement does not do. [We are] creating fellowship [and] should not be ready to say goodbye to anybody on the round earth."[28]

By the late 1950s students found group work to be undervalued in human service; we hear their complaints in the "Grins 'n' Gripes" section of the college newspaper: "George Williams College Graduate? So What!"

Carrying On the Group Work Tradition

"George Williams College Graduate? So What!"
Student voices in "Grins 'n' Gripes," 1952

> There seems to be a real question in some of the students' minds here at the school as to the value of a degree from George Williams College. Various queries and opinions have been voiced around the school in such terms as: "A George Williams student is not accepted into professional social work and group-work organizations. Isn't the school too small and its curriculum spread so that it does not adequately prepare a person for a particular field?" . . . It would be of real value to the morale of students and the growth of the college if these opinions could be clarified with actual facts.

President Coffman's response:

> George Williams is an accredited member of the North Central Association of Colleges and Secondary Schools . . . whose purpose is the establishment of definite scholastic standards. George Williams is a member of the Federation of Colleges of Illinois, the American Council of Education, and the Association of American Colleges. These educational bodies must meet definite standards recognized nationally. Our graduates are accepted into professional group-work organizations, and in some instances, social work organizations.
>
> The ambiguous position of the George Williams College graduate in respect to professional social welfare circles is not a reflection of any level of scholastic achievement of George Williams students, but rather it represents the insistence of many social welfare agencies that their employees be case work-oriented. Curriculum at George Williams is primarily centered around a group-work orientation.[29]

The next decade of the 1960s saw student activism on college campuses. In some ways George Williams College saw itself as differentiated from the trends. They entered, and won, a contest for an ad in the *New York Times*.

"What ever happened to altruism?"
New York Times ad contest winner, 1967

> We've been hearing lots about militancy, rights, affluence, security, and rebellion, but what ever happened to altruism? Altruism, "unselfish concern for others," somehow doesn't grab the headlines, but it's part of the campus scene at George Williams

College. Our graduates for seventy-six years have entered careers with voluntary community organizations—primarily the YMCA—which have as their objective some form of education in values. It is this unique quality of concern for others that makes the George Williams College student. Traditionally the college has educated by crossing barriers that separate persons—the major reason the school is genuinely interracial, international, interconfessional, and interdisciplinary. We believe that it is our job to attract, educate, commit, and help place the finest young people for careers of service in society's constructive agencies.[30]

In this same decade of the 1960s, as urban areas were in crisis, there was some return to the value of group work, seen as "prevention" programs, and programs dealing with youth gang violence. Dewey Cedarblade tells us his story of working with gangs in Chicago. He came to George Williams College at just the time the college was moving to the suburbs and began to take on a more inward looking "sensitivity training" approach to group work, emphasizing self-awareness.

"The heck with playing games, let's get into the real group work"

Duane "Dewey" Cedarblade, student, ('69)

It was a chilly afternoon in Minneapolis when I met Duane "Dewey" Cedarblade. He walked in to greet me decked in a Norwegian sweater. "Perfect fit," I thought. Dewey was born and raised a Minnesota Y guy. Like so many others, his father was a Y director, and Dewey grew up on camping experiences in the fresh, wholesome, Scandanavian-Minnesota air. At dinner the night before, Dewey had given a brief prelude to his story, which started out as a Minnesota camping story. Dewey was following in his father's footsteps, headed into Y work and camping experiences. He already had his role models from George Williams out of those experiences—Lyle Johnson (faculty and alum '79), Whitey Luehrs ('46, '48), Armand Ball ('60). But then Dewey gingerly touched a vulnerable spot, a moment in his life that turned things all around. His two-year-old son drowned at camp, toddling off to follow his dad and friends on a boating expedition, while mom turned her head for just one moment. Thrown into a state of anger and spiritual testing, Dewey took on the hard questions about life, direction, and meaning. That was when he decided to enroll in graduate school at George Williams College. The next day I expected to hear more camping stories from this group-work major of George Williams College. But that was not what I was to hear.

Have you talked to Ernie Jenkins? Ernie was a gang worker with the Chicago Youth Centers. When he came to George Williams he came with a lot of experience about how a group worker really does work. He was a classmate of mine. We were both older students coming back to school, and we just hit it off right away. We met at Orientation Practicum as first-year graduates, and we became a team through our time at George Williams. Ernie had the same attitude toward the kind of group work we were getting at Practicum. The heck with playing games; let's get into the real stuff, the meat and potatoes in the real world. In informal moments up there, we would go out for a drink together. We became good friends.

I wanted my field experience to be in the inner city, on the South Side of Chicago. They assigned me to Parker High School in Englewood. At that point Ernie and I made a pact to get us through the program. I had a strong background in statistics and things like that, and that was very easy for me. I said, "Okay, I'll help you get through statistics. It's your job to keep me alive, while I go through my field placement." I was to work with a group of potential high school dropouts. These were sixteen- and seventeen-year-old kids who were two years behind grade level. My function was to find alternate ways for young people to get involved in a constructive life and continue education through the Chicago Y educational system. They could take classes at night, work in the day, whatever plan would work for them. We would provide tutoring, whatever resources we could.

Well, I met some of these guys at Parker, about five of them. We got along really well. A group worker gets to know your individual people, see what their strengths are. Then you meet together as a group and say, "Okay, what do you want to do?" After about two or three weeks, they invited me to be their basketball coach. They asked me to get the gym opened up at this Catholic school. Once the grade school moved out of the neighborhood, the church shut down the gym. So I met this priest, Father Murphy. I said, "These guys are really needing a recreational outlet. I'll be responsible for them." He said, "Well, we don't usually turn over the gym, but there's something about you I like." Of course, I knew he liked my [white] skin. And I looked pretty convincing as straight middle class. I think I had a crew cut at the time. I always made it a point to look middle class. It makes it easier for them to figure out what you're doing, rather than trying to blend in.

I was prepared for twelve or fifteen guys showing up. But just to cover my bases, I went to see Wardell Hilloway, who I knew through Ernie. Wardell was with the Chicago YMCA, the street gang supervisor for that area. I told him, "I got the gym opened. But I don't know who these guys are connected to." I thought it might be wise to have someone there with me. I would have gone to Ernie, but Wardell was the supervisor of this territory. Wardell said, "I can't come in, but if you need help, I'll drive by to see what's going on."

That night I arrived early. In no time, 130 guys showed up, loaded for bear. They were the Imperial Pipers. I had no idea all five of the guys I was working with at the high school were the leaders of this gang. Maurice, the head of the gang, was at a table, playing with a little toy car, rolling it back and forth. Things got real quiet. I thought, "When does the basketball begin? Well, if this is the end of my life, let's make the most of it." They knew they conned me, but I didn't get upset with them. I was going with the flow. First thing on the agenda was whether they were going to go to war with the Disciples. Then they asked me what I thought. I said, "I think it's a bad idea." They asked me why. I said, "Because your little brothers and sisters are going to get killed. Once you confront the Disciples, you're into a turf battle." They hadn't confronted them to that point. They put it to a vote. They voted not to go to war.

Later, when I went to Ernie, he took this apart piece by piece, what happened that night. He said, "You did exactly the right thing. One of the roles of the worker is to get the group to take on the kind of motives and ideas they want to act on anyway, but they may not when they're in dangerous situations. At least they can blame it on you if things go wrong." They had to take that stance, but I gave them the rationale for what they wanted to do all along. Then I went to Wardell, and I said, "Where were you?" He said, "I rode by and it was quiet!" I said, "Yeah, you ought to have heard how quiet it was inside! The other thing you could hear were my bowels moving!" Wardell laughed. Wardell and Ernie both sort of adopted me then.

Ernie told me a few more things about my induction into gang work. "The first thing gang workers get is the physical test. They'll pound you, threaten you. If you back down, you are now lost." Knowing that, I went back to the guys and I said, "Look, I go down really easy. I've never beat up anyone in my life and I never will. I don't believe in physical abuse. If you want to take a poke at me, have at it, but I'll go down real easy." One of the guys confided to me, "The guys think you're packing heat. No one would be that bold, without something to back it up." I said, "You know what I've got to back it up? I care. I care about what's going on. Kids out all night. Glass all over the streets. Babies walking on it. That's what gets me bold!"

Late one night a kid came running out. A little child had walked on glass and was badly bleeding. We put the kid in the car and rushed to the hospital. The nurse was all taken up with doing a medical history and wondering who's going to pay for it. I said, "Look, this child's bleeding to death. Do something now!" It helped that I was a white man demanding attention. It shouldn't be that way, but it is.

After that, I said to the guys, "How can you live like this? Glass all over the street. Little kids getting hurt." They said, "We don't own the property. The man does." We got to talking about that. We came up with something to get credibility with the power structure. Let's have a cleanup of a two-block area. We sought newspaper coverage. Leadership began to develop around the cleanup. They called themselves Operation NOCRAP. It stood for Neighborhood Organization Cleaning Up Refuse from Alleys and Parkways. It was something to take the pressure off the negatives about them. They were viewed as a positive organization.

The night Martin Luther King [Jr.] was assassinated, things changed. The streets were going to hell in a handbag. There were baseball bats, White people dragged into the street, buildings burning, looting. I had my guys in the car with me that night, going up and down the streets. Some people saw me, saw them, and went on. I felt I was the safest person on the street, because they were with me. They protected me. In the middle of it all, the guys said, "Everything's changed." That was the last night I met with them formally. Some gravitated out of the neighborhood. Some went into the military, the Vietnam War. Some made it through the university high school and went on to college.

Back at George Williams, Ernie Jenkins and I kept our word with each other. I helped him through statistics, and he kept me alive. Ernie had a lot to do with what I learned about group work in my years at George Williams. There were others: Lyle Johnson was the intellectual, Ann Hyman good for learning about treatment, there was Duane Robinson. But through Ernie I learned about group work in the inner city.

Dewey got up and buttoned his Norwegian sweater to return to the bright, chilly Minneapolis air, leaving me with a parting word. "If you talk to Ernie, say hello from someone who loves him very much."[31]

While Dewey was doing the hands-on work on the ghetto streets, another alum, John Root, was working from an administrative leadership role to make it possible for Dewey to access the resources needed to help his kids. John was the chief executive officer of the Chicago Metropolitan YMCA in this same period of urban crisis.

"My greatest achievement"

John Root, student, ('46) and Chicago civic leader and trustee, 1960s–70s

John Root came to George Williams College to major in physical education in 1939, when the college was located in Hyde Park of Chicago. At the time the physical education degree was a five-year degree. His degree completion was interrupted when he was drafted into the service in the World War II. He put his educational preparation to use in the medical corps as a physical training officer, then as an officer of vocational and educational guidance. He returned to George Williams College with the military rank of major. He completed only a few remaining courses and received a bachelor's degree in physical education in 1946.

In the decades to follow, John left his mark on the city of Chicago. In 1954 he took charge of program services for the YMCA of Metropolitan Chicago. He reached out to provide support services to urban youth, street gang workers like Duane "Dewey" Cedarblade, then to youth of the suburbs. During this period he was an innovator in partnership development between corporate and community leaders and public and private agencies to address major youth problems. In 1963, when John Root became president and chief executive officer of the YMCA of Metropolitan Chicago, he developed the Central YMCA Community College Program, founded in 1961, to become a vibrant educational program, enrolling some six thousand inner-city students who were economically disadvantaged and educationally unprepared. In 1967 he established a JOBS NOW Program in conjunction with the Chicago Urban League and thirty other public and private agencies to train thousands of Chicago's youth and hard-core unemployed. The JOBS NOW Program became a national model, recognized by President Lyndon B. Johnson. Root collaborated with the public sector in organizing and funding preschool and after-school day care centers, services to the aged, and prevention programs for troubled youth. He developed a racially diverse professional team, comprising more than 50 percent minorities, who became consultants on fiscal management, personnel training, and planning services for public and private groups. His technical assistance model was adopted by the National Council of YMCAs of the U.S.A. John created a powerful board of trustees, consisting of corporate, social, community, educational, and ethnic leaders of the city of Chicago.

While providing active leadership in the city, John did graduate work at George Williams College in group work administration. Throughout the years, he gave back to his college, through active participation on the George Williams College Board of Trustees.

John participated in one partnership called the Chicago Alliance of Collaborative Effort (CACE), which worked to create "a sense of neighborhood" and job opportunities for youth in Chicago's public housing projects and troubled neighborhoods. He forged this partnership with his George Williams College colleagues Fred Lickerman ('51), director of Chicago Boys and Girls Clubs, and Russ Hogrefe ('41), director of Chicago Youth Centers. Working together, these three giants in youth service programs had a strong influence for good with Chicago's disadvantaged youth. In chapter 3, "Building Community Inside and Out," we will hear from Fred Lickerman, who also speaks of the CACE partnership. According to John Root's wife, Betty, a graduate of George Williams College herself, John wanted it known in the writing of these memoirs that he regarded as his "greatest achievement" this partnership that he and his colleagues from George Williams College created.[32]

In the 1970s and '80s, when the college was located in the Chicago suburb of Downers Grove, Illinois, the fields of professional human service practice expanded and diversified well beyond the traditional contexts of group work, recreation, and physical education, which had been the bread and butter of George Williams College. The college also was beginning to model itself after the surrounding liberal arts colleges in the community. By the mid-1970s it seemed expedient to alter the college's statement of purpose to be more inclusive of these expanding fields, professional identities, and academic preparations. Changing a statement of purpose was monumental for this college, which always took pride in its distinctive mission. The faculty settled for a stated purpose to prepare students for "careers of humanitarian responsibility," admitting that "you can't please everybody."[33] Many hoped that the spirit and distinctive philosophy of human service would remain, but no one could be sure. Focusing on people's strengths as resources; building group connection, support, and solidarity; encouraging mutual aid; empowering all people to have a voice in the groups and communities of which they are a part; engaging in physical activities to promote healthy development and esteem of individuals—when applied in practice, these principles were almost a radical departure from the direction professional social services had turned. The notion that one has to "be a whole person in order to serve people as whole persons," the old YMCA principle of body-mind-spirit and social wholeness, seemed buried somewhere in the college culture but not well articulated or highlighted. Speaking in the mid-1980s, faculty member Mary (Ryba) Knepper, presents a case for the liberal arts in preparing people for the field of human service.

A case for the liberal arts

Mary (Ryba) Knepper, professor, 1985

If you think when you graduate your job will be a simple little task of running a camp or a YMCA, or an agency, or working in a group home, or nursing a patient back to health or becoming a professional in the traditional fields, think again. Any time you try to serve people, it makes sense to understand the subject. If you don't, you will go to battle unarmed. I am making a case for being the best you can be in the human service area. I am talking about being a full professional by becoming a full human being. And I am suggesting that part of that becoming is participation in the performing and visual arts.[34]

"Two very high callings:
Be excellent and be uniquely excellent"

John Kessler, student, ('49) and GWC president, 1985

In 1985 the new president of George Williams College, John Kessler, also an alum of GWC ('49), was not in office more than a few months when he gave the following charge and warning:

> A concern I have that the college has unwittingly strayed a little distance from its mission does not issue from any desire to return to a narrower view of who should be the recipients of human services or in what organizational context they should be performed. Rather it emanates from the logic that a traditional education does not do as good a job in preparing for a career in human service, as does one specifically designed for that purpose. . . . That logic better be persuasive or we have no argument for our distinctiveness as a school. . . . The college has two very high callings: to be excellent and to be uniquely excellent, if it is to be the preeminent institution for leadership in human services . . . even if it risks enrollment decline.[35]

A few months later, in December of 1985, George Williams College closed, due to financial hardship. The social work and recreation programs of the college eventually transferred to Aurora University. Having survived a monumental crisis, the programs reexamined their fundamental identity and worth as carriers of the George Williams College history and traditions. A renewed professional interest and spirit to "get back to roots" grew. At the same time, by the early 1990s, the city of Chicago was beginning to miss the old group-work approach to human services, now referred to in some circles as "primary services" or "youth development." Certain civic leaders and academics, like members of Chicago Community Trust and the Chapin Hall Center for Children at the University of Chicago, advocated for a return to the professional training of human service workers with the philosophy and purpose of group work.[36] Some even chastised such professions as social work for abandoning group work and its early purpose. In 1992, when Aurora University celebrated an affiliation agreement with George Williams College, guest speaker Dr. Harold Richman from the Chapin Hall Center for Children personally challenged me, as dean of George Williams College and the School of Social Work, to return to our roots and focus on group work for youth and community development. It was the recognized tradition of George Williams College in the past, and the need was great.

George Williams College responded. In addition to teaching group-work methods, the entire graduate-level curriculum was infused with a group-work approach to all forms of human service (called the "group-centered perspective"). While continuing to offer the more traditional knowledge and skills required for professional practice, GWC ventured forward in some experimental programs by returning to roots. In 1992 the programs of the newly established "George Williams College of Aurora University" returned to Chicago to engage in the Chicago Youth Agency Partnership (CYAP); the aim was to educate and train youth workers. Three giant youth service agencies—Chicago Youth Centers (under the leadership of Del Arsenault ['62, '66]), Chicago Boys and Girls Clubs (directed by Robert Hussein), and Chicago Area Project (directed by David Whittaker)—provided the foundation of more than eighty community-based agencies serving youth. Alumnus William Conrad ('60) led the initiative. Faculty member Mary Nelums tells her story of her involvement with the CYAP.

"While you're looking at us, we're looking at you": Role modeling

Mary Nelums, professor, 1980s–90s

That was what Chicago youth had to say in a "fishbowl" focus group in the presence of 125 youth workers, youth agency directors, academics, and a nationally prominent youth specialist from Washington, D.C., Karen Pittman. They were attending a visioning conference, a first step in the development of a training curriculum for youth workers. Perhaps it would lead to a college degree specialization or a certification process for youth workers. All were poised in rapt attention to hear what these young people had to say. What kind of educational preparation would it take to be an effective youth worker? What courses should they take? But the youth were taking the focus in a different direction.

"They were doubtful," Mary said, as she recalled her role as the focus group facilitator. "Doubtful whether they would be heard about what really mattered to them." These youth were looking for something from their youth leader that you don't get from books or methods and skills.

> That's what led them to say "Don't forget, while you're looking at us, we're looking at you." . . . Group work is supposed to be about character development. But does the youth worker walk the talk? . . . If they say they need someone to insist they get to school on time and do their homework; if they say they need someone that expected responsibility from them; if they tell their youth worker, "This is what I need from you," and the youth worker shows up an hour late for group, what does that say? . . . The bottom line for youth workers is to become more aware of themselves and their impact on others. Group workers need to be aware that who they are speaks louder than words. The worker must be aware: What lesson am I trying to teach? Then you model that behavior all the time, in group, out of group. In the beginning they'll do things because of the relationship. That's okay. Eventually they'll do it for themselves.

Mary learned the power of role modeling from her own family and community.

I grew up on a dirt road in a small rural town in Wayne County, Mississippi. My family was poor, but I never felt that way. My mother made all my clothes, and she didn't even have a sewing machine, but I'd go to school looking fine. Mother was the manager of the school cafeteria, a good cook. Everyone in neighborhood called her "Ma Mary." In our house, the door was always open. Anyone could come in and share a meal anytime. Anyone could walk up and down that dirt road, and you could go to anyone's house to eat. "Come on in," they'd say. "I have a hot meal here waiting for you." Everybody cared about each other in the neighborhood.

I was the first person in my community to go to college. It was like I was everybody's daughter going to college. When I got ready to go, everyone in the neighborhood brought something. They'd say, "Girl, you got to have this now. You're going to Jackson State [University]!" In time, many young people from that place in Mississippi went to college. I was a role model for the community. . . .

GWC at Aurora University was where I wanted to teach, because George Williams College has a history so rich in terms of working in communities. Unless we move outside the ivory tower of the academy, we lose touch with what we really need to be teaching students. Unless we're in touch with the community, how do we know what works? We know from what we learn from them.[37]

Listening to Mary's story reminded me of the words of Henry Kallenberg, the dean of physical education back in 1913. He used different words but shared a meaning with Professor Mary Nelums. Kallenberg spoke of the "efficiency" of the human service worker, "incorporated qualities of character," evidenced "in the everyday life of the man, so he is able to put things across," "more important than skills." We might call it "role modeling" today. You have to be a whole person to effectively serve the whole person. That was Henry Kallenberg's point, and that was Mary Nelum's point. Mary's focus group of youth brought us back to what was most important to be an effective youth worker.

"Serving those who serve others"

Dovetta McKee, professor, 1990s and the first decade of the 21st century

At Aurora Unversity, faculty member Dovetta McKee picked up the beginnings of a group work degree for youth workers in the city of Chicago that saw its origins in the work of Professor Mary Nelums and others from George Williams College. It became a special kind of human service degree. Dovetta tells her story of how she got into this kind of work.

The legacy of George Williams College was about serving those who serve others. I grew up in Chicago. I came out of a family of ten children. Dad and Mom moved to Chicago from Arkansas in 1944. I was born on the South Side, but when I was three years old, we moved to the west side. At that time we moved into a community that was racially mixed. It was a wonderful thing to be in this community in my formative years. On the corner, there was a pharmacy. This pharmacist and his daughter had a magnificent library of books. They would give us books and encourage us to read. They distributed books to everyone in the community, right there in the drug store. You could sit at the soda fountain sipping Green Rivers and talk about the world, opportunities, and college experiences. We constantly heard, "You can do this." My dad was an avid reader. My mom worked for the Park District as an arts and crafts teacher. She was working with youth in community, motivating them, encouraging them, cautioning them about being in trouble.

I was involved in church youth work, then went on to Howard University, where I did neighborhood youth work on the side. When I came back to Chicago . . . I went to law school, where I got a degree. I burned out in the legal profession. It wasn't always about justice. It was more about money, and that was discouraging to me. I began to look for other ways to make a contribution, to have a broader impact on the development of youth.

I was introduced by David Whittaker, [director of Chicago Area Project], to Larry Hawkins [who tells his story in chapter 2, "Developing Body with Mind and Spirit"]. Larry—we called him "Doc"—was assisting young people to have an early appreciation for educational opportunity and what that meant for the rest of their lives. Early on, some youth don't get the reinforcement and motivation like I had in my family and community to appreciate a solid educational foundation. It's amazing how many lives Doc touched. Young people who moved through his program have gone on to be doctors, lawyers, judges, accountants, you name it. Larry Hawkins is a tremendous supporter of the George Williams philosophy to give young people the opportunity to prove themselves, that they have the ability. I'm not a sports person as he is, but he'd always say, "I use sports to get their attention."

The focus of the [Aurora University degree] program, [which started out as the Chicago Youth Agency Partnership training program], was for adults who had been working for a number of years in youth work programs at the street level. Many of them have their own self-esteem issues and as many concerns about their own ability as the young people that they were working through. The program was to encourage them to do their best academically, to build a level of self-esteem, to say, "I have the ability to do this if I work hard." They didn't believe the degree was important, didn't see the relevance. They thought they were successful. . . . They had been doing youth work for an average of fifteen years. They relied on their day-to-day experiences in youth programs, community activity, sports programs. They didn't have an appreciation of the theoretical foundation. [When they entered the program] you could watch that light bulb go on. They would say, "Okay. Now I see why when I did this it worked; when I did not do this it didn't work." Students were excited because they gained understanding by going back to apply what they were doing. They also gained a level of understanding about themselves and the world they worked in. Teachers were practice-based professionals with academic credentials who brought to the table the ability to understand the experiences the students were having, relating it directly. They had insight because they were familiar with the areas where they worked. Many of them had worked in the very same organizations themselves.

Young people are more apt to challenge you on what you do, not what you say. How do you encourage young people to go to college if you haven't had that experience yourself? Many of my students have actually heard the youth they are working with, say, "Why didn't you go to college?"

People do not see youth development as a professional track. Get a ball, throw it out, get a youth program going, and that's all you have to do. Now we're much clearer about working with people: issues of self-esteem, self-awareness, motivation, bridging over into adulthood—how to do that in a professional way? The GWC legacy is at the forefront of all of that. What greater calling can there be than to help, motivate, encourage, develop people who then turn around and say, "I'm going to give back to my community. I'm going to encourage and motivate others as I have been encouraged and motivated." To me, when I think of George Williams, I think: "Serving those who serve others." That's the legacy; that's what George Williams is about.[38]

A renewed George Williams College spirit showed itself in the desire of faculty to break out of the professional silos that academic disciplines had confined themselves to, to once again collaborate in interdisciplinary community work to meet the "whole person" needs of schoolchildren. Faculty member Chris Ahlman tells us the story of how the social work and recreation programs, along with the physical education and education programs, creatively designed and provided leadership to an experimental, interdisciplinary program operating out of a local elementary school. The project, which reflected the traditional George Williams College principles of human service, proved to be successful. This time the location was the east side of the city of Aurora, an economically disadvantaged community struggling with school dropouts and gangs. A United Way community survey identified the lack of parental involvement in the schools and their children's education as one of the top community concerns. In their frustration, teachers and community leaders wanted to "solve the problem" of children's poor performance in school by placing more punitive measures on parents who did not get involved in the school.

"If the kids come, the parents will come"

Chris Ahlman, professor, 1990s and the first decade of the 21st century

"If you can get the kids involved in some activities they enjoy, the parents will come." Those were the words I heard from a PTA president of Bardwell School, [a K–5 school in the East Aurora community]. The school population was 50 percent Hispanic, 30 percent African American, and 20 percent Caucasian. I was thinking about this when we had our first faculty meeting of [the newly organized] George Williams College [at Aurora University]. The pieces were coming together in my mind. I looked around at the new GWC faculty, and I wondered, "What do we have in common that can bring us together as GWC faculty?" Then, I thought, "What about the children?" We have people here committed to the development of everything about children: their physical, social-emotional, educational, and recreational development. We agreed to an interdisciplinary community demonstration project. Whatever project we came up with had to incorporate all these pieces. Roberta Naumann, [professor of education]; Alicia Cosky, [professor of physical education]; Sandra Hupp, [professor of recreation administration]; and I [professor of social work and a school social worker] agreed to be faculty mentors and work with a team of students from each of our disciplines to see what we could do together to attract kids and parents into the school. All of our students have requirements for a field experience in their separate disciplines, but we wanted this to be different. We wanted students to learn from each other. What would happen if the same child had experiences to grow in every area of their lives at the same time? If we create something that attracts the kids, will the parents come and get involved?

The project started with five student interns from GWC. They started with activities before school, at lunch, and after school. They focused on a group of forty fourth- and fifth-graders, setting up activities mostly in tutoring and recreation. Soccer was the first thing that worked. The recreation students said, "This is not about sports; it's about developing social skills and team building. Sports are the way we get there." Soccer also worked to bring the parents in. At first, parents were only involved in dropping students off and picking them up at the end of the day. Pretty soon, fathers were showing up, not just to pick up their kids, but to watch them play. The fourth- and fifth-graders were beginning to attach to the GWC students as their leaders.

We decided it was time to launch a Fun Night for parents and kids at the school. Usually the older students are the hardest to reach. But these kids wouldn't miss Fun Night because their leaders encouraged them to come. Because the older kids were excited about it, the younger students got involved. The Spanish language barrier was overcome because the student interns were mostly bilingual, and the fifth graders assisted in translating for other parents. At the first Fun Night event, an unprecedented six hundred parents and students came. Social agencies in the community asked if they could come to future Fun Nights to set up information booths, so they could reach the families about their services.

The GWC students worked hard as a team to plan the activities for the night. Some ideas came from a book of activities, but the most fun was the team brainstorming activities coming straight from the imagination of the GWC students and faculty, planning activities that would meet the objectives. A teacher intern who wanted to see parents and kids enjoy reading together proposed a reading room with a big easy chair and a bunch of books parents could choose from to curl up with their kids and read a story. There was a long line outside the "reading room." There was a treasure hunt to find vocabulary words in books. There were activities designed to learn how to problem solve and work as a team. A walk around the block became a math and history lesson—Where were your parents or grandparents born? How far away is Mexico City? They translated the miles into relative lengths of city blocks, and they had to walk that far. Before each activity the student interns explained the purpose of the activity, and after each activity there was time to reflect on what they learned from the activity. There were suggested activities families could do at home to have fun together.

It worked! "If the kids are interested and they come, the parents will come!" This was never in my academic preparation. I thought I did group work when I ran little discussion groups with kids. I now know learning happens when your body is up and moving. Teachers have violence prevention programs, a "peaceful schools" curriculum they are required to teach. After Fun Night and other project experiences, I looked at the sterile ditto sheet where children were supposed to fill out the "right answer," and I threw it away. This is not the way to prevent violence. They need to experience the choice points for violence and problem solve other ways. So I taught the curriculum but designed all experiential exercises to illustrate the points. I also learned the antidote to bullying has to be experienced. I tried to design activities where kids would learn empathy. I created physical activities where the chubby kid in the class who is the brunt of jokes eventually gets to be the one who everyone needs to solve a problem.

No one went away from that project untouched. We continued it for several years. Faculty members from each discipline presented professional papers for conferences in their academic disciplines: social work, recreation, and education. They also presented as an interdisciplinary team at each others' professional conferences.[39]

Comparing the "modern" with the "old"—prove it!

Social work educator, 1997

Today we see a certain nostalgia for group and community-oriented values within society and the human services. It surfaces in such bestsellers as Robert Putnam's *Bowling Alone*[40] or Fabricant and Fisher's *Settlements Under Siege*.[41] In 1997 three social work faculty from George Williams College published an article in the *Journal of Social Work Education* called, "Empowering Community-Based Programs for Youth Development: Is Social Work Education Interested?" The article described the Chicago Youth Agency Partnership between Aurora University and youth service agencies to illustrate. One "blind" reviewer made further comments.

> [The article] urges the social work profession to resume its historical leadership in community-based programs for youth and identifies current societal and professional trends that support a revival of social work's involvement in youth development. Being an old group worker, I am inclined to applaud its focus. However, the article . . . stops short of evaluation of a fully operational program. Why is it that group work gave way to group and individual talk therapies? One answer might be that the former were unable to demonstrate their effectiveness. . . . It is too bad there isn't good data comparing the modern with the old. . . . If we could show that it was a mistake to have given up the old, we would have a stronger case for going back to it.[42]

The comments capture the dilemma in professional circles today about the value of the historic group-work philosophy and tradition that branded human service at George Williams College. The scientific question still lurks, Can you prove it's the better way to serve others?

Chapter 2
Developing Body with Mind and Spirit

"You become **physical educators,** *not peddlers of physical activity, when you use activities as means toward greater ends, . . . an* **influence for good** *in mind and character as well as body."*

(Professor Arthur Steinhaus, 1968)

*C*oming from George Williams College, Dr. Arthur Steinhaus is nationally recognized as a pioneer researcher on the physiology of the human body, health, and physical education. Yet those who knew him say that he spoke as much as a philosopher as he did a researcher and educator. All his work was driven by a big picture of purpose; he even called his mission "building a cathedral."[1] His words that introduce this chapter could sum up the educational mission and purpose of George

Williams College in the area of physical education since its beginning. The college saw training in physical activity as "a means toward greater ends . . . an influence for good." We also see the holistic perspective: ". . . in mind and character as well as body." The three dimensions cannot be separated. Otherwise we are merely "peddlers of physical activity."[2]

Although this concept of holism is familiar today, it was not the case at the end of the nineteenth century, when the college came into being. In Western culture a huge paradigm shift was going on, and the YMCA, along with its training school (George Williams College), was at the forefront. Throughout the preindustrial Agricultural Age a conflicting dualism of "body" and "spirit" prevailed. Today we think of "working out" and the "sweat of one's brow" as an indicator of something good—the healthy maintenance of the body. In the past sweat was an uncomfortable reminder of original sin and the curse of Adam and Eve: "By the sweat of your face you shall eat bread until you re-turn to the ground."[3] In contrast, the Sabbath was a day of rest from physical activity, a holy day. Rest was also seen as a curative factor for physical illness and mental depression. The Industrial Age brought with it "sweatshops," where sweat was not as much related to physical activity as it was poor working conditions, such as long hours in poor ventilation in a sedentary environment. In the late 1880s, when the college was in its infancy, there developed a rejection of the idea that physical activity was a "necessary evil"; the body was now glorified as God's spiritual "temple" that needed to be well maintained and developed.

Theodore Roosevelt embraced this new paradigm. He became not only the American president but a leader and role model for physical exercise, having overcome frailty in his own life through tough, disciplined exercise and the strengthening of his body. His 1900 book, *The Strenuous Life,* was popular and made physical exercise a virtue. Roosevelt criticized the "overcivilization" of America's white-collar, educated classes, who did not balance the development of body with the development of mind. Roosevelt claimed, "[There is] a general tendency among people of culture and education . . . to neglect and even look down on, the rougher and manlier virtues, so that an advanced state of intellectual development is too often associated with effeminacy of character."[4]

the Christ figure as an emaciated, suffering, detached victim-martyr were replaced with a strong, muscular youth, a dominant, engaging presence, a shepherd leader-guide. Sermons featured a virile Jesus the carpenter, who spent his youth engaged in demanding physical activity. As cultural representations began to portray a "manlier" Christ figure, the follow-

"The body was now glorified as God's spiritual 'temple.'"

Since paradigm shifts are revolutionary, they stimulate ripple effects in the culture. The breakdown of the dualism of body and spirit showed itself in a societal movement in Protestant Christianity toward "muscular Christianity." The new glorification of the body with all its intricacies and potential needed to find its expression in the church to attract men back into its fold, since attendance of men in church and in church leadership roles was slipping. Stained glass windows representing

ers of Christ were to take on these "manlier" virtues as well. Sports heroes who professed to be Christians became magnets that attracted men to the Christian faith.[5]

Photograph, page 35: In the early years of the Hyde Park campus, students displayed their physical skills to the community in an annual "Gymnite" event. (1917)

The Emerging Paradigm: Development of the Body

At this juncture in history, the YMCA, its institutes, and training school (George Williams College) in Williams Bay, Wisconsin, and Chicago, Illinois, developed strong relations with "muscular Christians" and spawned a few of their own.

The "Muscular Christians"

Dwight L. Moody, evangelist, circa 1886

Evangelist Dwight L. Moody was closely associated with the Chicago YMCA. He spent his early adult years in Chicago supporting the work of the YMCA there, including the building of a YMCA structure that eventually burned down in the Chicago fire. Moody was one of the most popular evangelists of his time. He was one of the first to bring athletic heroes with him on his tours demonstrating the attraction to being both "muscular" and Christian.[6]

Moody first started the Northfield conferences for college students in 1885. The next year GWC founders Robert Weidensall, and I. E. Brown sought to replicate the student conferences in their new Williams Bay facility. They asked Moody to be the guest speaker, putting off their first conference until 1886 to accommodate him. It is unclear whether he ever came. The purpose of the student conferences was for college students throughout the country to come together to hear inspirational evangelists and Bible teachers, and the result was a massive commitment to "foreign mission work." It became known as the Student Volunteer Movement, with most of the "volunteering" involving commitment to foreign mission work. International YMCA leader and Nobel Peace Prize winner John R. Mott became the leader of the popular student conferences in Williams Bay, as the conferences took on their own identity.[7]

Billy Sunday, evangelist and first student, 1890

Well-known evangelist Billy Sunday was another icon of "muscular Christianity." Born in Ames, Iowa, in 1862, William Ashley Sunday came to Chicago to play professional baseball, a center fielder for the Chicago White Stockings from 1883 to 1888. After stints with the Pittsburgh and Philadelphia clubs in professional baseball from 1888 to 1890, he "entered full-time Christian service as a worker at Chicago's YMCA."[8]

Billy Sunday was in the first class of George Williams College (then called the Secretarial Institute and Training School (SITS). It was the class of 1890. He was one of fifteen applicants who made the enrollment cut, reducing the enrollment of the first class down to twelve. Lacking the benefit of the Privacy Act, the college published not only the names of the applicants, but the names of those who were cut and the reasons for their cut ("unfitness for the association vocation," "lack of fundamental education").[9] William Ashley Sunday made the cut. Tuition was 50 dollars a year. However, his name is not among the rolls of graduates of the college.

Billy Sunday went on to have enormous appeal as a nationally known evangelist advocating for Prohibition laws. In the years to come, Frank Sinatra would croon, "My kind of town, Chicago is . . . Even Billy Sunday couldn't shut it down." Billy Sunday enjoyed the patronage of John D. Rockefeller and presidents Theodore Roosevelt and Woodrow Wilson. The Chicago Presbytery ordained him in 1903. Perhaps Sunday's appeal was as much for his "manly" presentation of the gospel, as for the message of the gospel itself. He was known to use "colorful, slangy language"; he was "entertaining" and loved to use "mimicry."[10] And he was a known athlete. He attracted men to his message, even as his message was heavily bent on denying the pleasure of the drinking man.

Amos Alonzo Stagg, Student Conference Athletic Director, 1890–1892

Stagg was an all-American football hero from Yale University in 1889. He transferred to Springfield College, (the YMCA sister college in Massachusetts) and was there from 1890 to 1892. While at Springfield, Stagg came to Williams Bay in the summers to direct the athletic program of the Western Secretarial Institute (GWC). "Under the leadership of A. A. Stagg, in charge of recreation, the famous Yale player, the students entered heartily into the afternoon athletics."[11]

One biographical account claims Stagg played in the first public basketball game as a faculty member at Springfield College in 1892 and that he is known for being the "brainchild" of five-man basketball: it is said "he took the game of basketball from Springfield to Chicago, where it became a major sport." (Perhaps the export of the game started with the summer conferences at Williams Bay, where he was athletic director from 1890 to 1892.) Stagg then became athletic director at the University of Chicago and remained there from 1892 to 1933. Stagg Field at the University of Chicago is named after him. He coached seven Big Ten basketball championship teams and six Big Ten baseball teams, and started the University of Chicago National Interscholastic Basketball Tournament in 1917.[12] Stagg initiated the huddle, the lateral pass, and "man-in-motion" in football.[13]

Medical doctors are physical educators

Many of the physical educators at the college were trained in the medical profession, where the study of anatomy and physiology expanded from the study of disease and pathology to an understanding of wellness and the holistic development of the body. A glimpse of the college faculty profiles and curriculum in 1909 reveals the two-dimensional focus on "body" and "spirit." Five of eight faculty were medical doctors and theologians. Two of the faculty came from seminaries: (George Robinson from McCormick Seminary and Edward Harper from Chicago Theological Seminary). The rest were medical doctors.[14] The following are medical doctors who played influential roles in the college.

Luther Gulick, MD, summer institute instructor, 1889–1902

Luther Gulick is perhaps most recognized for promoting the symbol of the triangle to represent the YMCA purpose of integrating body, mind, and spirit. Gulick's academic career was based at George Williams College's sister college, Springfield College in Massachusetts. In 1887 he founded the first training course for gymnasium instructors at that school. This event is widely accepted as the first attempt to educate leaders for physical direction and recreational purposes. Luther Gulick also had a strong association with George Williams College. He first became associated with the college during the summer of 1889 to lead the institute mostly in gymnasium floor exercises. The following year Dr. Gulick founded the Western Summer Training School in Williams Bay, patterned after the one he began earlier in Springfield. Between 1889 and 1902 Dr. Gulick was a frequent lecturer at the college and served as an instructor for the summer sessions at Williams Bay.[15]

James Naismith, MD, summer institute instructor, 1900–1902

Luther Gulick was instrumental in bringing three pioneers of the physical education movement to the George Williams campus on Geneva Lake from Springfield College: Amos Alonzo Stagg, Henry Kallenberg, and James Naismith. James Naismith taught anatomy, physiology, hygiene, and first aid during the summer sessions at Williams Bay from 1900 to 1902. He is widely credited for an astounding contribution to American sports. He introduced and implemented the idea of hanging peach baskets on the gym floor of Springfield College for a game that quickly became basketball. As athletic director of Springfield College, Naismith created the original "13 rules" of the game. He went on to become a renowned basketball coach at the University of Kansas, developing the sport there.[16]

Henry Kallenberg, MD,
athletic director and dean of physical education, 1897–1917

Less well known of the people Luther Gulick brought to the college was a classmate of James Naismith's at Springfield College, Henry Kallenberg. After graduating from Springfield College in 1891, he went to the University of Iowa where he tested out some of his ideas about basketball. In 1897 Kallenberg came to George Williams College (called the Institute and Training School of the YMCA, or ITS) while he was pursuing a degree in medicine at Northwestern University in Chicago. He became the athletic director of George Williams College and eventually dean of physical education. Henry Kallenberg taught physiology, physical diagnosis, gymnastics, and athletics. Reports of the role of Kallenberg in the invention of basketball differ, but the fact that he played a role is undisputed.

> Kallenberg suggested to Dr. James Naismith . . . that they should make up a game to be played between football and baseball seasons. The two were classmates at Springfield College. Kallenberg was former dean of athletics of George Williams College. He was one of the pioneers of modern basketball.[17]

> At first, the baskets had no holes in them, so someone had to climb up and get the ball whenever a goal was scored. Then Dr. Henry Kallenberg, a friend of Naismith's, suggested cutting holes in them. . . . It wasn't until 1906 that open baskets were used to let the ball fall through.[18]

> In the fall of 1891 James Naismith attempted to devise an indoor game that would interest his bored physical education classes. What he came up with was basketball. After he tried it out with his own students, he wrote to many of his friends around the country, sending them the rules he had devised, asking them to try it with their own students and to let him know what they thought of it. Among those to whom he sent the rules was Henry Kallenberg. According to Kallenberg's daughters, he introduced the game to his YMCA classes [at the University of Iowa] during the Christmas break in 1891, very shortly after he received Naismith's letter. . . . Iowa City was one of the first places to experiment with this new game. The first intercollegiate game between five-player teams was between the University of Iowa [an unofficial YMCA team] and the University of Chicago [where Amos Alonzo Stagg was coaching].[19]

Charles Kurtz, MD, professor, 1900–1917

Charles Kurtz, also a medical doctor who taught at the college, recalls Kallenberg:

> At that time [1900] the faculty consisted of Mr. Hansel; I. E. Brown; Sidney Hotton, business manager and teacher of business administration; and Dr. Henry Kallenberg, who was an assistant physical director at the Central Y and had put himself through the medical school of Northwestern, graduating about 1901. Since he had been teaching anatomy, physiology, and all physical work at the school, he asked me to add anatomy to my portfolio.

Kurtz reflected on the lighter moments with fun-loving Kallenberg in Williams Bay, Wisconsin:

> Sometimes in the afternoon Dr. Kallenberg might take out the Hummer sailboat, a craft that could not tip over because of the heavy iron keel [that] made a noise when going, and a group of us would go with him to a sandy beach for a picnic. On Saturday nights, the faculty, with the help of the tent girls, waiters, and guests, usually put on a show or some other entertainment. One of the favorite programs was Dr. Kallenberg's imitation of the noise of the hog-train or his cork leg dance. Someone always had a good suggestion for the Saturday night show. Much later on the Saturday night affair became a professional entertainment.[20]

John Fuhrer, professor, 1920s

Faculty member John Fuhrer told a story of Arthur Steinhaus when he was a student at George Williams College in the 1920s.

> Steinhaus played football and enjoyed the zest of competition. In intramural sports Dr. Henry F. Kallenberg devised a scoring system to encourage participation by awarding points for using all available players. As team captain, Steinhaus discovered that by making frequent substitutions of different players, he could run up the total points of his team, actually winning, whether his team won the game or not. He employed this practice to the limit.[21]

Arthur Steinhaus, student, ('19, '21, '26) and professor, 1967

Steinhaus became a renowned professor at the college, and on the occasion of his retirement gave tribute to his mentor, Kallenberg.

> When we look back, we think of one of [Luther] Gulick's classes at Springfield College. There sat Amos Alonzo Stagg; there also sat James Naismith; there also sat a fellow named Henry F. Kallenberg. He came to this college in the middle 1890s to organize the physical education program here. So you see a direct line of descent from Gulick to Kallenberg to George Williams College. Kallenberg played football

in the days of the flying wedge. Before coming to us, he was a coach at Iowa and thus helped to bring football and basketball into the Big Ten; but he found himself most useful as a leader of the curriculum in physical education at GWC. . . .

Long before we had intramural sports, it was called "mass athletics." I don't think he ever got full credit for having introduced the idea of intramural sports. He spoke also of the water gymnasium as a place where you do more than just swim. What are we doing today? We are walking on the bottom of pools, and we are using the swimming pools for dancing. . . . There are other ways in which swimming pools can be used. Also, Kallenberg was responsible for stimulating YMCAs to put in health clubs. . . . All of this is part of your heritage when you come to George Williams College.[22]

Charles Kurtz, MD, professor, 1900–1917

Charles Kurtz served on the faculty of the college, called the Secretarial Institute and Training School of the YMCA (SITS) at the time, as professor of physiology from 1900 to 1917. He became a medical doctor through training at Northwestern Medical School, where he was one of Dr. Winfield Scott Hall's assistants. Hall recommended Kurtz to President Hansel for someone to teach first aid. Kurtz was no stranger to the college, having been introduced to the summer student conferences in 1892 by A. S. Wegner, one of the first students of the college. Kurtz was thrilled to meet John R. Mott at the summer institutes in 1889. Also, his brother participated in the Student Volunteer Movement conferences (student conferences) in Williams Bay and eventually became a missionary to India.

The professional ties of George Williams College to Northwestern University Medical School were strong. Not only were many faculty former medical students; medical school faculty were guest lecturers, and even the equipment was loaned to the college, when the college was still in a fledgling state.

Of course [in 1900] the YMCA institute had no laboratory equipment, so I borrowed microscopes from Northwestern's medical school, transporting them from the Chicago campus at 25th [Street] and Dearborn [Street] to 19 South LaSalle [Street]. Dr. Hall was most kind and let me have whatever I wanted, and so I used a number of medical students. E. H. Foster ['02 and professor at ITS in 1902] assisted Dr. Kallenberg while putting himself through medical school and then took over the physiology and histology courses until Charles Elder came to the school, graduated, and with my help took over the teaching of these medical subjects, until Arthur Steinhaus became a part-time teacher in 1918.[23]

Kurtz was also the camp physician at Williams Bay, in the days of the summer institutes. It brought to mind this memory of "a day at Lake Geneva":

> The day began with morning prayers, followed by classes [on association work] until noon. Afternoons were for swimming and athletic sports on the hill. . . . In 1892 . . . the gym was a platform where the older dining room now stands. The parallel bars, horse, etc. were covered with tarpaulin. The dining room was a barnlike structure about forty feet long located just south of the Railroad Building. The kitchen was in a lean-to; the tables were long; the seats were planks on logs. The meetings were held in the Lewis Auditorium, which, with the office building and tents, covered only about ten acres. Later, when the first dining room was built, the old eating place became the gym.[24]

Winfield Scott Hall, MD, guest lecturer, 1900–1917

> Dr. Winfield Scott Hall was another academic connection between Northwestern University and the college. Hall was professor of physiology at Northwestern University Medical School and guest lecturer at the training school (GWC) from 1900 to 1917. He was a brother of the famous G. Stanley Hall, psychologist and promoter of the theory of recapitulation, a way of understanding child and adolescent behavior that was used in YMCA programming in the years to come. Winfield, the medical doctor and physiologist, became a mentor for both Dr. Charles Kurtz and Dr. Henry Kallenberg, who trained under him at Northwestern Medical School.[25]

Besides the medical doctors, many leaders in the recreation and playground movement contributed to learning at the college as guest lecturers.

Leaders in the recreation and playground movement

Jane Addams, guest lecturer, 1890–1920s

In Jane Addams' time, the late nineteenth century, it was thought best to treat depression through rest and, if you had the means, to "get away" somewhere. Jane Addams suffered from depression. She traveled to England for rest, personally discovered Toynbee Hall there, and returned to this country to pioneer in the settlement house movement by establishing the Hull House settlement in Chicago. It was during this period that new vistas were opening on the value of physical activity to treat not only the physical state, but the mental and emotional states of people. Addams eventually became a leader in the recreation movement.[26] Addams spoke of the influence of the college students on Hull House in chapter 1, "Serving Others."

As early as 1895, the college placed a student physical director at Hull House in Chicago. The school's association with this historic settlement house continued well into the twentieth century. Jane Addams, a Nobel Peace Prize winner, spoke at the college on numerous occasions, and students were placed at Hull House as interns from 1895 well into the 1920s.[27]

Edward DeGroot, faculty, 1909–1913

George Williams College recognized the need for educating leaders on the various aspects of play as early as 1900. The concept of play in our culture was an integral aspect of course work for physical directors. In 1902 courses were expanded to included discussions on the philosophy of play, play as a factor in character development, and public playgrounds. Edward DeGroot continued his association with the school as a regular faculty member through the 1913 school year. He established a course on play and playgrounds for the curriculum.

As early as 1904, Edward DeGroot, best known for his innovative leadership as director of the South Park District in Chicago, spoke to the school on the topic of public playgrounds in Chicago. In the following year the South Park District completed ten neighborhood parks and community centers. George Williams College began placing field students in positions with the West and South Park Districts in that same year.[28]

Clark Hetherington, summer institute instructor, 1909–1910

As the playground movement developed, the college invited various well-known national leaders to teach during the summer sessions. Coming from the University of Missouri, Dr. Clark Hetherington taught for two years at the summer institutes. His main contribution to the field of recreation was his role in helping to develop the "Normal Course on Play" for the Playground Association in 1908 to provide adequate training for playground leaders. This course was taught at the Williams Bay campus by Drs. Henry Curtis and Edward DeGroot in the summer of 1910.[29]

Charles English, student ('12) and lecturer, 1912–circa 1920

Charles English graduated from the college in 1912. English would later gain fame for his work with the War Camp Community Service during the First World War, when the YMCA was commissioned by the president to provide recreational services and to boost morale for soldiers in the armed services. English directed the Playground and Recreation Association in Philadelphia from 1927 to 1945.[30]

Pioneers in Health and Physical Education: Science and Service

The "character builders": The ITS college traditions

Students, 1906

In 1906 Henry Kallenberg thought "it is very important that a school such as ITS [Institute and Training School of the YMCA, later George Williams College] should guard with care the traditions that are being formed, since they will determine to a considerable extent, the future usefulness of the school." And so the students came up with this definition of traditions that characterized the spirit of the college:

> Tradition 1: Heads up, with shoulders squarely set! The ITS student walks, stands, and sits erect, for only the sick or defeated man slouches. "Chin, chest out, abdomen in" means health and indicates a victorious life, and the lungs are given a better chance to do their work.
>
> Tradition 2: God's laws control his physical life. The ITS student eats slowly and chews his food thoroughly, drinks plenty of water between meals, works and sleeps in a well-ventilated room, takes time for wholesome recreation.
>
> Tradition 3: He is dominated by the spirit of Jesus. The ITS student is full of help for his fellows, is gentlemanly in speech and conduct, is charitable. Do not judge too hastily the man who yields to temptation. You do not know the circumstances of his life, nor how hard he has fought, nor how often he has successfully resisted the Tempter.
>
> Tradition 4: He is dominated by the spirit of clean sport. The ITS student plays fair in all contests, does honest work in preparation of school lessons, does not "crib" during recitation or during written examinations, and deals fairly with his fellows at all times.[31]

This simple, amusing student description of the traditions of the college in 1906 shows the close association of health and physical activity with godliness and character: "body" and "spirit" are the defining characteristics. "Developing body" meant taking responsibility for healthy habits of living. "Spirit," while still connoting the spiritual ideal of a life "dominated by the spirit of Jesus," begins to be infused with something more than soul salvation. Through terms like being gentlemanly, playing fair, treating other fellows with charity, being nonjudgmental and helpful, and being an honest (no "cribbing") and conscientious student, we begin to see how the concept of spirit was evolving into what has been called "character building." It became the dominant purpose of physical activity, both in the YMCAs and in its training institute, George Williams

College. There are some critics of the notion of character building, implying that it was nothing more than a means of social control by white, middle-class, Christian males to mold young people into their own image.[32] It was not the case of this urban-based college, providing physical activities for character building to the poor, the working class, the immigrant, the international, the African American. Many became students of the college. When they graduated, they became the character builders of the future. The youth they served identified with them as their role models who went to George Williams College. They followed in their footsteps to seek an education at the college. They would give back to the communities where they were raised. This kind of character building was not intended to screen, protect, or mold into a white, middle-class image. It was about providing opportunity and hope, building self-esteem and teamwork, becoming the unique and best person one can be.

In his first decade at the college in the 1920s, Arthur Steinhaus not only performed groundbreaking research in physiology, but he was a national spokesperson for the direction of physical education as an emerging profession. Whenever he addressed a group of physical educators, he highlighted the idea of physical education for a purpose; he saw that purpose as "a means for good in mind and character as well as body." He was steadfast in that purpose until his retirement in 1967. Halfway through his career at the college, he and his wife, Eva, wrote a three-act play, "The Romance of Service," in 1940, celebrating the college's human service mission.[33] Always colorful in his presentations, he frequently resorted to metaphors to drive home his philosophical point.

Steinhaus was appointed to the faculty on May 23, 1920. He was no stranger to the college, since he was fresh out of the classroom as a student. Charles Elder and G. C. Hawk, his professors, remember him as having an "insatiable interest in biology" when he was their lab assistant. He also became familiar with the laboratory instruments that the college had and did not have. The new faculty member was "a young man with abundant hair flowing high over his forehead, combed in a pompadour." He was a bit nervous meeting with his first class, but was soon relieved to interact with a group of students who already knew him on a first-name basis, because of their prior experience with him in classes.[34]

"Building a Cathedral"
Arthur Steinhaus, student, ('19, '21, '26) and professor, 1928

In an address to YMCA physical educators, he made it clear that they could no longer be a "jock of all trades, master of none"; the age of specialization had come. They would have to become experts, perfecting not only their skills but their scientific knowledge.

However, they were never to think of their specialization, physical education, as an end in itself.

> Think of building a cathedral. The expert stonecutter should never forget, when he is really great at his job of cutting his stones, [that] he is really about the business of building a cathedral. And the physical educator . . . is in the business of helping to build manhood—character, if you prefer. . . . If we physical directors are to function as specialists in the associations' program of manhood building, what shall be our contribution? . . . To live most and serve best should be the end of health education. . . . The cathedral is not a preformed thing. The stones we cut are making it, not molding it. Let us think of character forming by accretion. There are many builders. Let us stick to our task not unmindful that others are also at work. Our stones will not change the shape of the other stones but they will add or detract from the beauty of the total structure.[35]

"Thermometers and thermostats"

Arthur Steinhaus, student, ('19, '21, '26) and professor, 1949

> A biologist who has enjoyed thirty years of close association with some of the best thinkers in group-work theory cannot help getting some ideas about it. Scientists are like thermometers. They merely discover and record facts—about temperature, the composition of food, a person's needs, or anything else. Professional workers, on the other hand, are like thermostats, they do something about temperature, meeting the needs of people. Obviously the thermostat is the more helpful instrument, but with a good thermometer to guide its actions.[36]

"We look not into the narrow end of the funnel"

Arthur Steinhaus, student, ('19, '21, '26) and professor, 1967

> The funnel has a big end and a little end. . . . Too many people learn all their physiology by looking down the narrow funnel end of physical fitness. . . . If you only see it from the little end down, you have a very narrow viewpoint. This is one of the curses of physical education today. . . . This is your opportunity [at GWC], because we look not into the narrow end of the funnel. . . . You have a broad foundation [that] allows you to point the narrow stem of the funnel in many different directions.[37]

"Physical education as a means toward greater ends"

Arthur Steinhaus, student, ('19, '21, '26) and professor, 1967

> Physical education is that which sees, in measures [ensuring] bodily health and the right kind and amount of motor activity, an avenue of approach through which the whole individual may be an influence for good in mind and character, as well as in body. See—mind, character, and body, the triangle appearing there. . . . You become physical educators when you use activities as means toward greater ends. As long as we are thinking of activities as ends in themselves, we are nothing but peddlers of physical activity. . . . You are here in this institution [George Williams College], in an environment [that] has always recognized this basically.[38]

With statements and works such as these, Steinhaus was the interpreter of the philosophy of physical education at George Williams College. On a national and international level, he was known for groundbreaking research supporting health and physical fitness, and for his advocacy for public health. As his research career was launched in the 1920s, students called him "The Pavlov of G.W."

"Arthur Steinhaus: The Pavlov of G.W."

Arthur Steinhaus, student, ('19, '21, '26), professor, circa 1920s

Steinhaus reflected on the research heritage of the GWC student in 1967:

> We started a research program in the physiology of exercise here in the early '20s. At that time there were only three or four institutions that had done anything at all in the area of research in physical education. James Huff McCurdy, brother of the former president of this college, did the first research in physiology of exercise in America.[39]

So early in his career Steinhaus initiated research where his passion for inquiry led him. On a Rockefeller Foundation grant, he focused on research in exercise physiology. His initial project involved a controlled experiment on the effect of exercise on basal metabolism of dogs. Faculty colleague John Fuhrer tells this story of Steinhaus and his early research project:

John Fuhrer, professor, circa 1920s

> His frequent trips to the dog pound in his air-cooled Franklin automobile were followed by students and some faculty members with mixed amusement and misgiving. . . . His students, out of respect, dubbed him "the Pavlov of G.W." He

developed a charter to guide his undertakings: "Anything that throws light on how the habits of living affect health and performance."[40]

Over the span of his career, Steinhaus produced voluminous studies on the physiological processes that contribute to health. His research studies include: the effect of exercise on basal metabolism and weight reduction; the effect of exercise on the digestive tract; the effect of exercise on the heart; the influence of fatigue on acid balance of blood; the effect of smoking, drinking, eating, and sleeping on physiological processes of body; the physiological processes of stress; the effect of coffee on the spontaneous activity of rats; the physiological consequences of relaxation exercises; and the physiological processes of performance enhancement and public education to use relaxation exercises.[41]

However, Steinhaus was not content to keep his research in an ivory tower. In 1967, he said, "This college is the fountainhead from which neuromuscular relaxation is finding its way into education. Previously it was confined to the clinic and the practice of psychiatry. Now we can teach a person to fall asleep in five minutes or less and to blank his mind at will. . . . Tense muscles keep the thought processes active. Neuromuscular relaxation is something anyone can be taught to do."[42]

"Struggle for human well being": Steinhaus, the advocate
Arthur Steinhaus, student, ('19, '21, '26), professor, 1968

Steinhaus was a relentless advocate to promote awareness of health issues. He served on the Federal Trade Commission, addressing concerns about the danger of smoking and the influence of cigarette advertising. He was way ahead of his time in this area. In 1967, an age of war protest and demonstrations, he had this to say to George Williams students:

The real work of helping people to stop smoking or persuading them not to start must be done in every home, in every school, in every college—yes, also at George Williams College. Dr. [Henry] Kallenberg was an advanced thinker in this field. He often expressed the hope that George Williams College, which trains leaders of youth, would make more positive moves on this front. I often wonder if a group of students somewhere will initiate demonstrations against smoking. Today such a group would have more facts and many more supporting organizations than had Dr. Kallenberg to back their convictions and actions. . . . Is it too much to expect a group of young people to march against men who by smoking deprive their families of five to ten years of fatherly care, to stage "walkouts" from classrooms where instructors permit the pollution of air with tobacco smoke? . . . It would take a good deal of guts to fight against a habit that is nurtured by 328 million dollars of advertising in a year, but it would be a struggle for truth and human well being. It would take militant imagination and some strong slogans, such as "This is Marlboro Country" pictured in front of cemeteries, and in powder rooms the reminder "Smoke a cigarette and smell like a camel."[43]

With similar passion, he advocated the ban of dangerous exercise devices and dangerous "weight reducer" programs, and he addressed various groups on national and local television on the dangers of boxing.

"On the Wheaties Box and elsewhere": Steinhaus kudos

Steinhaus and his name appeared in many places for his contribution to health, fitness, sports performance, and sports medicine. He was a founder of the American College of Sports Medicine. He was in good company, when at Springfield College he was on a panel discussing human behavior with Dr. Aldous Huxley, Dr. Norman Cousins, Dr. Huston Smith, and Dr. Margaret Mead.[44] In 1959 his name appeared on America's morning cereal box, Wheaties, "the Breakfast of Champions." He was special advisor to Olympic champion Reverend Bob Richards and the Wheaties Sports Foundation, which "brought his exercises and the college name on scores of millions of Wheaties packages."[45]

Colleges across the country and the world were quick with words of praise for Steinhaus, as were students within the college.

W. W. Bauer, MD, director emeritus, American Medical Association

Arthur Steinhaus combines, in an unusual manner, the important qualities of sound scientific integrity and refreshing originality, and an ability to go straight to the heart of the matter. Steinhaus points out that "onc who sleeps like a log wakes up feeling like one." The cause of health education owes a deep debt to Arthur Steinhaus for his solid research, his original and refreshing approach to communications, and, above all, his courage and integrity and his refusal to compromise or resort to expediency.[46]

Jay Nash, physical educator, teacher, and writer

His conclusions relative to professional boxing and cigarette smoking are now being widely accepted. He has always been a pioneer, ready to accept the responsibility and defend his conclusions, regardless of their popularity.[47]

Mabel Lee, director of physical education, University of Nebraska

> Arthur Steinhaus . . . was the most sought-after speaker by women's groups. A glance at the conference program of the National Association of Physical Education for College Women . . . throughout the past thirty years will reveal no other speaker's name so frequently repeated.[48]

Emery Nelson, ('24), GWC development officer, 1970

> As I traveled across the country for the college and ran into former students of Arthur Steinhaus, they would always inquire about him, about his health, what his program at the present time might be, and always they would say, "Arthur Steinhaus was my greatest teacher."[49]

William Rowe, ('24), YMCA executive, GWC board member

> I was one of Dr. Steinhaus's early students. I entered college in the fall of 1920. It was that year he started his full-time faculty career. I recall some very good teachers I have had in high school and college, but Arthur Steinhaus is the best of them all. My knowledge of biology and physiology, particularly, goes back to him.[50]

John Fuhrer, faculty

Regarding the seat outside his office:

> Students came to feel that it was a privilege to sit in the chair. Few were summoned to sit in it; most students sought to occupy it—they came voluntarily. The few who received a formal call to sit in the chair never felt, on reflection, that they were unfairly dealt with. Often, when a student sat down in the chair, the voltage was high, but when the interview was over, the voltage was low. Desire had been kindled and eagerness set in motion. He had the capacity to perceive ability in his students, to draw it out, and encourage it. He was a friendly counselor on the frustrating problems of students: financial, religious, marital, and vocational.[51]

"Your heritage, opportunity, and challenge"
Arthur Steinhaus, student, ('19, '21, '26), professor, 1967

> I envy you. . . . Sometimes I think of myself as having been like Moses. You know he led the Israelites for forty years through the wilderness. Then when it came time to enter the promised land, God said he was not allowed to get in. That's my fix, you

see, after having spent forty-five years with George Williams, I can only envy you for opportunities that are your promised land. Let me elaborate: a folk dance center of the Middle West, with an international reputation; a volleyball center with a national reputation; . . . with George Falussy here, you are going to set standards for gymnastics on video tape [that] will inspire youth of the nation; . . . the aquatic center; . . . Dr. [Jack] Joseph [leading] a center of emphasis on physical fitness; Jeanne Norris [leading] a center for teaching and research in neuromuscular relaxation, a new phase of physical education; . . . Dr. David Misner and his research to show with correctly designed physical activities a child's reading and writing skills can be improved. . . . When you get into that laboratory and see Dr. Helen Westerberg and her "cold men friends" [the cadavers] lying in that cooler, please remember you are favored. . . .

Be a friend, and find a friend for yourself. . . . I would say that if there is any one thing that can help to cut down on the increasing mass of mental ill health in the United States . . . it is having the right kind of friend at the right time. And by the way, Carl Rogers, who developed non-directive counseling, is the son of a man who was one of the early trustees of this college. Two of the old Roger's sons, brothers of Carl, are now on the board of this college. . . .

Your chances of becoming the general secretary of the largest YMCA in the world are much better. . . . Almost all general secretaries of the Chicago YMCA have been teachers, trustees, or alumni of this institution. Your chance of becoming head of the recreation program in the Chicago Park District is very much in your favor because most of the top and secondary heads of that body have been graduates of this institution. And those who are on the "in" regarding work with delinquent youngsters know that the finest job that is being done anywhere in the country is being done by three alumni of this college [Russell Hogrefe ('41), John Root ('46), and Fred Lickerman ('51)]. I remember well when Johnny Root was a student and "Hogie" [Russell Hogrefe] was a student here, when Lickerman sat where you are sitting now. Are you any different? You have the same opportunities. Of course, we did not know who was going to do it then. They didn't look as important as they do now. They looked very much like you people. . . . There is another young man or woman in this audience who will do something similar in his day and his time. In fact, you must, because you are in George Williams College.[52]

Steinhaus reaches the bodybuilders:
"I wanted to excel at something"

It was the '50s, and pubescent boys across America were mail ordering programs from Charles Atlas, gazing on pictures of Herculean supermen, with advertisements suggesting that they had no idea of the muscular potential of their bodies and to just follow this program. The programs were selling like hotcakes. Ben and Joe Weider were marketing the best scientific foundation for their bodybuilding success, with terms like "professor" and references to their "research center." As the bodybuilding momentum picked up steam in the 1950s, contests like Mr. America, Mr. Universe, Mr. USA, Mr. Olympia, and Mr. World could hardly escape the attention of any adolescent boy. Such was the case for a boy growing into adolescence in Chicago. His name was Bob Gajda.

Bob Gajda, student, ('69, '73)

At age eleven or twelve I would read the Charles Atlas ads. I wanted to excel at something. When I played baseball, they wouldn't let me pitch; I had to be the catcher. I wanted to excel in football at Gordon Tech High School. I wasn't that big, and so I played safety. I thought weight training would increase my efficiency and strength. My coach discouraged it. In fact, my coach, along with my mom, forbade it. The coach brought me to the nuns and made me promise in front of them that I would stop lifting weights. I promised not to lift weights (but I crossed my fingers secretly adding "in the house"). I continued to lift outdoors. When I ended the football season, and things worked out pretty well for me, the coach reminded me, "Aren't you glad you didn't stay with that weight lifting?"

Bob felt his body, strength, and performance was improving, and with it came a fascination for understanding the physiology of the human body.

I was disillusioned with the so-called "science" of some of the body development programs out there. I once went to visit their so-called "research clinic" that I read so much about. I found the door with the sign reading "Research Clinic" led to a broom closet! I met the real thing when I attended a lecture by Arthur Steinhaus on strength and bodybuilding. Bob Hoffman [icon of the York weight-lifting dynasty and the York barbell industry] was there, too. Steinhaus introduced us to isometrics, and we went crazy with it. From then on I knew I wanted to follow the teaching of this man, Steinhaus. I first served in the air force, and when I came back, I worked as a program director for the YMCA. That earned me a scholarship to attend George Williams College, and I majored in physiology under Arthur Steinhaus. My first year I was disappointed, because Steinhaus was in Japan doing research. But when Steinhaus returned, I soaked up everything I could get from him. At the same time I was learning everything I could about physiology, and I was also competing in contests. I did it for the simple thrill of excelling at something.

In the competition area, from 1956 to 1969, Gajda won more than one hundred physique competitions and more than twenty-five weight-lifting titles, including Mr. U.S.A. in 1965 and Mr. America in 1966. He was a Triple Crown winner of the Mr. America, Mr. U.S.A., and Mr. Universe contests. In 1966 he beat Arnold Schwarzenegger for the world's most well-developed body as Mr. Universe.

In the physiology area, Bob learned from Arthur Steinhaus a training concept called Peripheral Heart Action (PHA). Gajda is recognized for this contribution to the science of fitness training, and he always gives credit to his mentor, Steinhaus.

Two familiar names related to fitness training are Bob Hoffman, founder of the York weight-lifting mecca, and Bruce Lee, martial arts expert and actor. In the book *Muscletown USA,* a biographical tribute to Bob Hoffman and the York, Pennsylvania, barbell center, Gajda is recognized:

> The 1966 Mr. America, Bob Gajda, influenced by his premedical training, introduced a training concept called Peripheral Heart Action (PHA), aimed at stimulating uniform development rather than focusing on specific body areas.[53]

Bruce Lee developed his own fitness training program, based on Gajda's PHA system for training:

> One of Lee's favorite strength training and bodybuilding magazines was *Ironman,* which during Lee's heyday . . . [was] constantly featuring cutting-edge training information and shied away from the commercial hype. . . . Lee was becoming more and more interested in researching the effects of a then-radically new weight training system he had read about in *Ironman:* Peripheral Heart Action. . . . The PHA system had been set up to diametrically oppose the more popular flushing or pumping systems of that time. In the late 1960s the leading exponent of the PHA system was a young bodybuilder named Bob Gajda, who explained through a series of articles in *Ironman* (which Lee clipped and saved) that PHA placed its main emphasis on "continuous circulation of the blood." From Gajda's writings (which in turn, were based on the empirical research of physiology pioneer Dr. Arthur Steinhaus), Lee reasoned that if he could keep his circulation at elevated levels throughout the course of his workout, it would tremendously benefit his muscle strength, endurance, and, if the exercises were performed over a full range of motion, flexibility—in other words, the three pillars of total fitness. . . . Exercise systems like PHA were actually forerunners of what is now commonly called circuit training. . . . To this end, Lee created his own program, which hit on these three touchstones of total fitness while still adhering to the guidelines or general principles of PHA.[54]

While Gajda acknowledges Steinhaus as his mentor in exercise physiology, he also acknowledges the entire culture of George Williams College for its philosophy of physical education; it was "a means to greater ends," as Steinhaus would say, the ends of human service. In 1978 Gajda said to a news columnist who was writing a story of him:

> My interest was in social work, and the titles I won were steppingstones for me. The kids were impressed with being around someone who was nationally known. I told them they had a choice between standing on a corner smoking a joint or doing something that helps the body.[55]

In a 2004 interview, when Bob was reminded of that statement, he said, "That statement still stands for me today. . . . And that's Arnold's concept, too."

"Arnold?"

"Arnold Schwarzenegger. We've talked and we share that idea."

Bob tried out his way of doing "social work" by started a weight-lifting group as program director of the Duncan Y. This became a group of men who took it very seriously and became nationally known. The story of the "Duncan Y lifters" is told in a biography of Bob Hoffman:

> So infectious was the spirit generated at York that it spread to Chicago, where Bob Gajda, seized with Olympic-lifting fervor, began to recruit lifters at the Duncan YMCA, dubbed the "York of the Midwest." Such standouts as Winston Binney, Mike Karchut, Fred Schutz, and Chuck Nootens from the upper Midwest . . . began challenging York. Most observers of the 1967 nationals felt that it had the highest grade of competition in recent years.[56]

In 2004 Bob Gajda had a reunion of the "Duncan Y" group at the old site.

> These guys were so nostalgic. They said, "When I walk in, I'm getting goosebumps." We did bodybuilding, weight lifting, boxing, karate, judo. People didn't understand. I had to defend the martial arts. Kids don't get more violent, they get less violent. One of these guys said to me, "Bob you saved my life. My brother got shot for dealing heroin; my other brother jumped in the river and committed suicide; and here I am, a dentist."
>
> At that time the Duncan Y did not understand my kind of "social work." One day a community advocacy group told me they were terminating my "hernia factory," and they were going to replace it with a prison release transitional program and Head Start program. So I went on to work in the public school system and as a consultant for a drug abuse program.

Gajda transitioned into owning and operating rehabilitation and performance-enhancement training centers for the public, including but not limited to a long string of high-profile individuals and teams: many players of the Super Bowl champion Chicago Bears (Jim McMahon, Mike Singletary, Gary Fencik), celebrity tennis athletes

(Jimmy Conners, Tracy Austin, John McEnroe, Andrea Jaeger), the Chicago Sting, the Chicago Blackhawks, the Harvard tennis team, and the 1984 and 1988 U.S. Olympic volleyball teams. He is widely recognized for these roles, but when Bob talks about using his reputation as a stepping-stone for service, he reaches back to his years at George Williams College.

> I remember Arthur Steinhaus and his wife. They would have me over for tea. They took a genuine interest in me and my future dreams. I wanted to become a doctor, and Steinhaus recommended I specialize in endocrinology, the research of the future. . . . I felt George Williams College was a place where everybody wanted to help people. I remember words used at the college, like "serving humanity" and "civilization builders." I remember I took a course at the University of Chicago while at GWC. It was a theology course, and I remember there were different Greek meanings for the word *love*. Among them was agape. "Where there is hatred let me sow love"— an ideal I saw in the college, the way I grew up, what I believe.[57]

"Physical education was the instrument . . . to do group work"

Henry Labatte, student, ('53), YMCA executive

Henry Labatte was a Canadian who came to George Williams College, like so many before him and after him, because the college was, in his mind, "absolutely unique" in living out this philosophy of physical education. It was about the integration of mind, body, and spirit, and it served a greater end, "an influence for good," as Steinhaus would say. Henry says the Canadians from the YMCA got the message:

> The folklore of the American YMCA movement was that George Williams College was kind of the West Point of the YMCA. It was the place to go. People came mostly from the West and Midwest to George Williams. Some of the YMCA people in the East went to Springfield, but George Williams was the outstanding educational institution for the Y, both in Canada and the U.S. Springfield prepared students to be teachers in physical education and such. George Williams had some of that, but not like Springfield. That was all in the East. George Williams was "group work." As a group worker you used many other disciplines besides physical education, but you used physical education also. Physical education at George Williams was not just about body. We were using a "method" called "physical education." There was a physical education focus, and a group-work focus, and they were both together. Physical education was the instrument we used to do group work, community work. In that sense, the college was absolutely unique. It had a philosophy of what it means

to be in human service. I wish we could create those educational environments today, not to duplicate the past, but the philosophy of what it means to be in the human services. It was a big loss when physical education got separated from group work.[58]

"A concern for human development"

James Brown, student, ('48, '49)

Henry was speaking of students in physical education who came before and after him at George Williams College. One was James Brown, a student of the class of 1949. Brown worked within the Chicago Board of Education for his life's work. For nineteen of those years, he was the coach of DuSable High School (on Chicago's South Side) where the basketball teams went to state competition. In 1970, as he reflected on his association with the college, he had this to say:

> I wanted to coach to stay close to young people, to suffer with them, to rejoice with them. In those years we sent two hundred kids to universities and colleges. Sixty-five percent of them were graduated. In 1968 I came on to the Chicago Board of Education. Among the GWC alums I see are Eugene McLean ['59], football coach at Gage Park High School; Jim Foreman ['58], basketball coach at Dunbar; Larry Hawkins ['56], at Carver High. McNair Grant ['50] was the first black district superintendent for the Chicago Board of Education. I remember GW as twenty to twenty-five years ahead of most schools in group work. . . . There was a human concern for human development and personality development.[59]

Physical education and human relations

James Gleason, student, ('57) and trustee

GWC trustee James Gleason, a physical education major, moved into human relations training, believing the college prepared him to do both well, prepared him for his life's work. First, he worked in the Wabash YMCA.

> After serving in World War II, I came to Chicago to work in the Wabash Y and started in graduate work at George Williams. I never had a better friend there than John Fuhrer, and of course I remember Karl Zerfoss and Hedley Dimock. When I came back as executive of the Wabash Y, I finished my master's at GW.
>
> I had one of the longest tours as a GW student—eleven years! My wife, Gloria Williams ['50] is an alumna of the college. After twenty-nine years with the YMCA, I was asked to come to R. Donnelley in 1969 as manager of personnel development. This was a new position in the company, growing out of the difficulties at the time

with the death of Dr. Martin Luther King [Jr.]. I refused, however, to take a job where I am restricted to working with Blacks alone. Personnel relations don't divide by Black, and White; they are problems of employee-supervisor relations. I'm bringing experience to this job, the whole range of experiences I've had in the Y and academic preparation at GW, especially in sensitivity training. I'm involving employees in the process to help them solve problems. I get a great deal of personal satisfaction in helping people deal out problems. I guess I'm hung up on that.[60]

Using sports to "get their attention": A day on the South Side

Larry Hawkins, student, ('56, '72)

What Larry Hawkins does perhaps best represents the "absolutely unique" philosophy of physical education that Henry Labatte and others said characterized George Williams College. If the term *character development* were used to describe the purpose of physical education, it would be targeted to disadvantaged youth, to develop self-esteem and values that would help them to move out of a cycle of poverty into a broader world of opportunity. One of those values was the importance of a college education: to consider college, to gain the skills necessary to get there, and to stay there. How could athletics and coaching be used for this purpose? Larry Hawkins saw opportunities in the role of "teacher-coach." He had ideas and the motivation to make them happen.

In 1968 student Al Boykin credited Larry Hawkins for influencing the direction of his life. After graduation from GWC, Hawkins became the basketball coach at Carver High School. Out of that experience, he initiated a youth development project to encourage disadvantaged inner-city youth to go to college and develop the skills they would need to get there. In 1967 Larry brought youth like Al to the Williams Bay campus for one summer month to prepare for the option of a college education. Students focused on testing, using standardized exams, tutoring in math, public speaking, and English. Al had this to say:

"I didn't think about going to college. I was going to join the marines. I didn't work on my grades at Carver High School. I didn't know how to use my time. But the coach's project helped me a lot. There ought to be ten more like him right now because programs like these are needed very much. Kids start to think about college and what they're going to do. They're not lost. I want to keep on doing this kind of thing—like the coach—maybe someday back in my old Chicago neighborhood at Altgelt. I found out that I'd better go on to school."

"I wanted to go to George Williams College, because the coach went there. If he went there and he's doing this program, I thought maybe I can too." Al majored in physical education, like his coach.[61]

Out of the Lake Geneva youth development project, Larry founded and directed the Institute for Athletics and Education in 1972. Building on this initiative, he became the director of the University of Chicago's Office of Special Programs to serve the surrounding community of the University of Chicago in Hyde Park [which was once the GWC neighborhood also]. Through Hawkins's program, hundreds of students took college-prep Saturday courses to find the motivation and to give them a better chance of success in college. Sports activities, which were a part of the Saturday program, were, as Hawkins would say, "a way to get their attention."

I met Larry Hawkins in March 2005 to hear his story of George Williams College and to get a personal tour of the old South Side neighborhood where George Williams College was located. Coincidentally "March Madness" had reached a feverish pitch in Illinois, as the University of Illinois basketball team defied seasonal expectations and were going to the finals. For a brief moment everyone in the state wanted to be in on the identity and the glory. It did not matter if you went to the university. Everyone wore orange, everyone was a "Fighting Illini." Everyone was living out Larry's idea of what can happen, not only to athletes, their parents, and coach, but also the entire school, community, and state, when you have a successful team. The idea of who actually "has" this successful team begins to expand. Everyone felt this team was "ours," and we were all feeling pretty good about ourselves. We were also wide open to the words and magical influence of "the coach." Whatever he said and did was golden.

Larry picked me up at the Ogilvie Train Station (the old Northwestern station), bearing trains coming from the western suburbs, the direction George Williams traveled after the college left Hyde Park in 1966. Off we went to take a fresh look at the old George Williams College neighborhood, the neighborhood where Larry grew up, a neighborhood that has defined the history, culture, and character not only of the college but the entire city of Chicago. The neighborhood is going through a renaissance and is proudly called by its historic name, the "Bronzeville" area.

Larry recounted: "Over here [on Thirty-seventh Street] was Phillips High School, where I went to school. [Wendell Phillips High School also produced the core members of the Harlem Globetrotters who came out of Chicago, not Harlem.] There were only two high schools for blacks in Chicago at the time. Phillips was one, and then there was what was called 'the new Phillips' high school or what became DuSable High School. . . . Over here [on Prairie Avenue and Thirty-first Street, now a surrounding park green of Douglas Elementary School] was where my house was, the place where I grew up. . . . My family migrated to Chicago in the '20s from the little town of Liberty, Mississippi. . . . From my home, my friends and I would walk 'the golden triangle' to play basketball at one of three gyms. The first point of the triangle was the Wabash YMCA, the only YMCA for blacks, a place whose leaders, for the most part, came from George Williams College. The second point was the Southeast Side Boys Club. Some of the Harlem Globetrotters came out of that gym. I played on the Brown Bombers, the team that competed with those guys on the Harlem Globetrotters. The third point of the triangle was the Elliot Donnelly Youth Center."

As we drove by each point of the triangle, Larry continued to point out the other neighborhood sites from his youth. There were the gyms in churches, the Bronzeville Military Academy gym. As I was getting a tour of Larry's world growing up, I was getting a tour of the neighborhood gyms. Of course, there were other sites.

"Over there was the elegant Sutherland. . . . Over there was the Regal. People would dress up, and hop from club to club. Later, those who could afford the nightlife moved further out. . . . Over here [on Forty-seventh Street] was the Chili Max, a little dive where all the performers from the Regal would come after the show, hang out, and play."

But Larry's world was basketball. Growing up in the '40s, it was what he knew best, where he excelled. His community seemed so vibrant, yet self-contained, walled off from the rest of Chicago by "the color line."

"In my days, it extended from Cottage [Avenue] to Dearborn [Street], east and west, and from Twenty-sixth Street to Fifty-fifth Street, north and south. Rarely did I move outside those boundaries."

We headed for Larry's office at the University of Chicago. (Larry is called "Doc" by neighborhood youth because he earned a PhD). Across the street was the School of Social Service Administration, where we stopped briefly. I noticed a university publication, *Working Together: A Guide to Community Outreach,* proudly displayed under glass, with a picture of Larry Hawkins on the cover. We crossed the Midway to his office. Down the hall, a map of the United States was on display, with lines reaching to outstanding colleges and universities throughout the country where all the students and athletes who had come out of his college prep program were attending. It was impressive. We sat down, and Larry told more of his story.

I came from Phillips High School, a totally black school. I went to George Williams College because a guy named Alexander McDade, who worked for the Chicago Area Project, suggested "that's the place you ought to go if you want to learn to do this kind of work." I followed him around a lot. He was a community worker. He coached teams, painted walls, managed the gym—he did whatever it took. The gym was in a big brownstone church called Hartville Methodist Church. . . . He would take me around to talk to parents. He argued that this was important to understand the work. He did some training at George Williams but didn't get a degree. . . . When I was young, McDade was my guy, but once I got to George Williams, I realized that maybe 80 percent of the people who were in group work or physical education in the public schools, YMCAs, or Boys and Girls Clubs were from George Williams.

I didn't have the money to go to George Williams straight out. So I went to a city college and got an [associate's] degree, but I ended up at George Williams. Always my aim was to get there, because that's what Mac said. He said, "I've been saving the money for you to go to George Williams, but if I read you right, you're never going to use it." He was right about that. I tried lots of jobs, and I continued to work with Mac a lot. In summers we would do a little camp in Marseilles, Illinois—five series of ten days each. I was the "assistant cook," which I learned meant cleaning the pots. Always my goal was to make enough money to get to George Williams. I finally got there in '51. Then I got drafted in '53 and went off for two years. I came back in '55 and finished my work in '56.

The first teacher that made a sharp impression on me was Karl Zerfoss. He was from Georgia, and he had this southern accent. He saw what my learning problem was and helped me, but he did it in a way I could understand. His whole point of view was not "you didn't do that right," but "how can I help you to do it better?" Then he engaged me in talking about basketball. . . . He used that as a way to get my attention. He knew that was what I knew about. He wrote in the YMCA *Journal of Physical Education* about "the guidance point of view." That is the basis of all I've talked about in the last thirty years. My point was that coaching is not so much winning the game, but using the game to get the attention of the youngster, to get your group together, to move them along. . . .

I liked Arthur Steinhaus. He took technical things and made them understandable. He had really sharp arguments with people about boxing. He could tell you about that bone in the base of the skull. All the instructors knew you by name. They knew everything about you. Helen Westerberg was very good. She was not so much a teacher, as a person who guided you through a project. William Fenstemacher was the guy who taught us professional values. The whole time I coached, I always wore a shirt, tie, and jacket. That came directly out of his teaching. If you want people to treat you as a professional, dress like it. He took an interest in you as a total person. Sylvanus Duvall, our religion teacher, would take us up to Lake Geneva, and we would talk about the riots going on. Then there was the music teacher, Harmon Bro [professor of humanities and English]. I was always crazy about music. We had a barber shop quartet. We would go out and sing at parties, things like "Daddy Get Your Baby Out of Jail." Casey [Ken "Casey" Clarke ('53)] was another whole thing. He came out of Gary, Indiana. That we came to be friends was kind of interesting—he from Gary, me from the South Side. We have a friendship that lasted our lives. Casey went to the [University of Illinois]. When we had meetings about athletics, I would call Casey to see if he was free. Two of the first kids that graduated from Carver High I sent to the University of Illinois for Casey to look after.

When I graduated, I went to Carver High School as a basketball coach Oh, it was like being in a bubble! We had a good relationship with the principal and the central administrative office. It was like working in a small town, a community. After 130th Street, you would have to go all the way down to about Sixty-fifth [Street] to find another kind of black community. Everything else was essentially white, straight up and down, in Roseland.

Early on, it [a philosophy about coaching] hadn't all clicked in. I'd been taught it but didn't understand it. You're into winning games. In 1962 we lost [the state championship] by one point, and in 1963 we won by a bad pass. Centralia and Decatur were the schools we played. Cazzie Russell was one of the guys who was on the team. Later he played in the NBA with the Knicks, and then the Bulls. I remember a researcher who interviewed students to find out how they felt after a big-game win on campus. She called it "BIRG," or "Basking in Reflected Glory." She found that everyone—the kids, the entire school—feels good about themselves after a win. [We paused to note on this day in March Madness that it seemed all of Illinois had an attack of "BIRG."]

Well, at Carver High, it was a matter of figuring out what was my real task there. Working in the school was one thing, and I enjoyed that. But what I figured is, we've got to be sure the kids get to see other kinds of things. Our kids always expected to be going somewhere. In our basketball schedule you were able to choose six or seven practice games. I wanted these kids to meet other kinds of people.

"Cookies and milk," Larry chuckled. "We started to put out cookies and milk for the two teams after the game. The first time, our guys ate them all. I had to explain they were the hosts. . . . Then it began to be what I thought it could be. The kids from the two teams would talk to one another. Recently I talked to a guy who was on the Carver team. 'What I remember about high school,' he said, 'is the cookies and milk. That's when I got a chance to talk to a guy [who] I only watched play before.'"

We would play in these little towns, like down in Pittsfield, Missouri. . . . We would bring our kids down there and there would be a big sign—"Welcome Carver High School." They would invite the kids for dinner, and they would socialize. We would go down to Christian Brothers [High School] in Quincy, Illinois, because the two teams would get together. The game was part of it, but the whole of it was the experience.

But then the kids went off to school, and they really weren't prepared for it. I thought it was my fault, because whatever it is I asked them to do, they did it. Not only they did it, but their parents did it. We had a parents' group throughout the time at Altgelt. [Altgelt Gardens is a public housing project whose students would go to Carver High. It also happens to be where Illinois Senator Barack Obama did community organizing in his earlier years.] We would tell the students, "I'm going to talk to your parents, and if they say you're not taking the garbage out or whatever, I'm going to give them your uniform. In order to get it back, you're going to have to do for them." Oh, they thought I was crazy. The kids didn't like it, but the parents loved it. Of course, then the parents came out a lot. . . . At the end of the game, I would talk to the parents. They would get in their two cents worth. "You should have done this, you should have played that." I got some pretty good ideas from them. The team was what the community had. And I didn't want the team over here, and the community over there. . . . Some of the kids were rough and tumble. I would argue to the principal, "We've got to let them in." "Yeah, but they're going to cause trouble," he'd say. "No, they're going to cause trouble if they're out there," I'd say. "Just bring them in. Give them a place." I remember one guy would say, "Look, my little brother, he's a good player. I want you to watch out for him." . . . It really was, at least in my lifetime, a community spirit—a small town and their team. After the game, if there was something students had feelings about, we would keep the students there to talk about it. They would all stay. You know, there was only one way in and one way out of the gym. This was about parents, a community, and kids. The feeling was "this is our team." Al Beals had a store. He would say, "What do you guys need?" I would make sure there was a seat for Al at the game. And there were others. When they see me as the point person, then I can talk to kids and parents about other kinds of things. If the team is successful, everyone feels good about the team, the school and the community.

In the thirty-five years to follow, Larry continued to develop what he calls his own kind of group work and community organization. As he began to focus on preparing athletes for college, he developed first the Institute for Athletics, where, as early as 1968, kids would combine summer camping and college preparation. At first he brought them to the Lake Geneva College Camp. Then the University of Chicago hired him under the Office of Special Projects to develop an ongoing college prep program for youth in the neighborhood. Many times the University of Chicago has named Larry Hawkins as their partner in "being a good neighbor" to the community surrounding the university, the same neighborhood where George Williams College was located. As a kid, Larry learned from his mentor, McDade, that working with the parents and supporting them was the key to community development. Larry founded the Parent Athletic Support Team and the National Parents Committee on Youth Sports to encourage parental involvement in their children's sports and more importantly in their overall development. For over thirty years Larry has had parent meetings; they occur every second Sunday.

There are about one hundred and ninety kids in the Saturday schools holding both classes and tutorials. The college prep program is not just for athletes now, but I still use sports camps and athletics as a means to get the attention of youth. We would get their attention early, when they are little kids. At the end of summer school, they would have a sports camp. The parents come, because they like to see their kids in sports camp. Many times this was the first time "the naturals" were identified. If you saw a kid who had a natural ability to run, the adults would sponsor a track club and encourage the kids. They developed a program in track and field with one hundred kids in it. These kids would stay in the program and become the future athletes. Once you have their attention, and the parents' attention, you can direct them to other things, like planning and working to go to college. . . . They stay for life. They come into a process. When they start at fifth grade, they have a lot of time on their hands. It keeps them from drugs and gangs.

Larry has been a spokesperson for his philosophy, and he has been heard for decades.[62] In the '70s a University of Chicago reporter did a story on Larry. When Larry described the skills needed by a coach, he said:

He must have far greater skills than only a knowledge of the fundamentals of his sport. He ought to be trained in the areas of guidance, counseling, community organization, and group work. The coach, in short, should be a sort of hybrid social worker, both teacher and athlete.[63]

In 1966 he wrote a column published in the *Chicago Sun Times* of his concern for community support of student athletes:

Higher standards, academic excellence, and stricter college requirements may be the phrases educators across the country are using lately, but for many students there are other more rudimentary concerns to resolve before we can even talk higher standards. Given the severity of the dropout rate in Chicago, there is something to be said for the near-zero dropout rate among athletes—even among athletes not performing so well academically. If finding ways to motivate people to stay in school is a primary goal, it is time to reevaluate school sports. We must be careful about how we penalize and prohibit a students' participation in the very school programs that have been proven to motivate young people to feel good about themselves, to stay in school, keep out of gangs, and be proud of their school and community.

Academic eligibility begins with the question: How can we help all students play on a team and achieve academically? The teacher, counselor, athletic director, principal, and parents provide the support system to help the coach achieve his goals with each athlete. The term "teacher-coach" is a fine name for coaches to live up to. The coach who views himself as a "teacher-coach" will produce student-athletes. . . .

When we can recognize the value of the student-athlete to his parents, his peers, and to the entire school environment we will have identified a potent motivational link between our youth and their school and community.[64]

In our interview Larry continued, "I would press the administration at high schools, 'Do you have a philosophy about what you do in sports and physical education? A philosophy that would guide you in making choices about what students need to learn for life? A philosophy of the same importance as math or English?' We don't have 'teacher-coaches' with a philosophy anymore, because George Williams is not here anymore. We can continue to grow teachers, but we lost the philosophers!"

"Whenever you have a sport or any activity where an adult and group of kids come together around a common interest, something good is going to happen—if the leader-coach has a clear role. You move kids from being an outsider to an insider, and then you can move them toward what they need for life. That's where the teaching occurs. . . . Of course I sound like a group worker. That's what it is. I tell everyone who asks what skills you need to become a teacher-coach. I tell them you need group work skills."

Larry noticed a picture I had with me, from the Hyde Park days. "Oh, there are Paul and Gretel." So many people I interviewed referred with great affection to the Dunsings, or more commonly "The Dancing Dunsings." Paul and Gretel were a German couple who demonstrated skill and passion for folk dancing, which they enthusiastically shared with George Williams College students. It seemed everyone was "dancing with the Dunsings."

The students were so good, they ended up touring Europe and appearing on *The Ed Sullivan Show* in New York on their way. But what would a young African American growing up on the South Side of Chicago, interested in basketball, surrounded by the very best of Chicago blues and jazz, see in a German couple teaching folk dances? That was my unspoken thought. Larry's only comment was, "Anyone with a box of records who could move people around had to be good." Then he became wistful. A picture memory came to him:

It was a perfect evening. I and another student were invited to the Dunsings' home for dinner. Afterward it began to snow heavily. There we were, gazing out the window, watching the snow fall silently, peacefully. It was a wonder.[65]

Our interview concluded, we hopped in the van. We drove to Fifty-third [Street] and Drexel [Avenue] to take a look at the "old shoe factory." Nothing was left of it. The building was torn down and replaced with rather chic looking townhomes. There was nothing concrete to grab onto, nothing to evoke memories of a past legacy. We quickly moved on, past Drexel Square, then past the Illinois Central Railway station. My mind quickly skipped to an image I read about. It was Emmett Till's mother kissing him goodbye at this station, as off he went on the Illinois Central to visit his grandfather in Money, Mississippi. The next time she saw him, it was a brutally disfigured body in a closed box. When she displayed that body to the world, the civil rights movement ignited. A tune was buzzing in my mind. Suddenly, in synchronous time, Larry and I were humming the refrain, "Riding on the City of New Orleans. . . . Illinois Central Monday morning rail. . . . "

Back on the commuter train traveling to the western suburbs, I tried to fit together the pieces of this day: Alexander McDade, the community organizer who would personally put up the money to see that a promising young man would get to George Williams College; Karl Zerfoss, the southern-accented white teacher of the college that connected to this African American from Chicago's South Side and opened him to learning through a shared interest in something the student knew about—basketball; cookies and milk; and the Carver High coach's desire to take his team to small towns across the state and elsewhere to meet and interact with "a different kind of people"— just as important as winning games, he says; town meetings with parents and community after the games. Pieces of a blooming philosophy were coming together, a philosophy about youth and community development—character development, if you will—and how sports fit into the picture. And then there were the Dunsings and the snowfall. What was that about? Could it be how they opened their home to students like Larry and shared what they loved and knew best through the movement of folk dancing? Is that how Larry became an enthusiastic learner? Was that the common thread—a philosophy of relationships and learning; meeting people where they are, in what they're excited about, and taking them to another level of development? Yes, that's what Larry said, "You have to meet people where they are and then help take them where you think they should and could be. You're not going to get to them by standing and yelling from the place you think they should be. You have to go to them."[66]

In 1972 Larry Hawkins went on to the new suburban Downers Grove campus to get his master's degree. Ten years after the college moved to Downers Grove, Larry mused, "The 'old' college and the current college seem to be very different philosophically. I am not sure how to describe the new college in terms of my undergraduate preparation."[67]

Larry thought the college was too influenced by its new environment, trying to be like their liberal arts neighbor colleges. Others noticed a developing chasm between the old and the new environment of the college, and wondered whether it was influencing the philosophy of the college, its reason for being. A deep-seated chasm between city and suburb also was developing. The suburb of Downers Grove, only twenty miles or so from the city of Chicago, seemed light years away in the late '60s. The suburbs were just beginning to spring from cornfields, marshes, and open land. The separate worlds were divided by multiple boundaries—boundaries of race, ethnicity, social class, and lifestyle, to name a few. Where there are chasms that separate, the action-oriented ones build bridges.

"Spanning the abyss" from city to suburb

Herb Smith, student, ('70)

Herb Smith was a student in the camping and recreation program in the Hyde Park campus. He was in his senior year when he moved with the college to the Downers Grove campus. Herb's personal experience, heart, and mission remained tied to his roots in the city of Chicago, though his feet were now planted in the western suburbs. He came with experience in the Chicago parks program and wanted to continue to serve inner-city youth through recreation. Now in Downers Grove he could envision a mission for suburban youth. Would there be some way to serve the whole Chicago community—city and suburb—and the youth growing up in two different worlds? Could a recreational program "span the abyss" and prepare both suburban and inner-city generations of youth for the world of the future?

Herb heard of a new program called Urban Gateways. Could this be a way that the newly transplanted GWC could participate in building bridges? The purpose was "to create bridges of communication between the inner-city and suburban youth" in a year-round program. In the summer of 1968 over 1,250 inner-city and suburban youth, ages five through thirteen, would learn, have fun, and share adventures together with art projects, recreational activities, and field trips. The campers were paired in a buddy system by age—one suburban with one city youngster. The counselors were neighborhood youth corps aides, suburban teen volunteers, and George Williams College students and other college students. Herb brought the city youth to the GWC Downers Grove campus for their suburban experience, and in the city they met in churches and schools. George Williams faculty were quick to give Herb a hand. Faculty member and swimming coach Ed Langbein led his staff in giving the campers swimming lessons at the college pool. Some of the teen junior counselors planned to enroll in GeorgeWilliams College and become college aides in the Urban Gateway project in coming years. The kids as well as the parents enjoyed the experience so much that in the winter parents sponsored "reunions" in both the city and the suburbs.[68]

"You can go home again"

Herb Smith, student, ('70)

When Herb Smith graduated from GWC's new campus, he returned to the South Side of Chicago to work. He helped set up a planned community facility and recreation program in its South Commons development. Then he went on to teach physical education at the University of Chicago's Laboratory School and coach basketball and baseball. At this time Herb became a graduate student in social work at the University of Chicago's School of Social Service Administration. While a graduate student, he was also an assistant to the vice president for planning at the university. He designed a year-round recreational program for youth in the neighborhood surrounding the university and "sold" the program to the University of Chicago's Board of Trustees for the university to sponsor. How did he do it? According to Herb, "I used the principles I learned from Jim Coleman and Jack Joseph and Bill Hughes at GW. . . . You can change anything, provided the resources and process are there, and the change will be meaningful."

Herb got to pick the site to implement his recreational program with a staff of twelve University of Chicago graduate and undergraduate students and other volunteers. And what site did Herb pick? "You can go home again." Herb picked the old swimming pool of George Williams College at the former Hyde Park campus. It was called Boucher Hall in 1971, when Herb initiated the program, but to Herb it was still the George Williams College site where he started his undergraduate work in health and physical education. And Herb was not just drawing on memories of the pool at George Williams College to implement his program. "I had to draw from everything I learned at George Williams," he concluded.[69]

Team Sports and Whole Person Development

The programs of Larry Hawkins and Herb Smith clearly represent the philosophy of physical education at George Williams College. The programs met important needs in the college's old neighborhood of Hyde Park in Chicago. The college's esteemed neighbor in the old neighborhood, the University of Chicago, recognized their worth and supported their efforts to carry them forward when George Williams College moved to the suburbs in 1966. As the college moved, so did the bar for excellence in team competition, physical fitness, skill development, and recreation as entertainment. The bar moved up. Now women wanted equal opportunity to develop their potential. This was a new era; higher and broader expectations made it all the more difficult to promote integration and balance in all things at once: educational development, holistic body-mind-spirit development, skill development, character development, team sport development, spreading the circle of competitive sports wider, and using physical education in the service of community development. The strains could be felt on the college campus.

A dilemma: College teacher or Olympic volleyball coach?

Jim Coleman, professor, 1968–1979

The legacy of George Williams College in the area of sports is probably strongest in volleyball. For many, if you say "sports—George Williams College," you say "volleyball," and then you say "Jim Coleman." There is one more word association with Jim Coleman and the volleyball world—"the Olympic Games." Jim was known worldwide as "one of the true American volleyball coaching pioneers of the modern age, particularly at the international level."[70] Overall, Jim took part in seven Olympic Games, eight Pan American Games, five World Cups, and six World Championships. He was part of the coaching/advisory staff during U.S. volleyball's greatest era, 1984–1988, when the U.S. men's team won the Olympic gold medal at both the 1984 Olympic Games in Los Angeles and the 1988 Olympic Games in Seoul, Korea. He was also on the coaching/advisory staff of the 1985 World Cup, the 1986 World Championships, and the 1987 Pan American Games. This five-year run of victories crowned the U.S. team as the best men's team in the history of the sport. Coleman has said that his favorite memory was the victory ceremony at the 1988 Olympic Games because it was the culmination of a great five-year dynasty.[71] Leaders involved with the U.S. men's national volleyball team and the Olympics see Jim Coleman as a pioneer leader and mentor.

Doug Beal, U.S. men's national team head coach in 2001 conveyed the following:

> Jim Coleman meant more to me personally than anyone I have ever encountered in the sport. He represented everything positive, and he motivated and guided so many people and so much that was good and joyous in our world. I can't think of any coach [who] hasn't been touched by Jim Coleman. I seriously doubt that we will ever see anyone again who will combine Jim's technical knowledge, his inquisitiveness, his personality, and enthusiastic energy. His contributions are timeless.[72]

Marv Dunphy, head coach of the 1988 U.S. men's gold medal Olympic volleyball team had this to say about Jim:

> I can't think of anybody that has done more for the sport in their time than he has. . . . It was just special to be around someone with that kind of passion. I think where we are and where we are going in this sport is due in large part to him. Everybody has their pioneers, and he was the guy.[73]

Finally, Al Manaco Jr., president, U.S. Volleyball Association offered this reflection:

> All of us who are in senior leadership positions with USVBA today were mentored in some form by Jim in our earlier years. Without Jim we would not have national

teams, statistical analysis, comprehensive rules, and the coaches, administrators, and officers that lead us today.[74]

In 1979 Jim Coleman had to make a choice: Did he want to continue teaching and coaching volleyball at George Williams College, or would he pursue his dream to develop the U.S. men's volleyball team into a gold medal contender? Jim was prepared and willing to do both well. Jim joined the faculty of George Williams College in 1968. He learned the game of volleyball from his father, George Coleman ('39), who was on the staff of the Springfield, Ohio YMCA. Prior to coming to GWC, he taught chemistry and other science classes at the University of Kansas, where he started a successful volleyball program. Before GWC, he already coached the U.S. men's team to the championship of the Pan American Games in Winnipeg, Canada. He also was the first American to go overseas to study volleyball in Poland, and as a result he became noted with European teams. He was on the national board of directors of the U.S. Olympic Volleyball Committee, tutored the U.S. squad that opposed the Soviet Union in a series of games in Canada in 1965, and competed in the world championships that year. He was already on the international rules committee. So before he signed on with GWC, Jim was already visible as one of the top Americans in the U.S. Volleyball Association.[75]

Jim had already spent twenty years teaching, with ten years under his belt at GWC, when he was faced with his decision. He was just as passionate about being a teacher of the sciences as he was about coaching volleyball. Jim's academic expertise was in chemistry and physics, and those were the areas he taught as a professor at George Williams College. Students who were attracted to the volleyball program at GWC because of his visibility in that area were going to get strong academic preparation in the physical sciences, because he was as strong a teacher as he was a coach. One of his students, Jerry Angle, commented:

> The curriculum was so demanding for a physical education major. . . . We were only three hours short of a premed degree! Jim Coleman was known to be a demanding teacher, teaching difficult courses in the sciences, but he coupled that with commitment and care for his students. . . . Jim would literally stay up day and night tutoring students so they could achieve academically. He was just as interested in their academic achievement as he was with how they were performing on the volleyball court.[76]

Jim had the same high standards for the sport of volleyball. He expected nothing but the best from the best athletes that the entire country had to offer. Preparing for Olympic competition was an opportunity to show that, with proper training, Americans were in reach of the gold medal, if not a gold medal dynasty. Jim would have preferred to meet both challenges—to be a college teacher and be an Olympic volleyball coach. He did it before, when he was the Olympic team coach preparing the team for the Mexico City games. However, that was only a three-month commitment he could fulfill in the summer, when he was not teaching at GWC. The expectations for an Olympic coach were higher, as were the expectations for the performance of the U.S. Olympic team. The U.S. Olympic Volleyball Committee wanted Jim, but they also wanted a full-time commitment from him for a year and a half to prepare for the 1980 Olympic Games. They wanted him to come to Ohio to engage in training for that entire period.

Jim requested a leave of absence from GWC for a year and a half. This put the college in a difficult position. The college administration explained they would have to make a decision. "With the students in mind" and "what was best for them," the administration told Jim that he would have to resign and give up tenure if he made the decision to go to Ohio. The college response did not sit well with some people inside and outside the college. The *Chicago Tribune* published an article in the sports section, commenting, "George Williams College was apparently not overcome with Olympic fever."[77]

Should the college have had the foresight that this would be good public relations for them? Should they have contracted with a temporary faculty member to cover Jim's classes, to coach, mentor, and advise graduate students on their thesis work? Should the Olympic committee have been a little more yielding, recognizing that it was a difficult commitment to pull anyone from a full-time teaching position to work full time for a year and a half commitment to the Olympic team? And what about the Olympic athletes? Was it a good idea for them to be dropping out of college for a year and a half to prepare for the Olympics? Was it wise for Jim to resign and go with being the Olympic coach for a year and a half?

A gaze into a crystal ball of the future would reveal a U.S. men's Olympic volleyball team dynasty brewing, with gold on the way in 1984 and 1988. At the same time, the entire Downers Grove campus of George Williams College folded in 1985, and his faculty colleagues there were scrambling for positions elsewhere. After the Olympic coaching stint, Jim secured positions at Whitman College and Washington State University as women's volleyball coach from 1981 to 1984. Hindsight might say yes, Jim made the wise decision.

Webster's dictionary defines *leisure* as "having spare time, not working for a living." *Recreation* means "refreshment in body and mind after work." *Sport* means "any activity that gives enjoyment or recreation; a pastime, a diversion." Beginning in the 1970s, the definitions do not hold. Jim Coleman's dilemma about sports and coaching had to do with the complexity and standards of excellence in sports, requiring full-time commitment. The Olympic athletes also were required to make full-time commitments to training for Olympic volleyball. Jim made a statement himself about the dilemma of what sports had become: "The game is definitely different than the one I played. . . . I wouldn't be allowed on the court today." He questioned the definition of *amateur* in Olympic competition.

Today, in an age where skill is what counts, requiring full-time devotion, questions of full and integrated youth development linger. In another sport, the National Basketball Association recruits the very young just out of high school to play professional basketball. They go to the Olympics. Questions arise: Can you play a professional sport when you are still a youth, still developing in body, mind, spirit, and character? And what are the "greater ends," as Steinhaus would say, of physical development and activity?

There were others before Coleman who brought the sport of volleyball to high visibility for George Williams College.

Other volleyball legends

Kenneth "Casey" Clarke, student, ('53)

Kenneth Clarke was a volleyball athlete at GWC before Coleman's time. Ken was a student at the Hyde Park campus. He was on the 1952 GWC volleyball team that went to the national championship. In 1981 Casey became a part of the U.S. Olympic Committee, serving as assistant executive director and safety officer. It was Ken's job to prepare the Olympic athletes for media attention. Players from lower profile sports, such as volleyball players, were not as familiar with facing the media, and Casey saw to it that they were just as prepared for media attention. "One of the biggest challenges was to give balance to all the sports," Casey said. "Something that doesn't bring in lots of spectator money should be given the same amount of attention that a sport with lots of marketability gets." Clarke showed his commitment to equal opportunity in another way also, through his involvement with the Paralympics, a competition for the world's top athletes who are physically challenged. The Paralympics follow the Olympic Games. Clarke, a member of the National Wheelchair Hall of Fame, worked with quadriplegics and was the head coach of the "Gizz Kids," a group of wheelchair athletes. "I was able to see what people are really capable of doing. It was a wonderful experience," Clarke said.[78]

Bill Neville, student, ('67)

Bill Neville also came from an era before Jim Coleman. Bill came to George Williams College from the great Northwest—Spokane, Washington—through a YMCA connection. Though he started on the Hyde Park Campus, Bill finished his group work and recreation degree at the Downers Grove campus. After graduating, Bill became the men's coach for a Canadian national volleyball team and went to the Olympics in 1976. He then became head coach of the U.S. team in 1982 and was the assistant coach of the 1984 team that won the gold medal in the Los Angeles Olympics. Bill became the head coach of the women's volleyball team at the University of Washington.[79]

Taras "Terry" Liskevych, student, ('72)

Jim Coleman recruited Terry Liskevych to GWC. Jerry Angle attests to the power of Coleman to recruit volleyball experts and coaches of the future:

> Terry was going another direction and gave up medical school to come into the GWC program and work for Jim. Jim had a men's club [that] met on campus. It became a strong recruitment strategy for future talent. Terry became assistant coach to Coleman in 1973, the year the team took second place in the NAIA [National Association of Intercollegiate Athletics].[80]

Along with Jim Coleman, Terry struggled with the bar being raised for sports performance, making it difficult to differentiate a professional from an amateur.

> The word *amateur* comes from the French word meaning "dabbler" or somebody that does something for an avocation. That's because in the past French society, the only people that had time to take part in athletics were an elite class. They were the only ones who could afford it. The rest of the people were working. Now anyone who does something for more than an hour a day is a professional athlete. Think about college athletes. They are not considered professional, but in a sense, if they get their education paid for by a scholarship, they are getting paid to play. I say open the Olympics up to everyone.

As coach at University of the Pacific, he brought them to the Final Four competition for the national championship. From GWC, he integrated and passed along character development values for his athletes, along with skill development. An Aurora University student reporter who interviewed Terry in 2000 was impressed.

> His coaching philosophy, which includes a potion of respect, discipline, talent, teamwork, and inspirational quotations, was the formula for building a winning team. . . . The number of concepts that can be applied to both the dedicated life of an athlete and the everyday life of a non-athlete is neck and neck. Aren't all of these sayings a reminder of something a parent would say to a child?[81]

Apparently Terry puts everything he has into making the "body-mind-spirit" focus work for his student athletes. His proudest accomplishment was that every player on his winning team graduated in four years, an impressive feat, since in 1986 only one-third of the students graduated in four years. Terry became the U.S. women's volleyball assistant coach in 1975, and in 1985 was head coach. Terry acknowledges Jim Coleman with these words, "I was qualified for the Olympics because at GWC, I got to work really close to my mentor."

Bob Gambardella, student, ('77)

Bob Gambardella played on two men's NAIA [National Association of Intercollegiate Athletics] national championship teams at George Williams College. He was head coach of the women's volleyball team that in 1980 successfully defended the NAIA title for women. Bob went on to be the volleyball coach for the U.S. Military Academy at West Point. Bob was with Jim Coleman on the U.S. Olympic Committee in Colorado Springs, developing future Olympic athletes.[82]

The coaching experiences of Jim, Bob, Terry, and Bill reveal some major shifts that were going in George Williams College in the decades of the '70s and '80s. All of them moved into major leadership positions coaching women's volleyball teams. Casey Clarke moved into coaching some of the world's best physically challenged athletes. Doors of opportunity in athletic competition were opening. At George Williams College, women were coming into their own, showing remarkable excellence in physical skill and competitive sports.

Women's athletics spells success

Nora Campbell, student, ('72), rhythmic gymnastics coach

Nora graduated in the early '70s, with a master's degree in physical education. She stayed on at GWC, becoming a faculty member and gymnastics coach. Nora broke ground in an athletic activity that was new to this country. Known only in Europe, it was called "rhythmic gymnastics." She was only a graduate student when she introduced rhythmic gymnastics as a competitive sport in the United States and ended up bringing it to Olympic competition in 1984.

> Paul Dunsing was the one who introduced me to the concept of rhythmic gymnastics, a German concept of movement that had not yet been introduced to the United States. I came to GWC as a graduate student and took a course called "Modern Rhythmic Gymnastics." Paul came from the Medau School in Germany that taught the concept of movement with light apparatus. It started with old wooden hoops. The hoop and ball enhance movement. The first rhythmic gymnastics clinic was held in New York, the first time it was introduced as a competitive sport. Now we

see hand apparatus used with all kinds of exercise. Pilates eight-inch balls were used for exercise equipment. Paul Dunsing was instrumental in the development of the concept. I took Dunsing's job when he retired at GWC.

GWC was the first college to have competitive rhythmic gymnastics. George Williams College hosted the first Rhythmic Gymnastics National Championships. The purpose was to select promising athletes for entry into the world championships. From that event, the first U.S. gymnasts were selected to enter the world championship competition in Rotterdam [in the Netherlands]. The national rhythmic gymnastics meet at GWC was May 5, 1973. The first time the U.S. entered the world championship was in October, 1973. One GWC student, Kathy Brym, was selected for the world championship competition. I was the coach for the world championship team. [Faculty member] Don Morrison was the pianist for the competition. Live music was a major part of the competition, combining music with sport. The sense of community [among colleagues] was strong. You have a music teacher that wants to do all he can to encourage you in your big idea, and so there he was playing the piano for us, an important part of the first competition for GWC.

GWC was so ahead of its time in many ways. When Title IX was introduced, GWC did not have to worry about catching up on opportunity for women in sports. They were already doing it. It was a leader in women development. Mary Langbein was one of the first women college athletic directors. The fact is, we were a small college. We didn't have to go through a million hoops to get things going. I got all kinds of support for my idea. Innovation was easy to implement at GWC.

What made GWC special was that it was strong in community. There was no place like it. And it was way ahead of its time in the '70s, supporting the development of women's leadership in competitive sports.[83]

The college encouraged talent and leadership from within its own student ranks, as they did with Nora Campbell. As the sport was widely received and organized, she became the chief administrator for the Rhythmic Gymnastics Association. Nora was the assistant director of rhythmic gymnastics in the 1984 Olympics, when it was introduced for the first time. Nora came to a similar conclusion about Olympic-level competition for athletes: "Athletic careers have morphed into a full-time job. . . . There really is little difference between a professional and an amateur athlete. In the new century, because of what the sports require talent-wise and financially, they are no longer part-time positions."[84]

Mary Langbein, student, ('69), coach and athletic director, 1968–1985

Mary Langbein was the women's basketball coach at George Williams College when the college first came to the Downers Grove campus in 1968. She held that position for almost ten years. By 1975 Mary became coordinator of women's athletics. The sports headlines were reading, "Women's Sport Spells Success"; "Women's Basketball Team takes Section Crown, Earns 5th in State"; "Breaststroke Champion Jane Ward Places 18th in Nation in 50-Yard Competition"; "Women's Gymnastics Team Takes State." At that time, Mary commented:

> Women haven't been saturated with sports since they were little, as have many men. The women are saying, "I wish I could have had this earlier, but since I didn't, give me!" I believe athletics is a real extension of a college curriculum, particularly in human relations and developing effective strategies for problem solving. Students will forget the scores, but they'll remember feeling good about their role in the team's success. We attracted quality student athletes who excelled in the classroom as well as in their respective sport. The strength of the athletic program was also due to the quality coaches who were not only experts at "their game" but also were committed to maximizing the potential of every student athlete. We have unusual cooperation. There's no "men first, and what's left goes to the women." I attribute our growth to this coordinated effort. I think that's a big plus.
>
> Coaches . . . need a strong background in behavioral sciences as well as physical sciences to understand the interaction of mind and body, above and beyond good sound knowledge of the sport. George Williams' courses in coaching and the athletic administration recognize this interdisciplinary nature.[85]

In 1980 there were only three women athletic directors responsible for both men's and women's sports at any college in the country. Mary Langbein was one of them.

"Leaders for Service"

Mary and Ed Langbein, students, ('69; and '65, '69, respectively), professors

Mary Langbein and her husband, Ed, were both leaders on the faculty in the Downers Grove era of George Williams College. Like so many others, they started as graduate students at the Hyde Park campus. Their appreciation for the college started with an appreciation for Arthur Steinhaus. Although Steinhaus never made the move to Downers Grove, it seemed Mary and Ed took his spirit with them to the new campus as they stepped into teaching and coaching responsibilities. Mary Langbein explains,

Arthur Steinhaus was the reason I came to George Williams from my home in Seattle, Washington. In Seattle I lived with a relative who was very involved, for health reasons, in a muscular relaxation program. Her physician was training her how to relax long before stress management was recognized as a health benefit. I met with her physician, and he told me that there is only one place in the country where you can go to school and learn about the scientific foundations and teaching theory for progressive neuromuscular relaxation: that's George Williams College. The beauty of it is it's an integral part of their physical education program. The fact that I was in physical education at the time only served to pique my interest in the graduate program at GWC.

Moving to Hyde Park was quite an adjustment, being so far away from home as well as living in an urban neighborhood, but what a great place. The culture, the diversity, the proximity to the University of Chicago library added to the richness of the experience. The majority of students attended classes in the morning, and in the afternoon everyone went out in the community to do their fieldwork.

Ed Langbein offers his story:

I had never heard of Steinhaus or George Williams College from my corner of the world in Dorseyville, Pennsylvania, outside Pittsburgh. I was a senior in high school, planning to enlist in the navy after graduation. My football coach stopped me one afternoon after practice and suggested that I meet with the physical education director at the East Liberty YMCA before committing to the navy. I began doing volunteer work at the East Liberty YMCA in the youth physical education program. That summer I worked in the Pittsburgh YMCA Camp Kon-O-Kwee as a cabin counselor. Toward the end of summer I was approached by the Pittsburgh Y and offered scholarship assistance to attend GWC. From these experiences I discovered that I liked working with youth, physical education, and camping. This relatively brief exposure to the YMCA and scholarship assistance had a marked influence on my future professional path.

So I went to GWC for an undergraduate degree in health and physical education. I then worked for four years at the Central Queens YMCA on Long Island, New York. I returned to George Williams College for a master's degree in health education. It was during graduate study that I met Mary. We were married by Dr. Robert Steiger at the chapel at the GWC Lake Geneva campus. After graduation we both taught in the health and physical education division and coached in the athletic program.

Mary continues:

Dr. Steinhaus set the tone. The other faculty who worked with him followed suit. He was very strong in his philosophy, and the YMCA philosophy fit nicely for him. His primary concern was for the well-being of humanity. In that era, it was very unique. He was an integrator. Of course it helped that we were all in one building [in Hyde Park]. Living in such close proximity, you couldn't help but interact with students and faculty. There was not the physical separation of departments and study or meeting spaces. The total environment helped to "see things through the broad end of the funnel." When we moved to Downers Grove, people were spread out in separate buildings and spaces. It was harder to get back to this integration of body, mind, and spirit. But the human service mission continued to flourish.

Steinhaus was an outstanding physiologist, way ahead of his time. He was always interested in what students were thinking. He'd frequently ask, "What do you think?" He wanted to hear different perspectives. I remember going to the physiology labs in the evening to complete an experiment, and Dr. Steinhaus would stop in and give us a hand or sit and discuss what we were learning. You weren't just there to learn from his perspective; he wanted you to demonstrate an ability to apply what you learned. You couldn't help but grow from his enthusiasm and excitement.

Ed adds:

He was always engaging students in research. "Let's try it out. See if it works." It was not intimidating. His approach to teaching was pragmatic. For example, using scientific principles to teach movement, one could ask a student, "What is the first step necessary to teach a child to hop?" Students versed in physics, biomechanics, and physiology would have to integrate all their information to solve a simple problem. That was the way he would approach teaching. Science was brought back to how to use it in our daily lives.

It seemed followers of Steinhaus were not afraid to break new ground. He encouraged innovative thinking and research, often to improve the quality of life for people. This was excellent preparation for the days to come for Ed. He became a research health scientist for the Department of Veterans Affairs at Edward Hines, Jr. VA Hospital in Hines, Illinois. It was here that his imagination and skills were directed toward program and equipment innovations in the service of physically challenged veterans. It all started when George Williams College closed its Downers Grove campus in 1985. According to Ed,

When George Williams College closed, I was building a laboratory to conduct my dissertation study of temperature regulation during upper-body exercise in persons with spinal cord injury. There goes my degree, I thought. Then [Loyola University Professor] Robert Wurster and I went to the Hines Veterans Administration

Hospital's Rehabilitation, Research, and Development Center, and met with the director. I gave him an overview of the background and said I was looking for a new laboratory location. The focus of this research program was to work with people with disabilities. He said to me, "Well, what is the immediate benefit of your research topic that will improve the health of the veteran with a spinal cord injury? What alternative questions can you come up with right now that have the potential to improve the health care of veterans within the next ten years?" I thought [that] because many of these vets have spinal cord injuries, they are vulnerable to heart disease. I came up with the idea of a wheelchair ergometer to improve cardiovascular testing and rehabilitation for them. That's how I began my research career at Hines VA Hospital.

While developing a lab and conducting research at Hines, Ed completed his PhD at the University of Wisconsin. His research in cardiopulmonary rehabilitation not only has been a significant contribution to the lives of the veterans but also to the body of knowledge in this area.

Mary further explains,

The college graduates' commitment to service was foremost in their decision to attend GWC. When I reflect on the contributions our graduates have and are making in the field of human service, their accomplishments are impressive. Our students stood above their peers in what they did because they gained more than the book learning. They are leaders for others.

Ed concludes:

I think when George Williams College closed, one of the things that the faculty and the students lost, and miss the most was the energy they shared with each other. Students energized faculty, faculty energized students. There were no barriers between them—an environment that was unique and not easily found elsewhere. I was, and I still am, kind of an addict to that atmosphere of energy sharing. When I retire, maybe I'll just dry up and blow away because I've been stealing energy from these young people all this time. When the college closed, you lost the buildings and the grounds and so forth, but I don't know of a faculty person who wouldn't have worked in a tent to keep what we all valued so highly alive.[86]

"Science and caring—what it was all about"
Jerry Angle, student, ('74, '76), GWC and AU coach

There was one coach from George Williams College who came to Aurora University some fifteen years after George Williams College closed in Downers Grove: That was

Jerry Angle, who coached women's volleyball at Aurora University. Jerry was a student at George Williams College, completing his undergraduate degree in 1974 and his master's degree in 1976.

I came to George Williams College for one reason: Jim Coleman. I got to know Jim through playing on a local men's volleyball club team, the Kenneth Allen Club. At first I thought of majoring in social work or therapeutic recreation, but I decided to focus on coaching. I stayed for my master's degree in physical education, with a focus on sports psychology.

When Jim Coleman went on sabbatical in 1975, I coached the women's volleyball team. In that year, the women's volleyball team won the first small college national championship. I remember Nelson Wieters packed the team in a van and drove them clear across the country to Pocatello, Idaho. He joined Russ Rose and me to bring them to the nationals. . . . Russ Rose became the volleyball coach at Penn State, and I assisted the Penn State women's volleyball team that went to Cuba several years ago.

When Jim Coleman came back, Jim brought the men's volleyball team to back-to-back NAIA national championships in 1977 and 1978.

In 1977 Armando Zabala was on the team. He was from San Juan, Puerto Rico. This time the team traveled to Graceland College in Iowa. Armando, . . . a big city guy, couldn't believe the only thing in a block radius was the college. Armando not only played championship volleyball, he had that strong science foundation as a physical education major and went on to become a medical doctor in Puerto Rico. The second year we traveled to George Mason College in Virginia to play for the national championship. George Mason eventually became Division I.

From George Williams College, Jerry went to Northwestern University to become women's volleyball coach and remained there from 1979 to 1993. From 1993 to 1996 he worked in Sports Performance, a volleyball club for men and women, and he assisted coaching on the U.S. men's volleyball team.

George Williams College was so far ahead of the times in physical education. Arthur Steinhaus was a pioneer in the field of neuromuscular relaxation. His courses on neuromuscular relaxation were open to students in the '70s, far before the public was educated on the possibilities of neuromuscular relaxation and its possibilities for monitoring heart beat and pulse. You had a superior science preparation as a P.E. major at George Williams. It wasn't just learning the skills of sports, but the science foundation that supports knowing those skills. All coaches were also faculty. Jim Coleman was the standard-setter for a strong foundation in the sciences. P.E. majors were only a few courses short of the requirements for a premed degree. Many went on to become medical doctors or academics. They were required to take physics, chemistry, anatomy (six students to one cadaver), and exercise physiology. Motor learning was science-based. Jack Joseph had a national reputation for the value of exercise and conditioning on health, long before the public knew much about its value. Wes Sime ['65, '67] worked with Jack Joseph in health science. He played volleyball in Jim Coleman's club. Now he has his doctorate and teaches at the University of Nebraska in the Department of Health. . . .

It was a caring community. Faculty really cared about students. They went out of their way to see that they succeed. Jim Coleman devoted endless hours tutoring students on his own time to see that they achieved in science. He had boundless energy. He could function well on three hours of sleep a night. September Camp contributed to this strong feeling of community. All physical education and recreation majors had to spend at least a week in Lake Geneva. Social work students came, too. Also, faculty retreats were up there. I plan to take the volleyball team up to Lake Geneva for team building before the season begins. I did that when I was volleyball coach of the Northwestern volleyball team.[87]

"Writing about grief"
Cindy Schendel, AU professor and coach

Several years ago a teacher and coach in physical education at Aurora University wanted some information about George Williams College. Cindy Schendel was writing a paper for a doctoral course in organizational development, and she chose to do her research on the closing of George Williams College, something that happened over twenty years ago.

I wanted to know about the grief process for faculty and students. When they heard their college was abruptly closing, were there processes to help people handle grief? And if so, what were they? I went to another college for my education in physical education. I heard a lot about George Williams College. I loved to read papers written by people who had come through the college, even papers by my colleague here, Jerry Angle. I knew there was a philosophy of physical education there; I knew it was about physical education for service.

When I came to Aurora University to coach and teach in physical education, I was excited that it was a part of the George Williams College of Aurora University. Rita Yerkes, the director of the program, worked diligently to instill a George Williams College philosophy in the program. We liked that service part; we really bought into physical education for service.[88]

In 1992 when George Williams College entered an affiliation agreement with Aurora University, an organizational structure called George Williams College was created. It included physical education with recreation, social work, and education. Dr. Rita Yerkes was director of the physical education and recreation programs. The coaches were organizationally located in George Williams College also. It was a little easier to develop a George Williams College philosophy within the social work and recreation programs, because they came to Aurora University with their leaders, like Nelson Wieters. But health science and physical education did not come to Aurora University.

Some efforts to get on the same page as George Williams College worked. The energy of a George Williams College spirit caught on. At first, we "learned by doing," trying out interdisciplinary service projects in the Aurora community (a fuller description of one is in chapter 1, "Serving Others"). But the Aurora University coaches had difficulty with the organizational structure and the philosophy. At one GWC meeting we had on campus, one coach said, "I think it's just great what George Williams College stands for and what it has accomplished in human service. But for the life of me, I don't get why we have to be here; what are we supposed to do?" It was difficult to respond. A philosophy never comes across easily in a simple, on-the-spot answer.

Cindy was not at Aurora in those times. But she knew the whole purpose of physical education and coaching at Aurora University had a different history from George Williams. Now Cindy wondered if that philosophy of physical education could continue on at Aurora. For her, that would be disappointing but not surprising. We got back to talking about that grief paper again.

From the closing of George Williams College in 1985, there were no carriers of the culture in the areas of health and physical education to Aurora University. Aurora University acknowledges the heroes of the college from other eras. A timeline of GWC sports heroes and accomplishments is displayed on walls. Distinguished GWC alumni in sport, health, and physical education are honored each year. Championship volleyball teams are reunited and honored. But it is the past that we celebrate.

Stories of Dr. Arthur Steinhaus; the cadavers in the laboratory; the inspired curiosity to find out more about the anatomy and physiology of the human body; the excitement of being on the cutting edge of research and practice in areas of exercise, wellness, and improved body performance; the techniques of neuromuscular relaxation and stress management that were moved out of the research laboratories into the hands of the people who needed it; the Olympic level excellence in sport competition—all these stories are told with a poignant sense of loss and grief. We speak of the past. Some people say it hurts even to talk about it.

An even greater loss was the philosophy, so painstakingly nurtured by Arthur Steinhaus. Body, mind, and spirit—you cannot separate them. Today the world has caught up with the YMCA philosophy. We build into our daily rituals actions to take care of our body, mind, and spirit in a holistic way. But the second part of the philosophy—physical education as a means toward greater ends—will that idea survive in our culture?

Chapter 3

Building Community Inside and Out

*"You walk here **not alone.**"*

(Hedley Dimock, Last Lap Ceremony, 1934)

*T*he commitment to build community is embedded deeply in the life of George Williams College, evident in the stories of a century of generations. The initial purpose of the college was to prepare people for YMCA leadership, and that community-building instinct was inherent in the earliest stages of the YMCA movement "to unite young men in fellowship."[1] The fourfold purpose of the YMCA was for the development and integration of body, mind, and spirit, as well as the social dimension of people's lives. That social purpose leads not only to a spirit of service to improve social situations that interfere with individual development but also to a resolve to help the individual build social ties in every context of life.

The college always took the view that community building was best learned by experience within the very educational institution they had created—from the training institutes at Williams Bay in the Lake Geneva area to a fully mature college. The lessons learned from building community within were extended and applied outward to neighborhoods, the Ys, and social agencies and the communities they served, and ultimately to the global community.

The title of a recent bestseller, *Bowling Alone,* provides a compelling picture of modern-day life in the absence of community.[2] Even bowling, a recreational sport designed for teamwork, can be practiced in isolation. Sports fitness centers suspend television sets above mechanical weights, bicycles, and treadmills; individuals screen out others to tune in to their iPods; a room full of people "parallel play" in isolation from each other. "Bowling alone" captures a cultural scenario familiar to all of us. It could also be the outcome of the YMCA triangle—to develop body, mind, and spirit—without a fourth dimension; the social dimension. Author Robert Putnam describes a decline of "social capital" in our culture in the second half of the last century into this new century. Social capital is all the rich benefits derived from genuine human connection, creating a web of social support necessary to survive and thrive in this world. Moreover, social capital is the desire to give back to community for what you have been given. The ties of social capital extend from personal friendships, to neighbors, to communities, to social institutions, to our country, and to the world.

George Williams College's richness in social capital has been a hallmark of the college throughout the generations. The first two-week summer institute was held on Geneva Lake in 1884 at a place called Camp Collie, now called Conference Point. The second and third institutes (1885 and 1886) were held in tents on a road leading to Congress Camp. All three were only a short distance from the permanent site of George Williams College. The institutes were well attended (54 people in 1884, 97 people in 1885, and 154 people in 1886). In 1886, the Western

and brush to create a permanent site for the Western Secretarial Institute, the students pitched in to do the work. By the time the dedicatory campfire was lit on the evening of August 12, 1886, students "were in this together"; they felt shared ownership in this new vision. They participated in creating something bigger than themselves that would be permanent for future generations.

"A resolve to help the individual build social ties in every context of life"

Secretarial Institute was incorporated, and land was purchased on the current site on Geneva Lake. At the conclusion of that summer session in 1886, the first hands-on action to create an institute that was to become George Williams College was an act of creating social capital among students. When it was time to clear out wood

Photograph, page 85: Students experience community at Orientation in Lake Geneva. Building community internally—within the college—was viewed as essential learning for building community externally—in neighborhoods and organizations. (ca. 1960s)

Community Building: Planting the Seeds

"The Clearing Bee of 1886"

James Austin, student, 1915

Student James Austin spoke at the annual commencement at Williams Bay on July 25, 1915. He had just completed his thesis research on the history of College Camp.

> One of the features of the session of 1886 was the clearing of the new camp grounds purchased by the committee in the name of William E. Lewis. Axes were provided by the committee on recreation, and the "secretary" [Y student leader] for the time being became a "woodsman." . . . On the evening of August 12, 1886, as a result of the "clearing bee," there was held in the new camp, on the hillside just above the spring, a campfire.[3]

When the college moved to Chicago, Illinois, in 1890, and a permanent new building was constructed for the YMCA College in 1915, students from the class of 1916 show that same spirit of "giving back for what you have been given" when they expressed their "obligation to the brotherhood" for such a "splendid" building created for their educational experience.

"Our Obligation to the Brotherhood"

Student statement in yearbook, 1916

> The college building stands not alone as a splendid training center for men, but stands as a lasting monument to the faith and hope of the YMCA brotherhood. . . . The brotherhood has loyally supported us in gifts, financially and otherwise: they have supported us in an unswerving interest and appreciation of what we are accomplishing, and what we are standing for; and they have supported us as men! What shall we give them in return? The answer is . . . men filled with a genuine love of work and fellow-man; and men of capacity and ability who are trained. This is our obligation to the brotherhood. Shall we not strive to meet it, men?[4]

The term *brotherhood* was frequently used to describe the student's feeling of unity and bond to a greater cause than themselves, one of service. The college reinforced this sense of community in many ways. Founder Robert Weidensall, who permanently resided in the Chicago Training School, was referred to as "Uncle Robert." The YMCA intention—to make its institutions and activities "homelike"—was an integral part of its original mission for young men who were relocated in unfamiliar cities, separated from their home and family.[5]

However, as early as 1886, when the dedicatory campfire was lit, the question arises: Were sisters included in the brotherhood? Women were present at the dedicatory campfire in 1886 and throughout that historic week of August before the campfire. Some were wives of the founders of the institute, but these women were up to something of their own. The three visionaries, William E. Lewis, Robert Weidensall, and I. E. Brown, believed something historically significant and permanent was unfolding on this day. They "preserved the three pencil stubs with which they wrote down their plans and policies, along with their notes in a sealed envelope" for posterity's sake.[6] But they missed the significance of what the women were doing. During that same week, August 6–12, 1886, the women were organizing the national Young Women's Christian Association. Two plaques remain on the Williams Bay campus site, commemorating both events. Though this historic "women's conference" did not go unnoticed, we read in I. E. Brown's historic sketches of what happened on August 12, 1886, the things that "linger in the memory":

> A reception was tendered by the ladies in place of the usual concert. The decorations of ferns, leaves, and flowers; the birch bark badges; the poem by the hero of Howlers Row; the tardy ice which came at last . . . linger in the memory yet.[7]

A full discussion of all the reasons why the YMCA and the YWCA became separate entities would be enlightening, particularly when their origins converged so closely. It will suffice to say, though women of the YWCA continued to meet annually in Williams Bay, the place of women in the college community dedicated to "the work of the association" did not really take hold until 1933, when women were admitted to George Williams College.[8]

Though the year-round college moved from the shores of Geneva Lake, Wisconsin to Chicago, Illinois in 1890 and to other sites in Illinois in the years to come, the Williams Bay campus on Geneva Lake remains the "soul" of the college community; it provides an abiding sense of place for courses, institutes, and other educational and cultural experiences. It remains, in the hearts of its sojourners, the site where community building takes place. The peaceful beauty of the Williams Bay campus continues to satisfy its promise to restore body, mind, and spirit, and strengthen relational bonds of students and faculty, as well as family, friends, and other guests from social agencies, churches, organizations, and groups of all sorts.

The Williams Bay campus has played a rather unique role, compared to other colleges that may not have a similar camp or conference site so congruent and supportive of the college's mission. Camping and the YMCA went hand in hand with experiential learning; holistic development of body, mind, and spirit; and community building. For well over a century, the site has seen annual rituals and programs like graduations, community building orientations for new students, "September Camp," social work "Orientation Practicum," experiential learning programs, faculty retreats, language immersion programs, high-challenge team building experiences, and alumni gatherings. As such, the Williams Bay campus continues to be a major resource for a unique kind of community building in an educational institution. In the last few years, entire academic programs have returned to the Williams Bay campus for their classroom work.

In 1890 the college moved to Chicago; in 1915 it built a permanent site in the Hyde Park neighborhood of Chicago. Six years later student Ray Johns tells the experience of a freshman who enters this learning community.

"How Association College Strikes a Freshman"
Student statement in yearbook, 1921

> Has Association College a spirit that "strikes" a freshman, or is it something a new man at school does not feel? . . . The average freshman's induction to Chicago was bewildering. He arrived at the college in a confused state of mind. But that welcome in the corridors, that hearty handshake helped to put him at ease. . . . A junior helped him to find a room; then to find "that job." He sensed the spirit so much that he wrote the folks that "everyone seems to want to help me get settled."[9]

There were "starting" and "finishing" rituals built into the college life that celebrated the meaning of community. Faculty member and Dean Hedley Dimock describes a graduation ritual after the ceremony in 1934. Students are to take a "last lap" around the quadrangle in front of the college building.

The Last Lap Ceremony—"You walk here not alone"
Hedley Dimock, professor and dean, 1934

> The ceremony of the "last lap" is symbolic of the life you have lived as members of this college community. The four sides of this quadrangle [at the Hyde Park campus] symbolize the four years which most of you have spent here. Each side may suggest experiences characteristic of these years. Our memories move back: To that eagerness of spirit of the first weeks which was soon tempered by the demands of new and complicated situations. Then to the sophisticated spirit of one who knows his way around a bit; then to the humble spirit of one who begins to discover the vast extent of his limitations: and finally the poised maturity of a professional worker eager to test his competence.

Dimock adds one more instruction: the "last lap" is to be traversed in twos.

> This ceremony also symbolizes the significance of friendship in human experience. You walk here not alone, but in companies of two. The genuinely satisfying life is always shared. He, who joy would win must share it, for happiness was born a twin.[10]

In the late 1930s the college conducted a daring experiment in community building. Professor Charles Hendry explains how this philosophy-in-action is a radical departure from traditional higher education. The experiment was called the "Community of Living and Learning." We also hear from Professor Karl Zerfoss on the value of the idea and how it is played out in the life of the college. Both professors hold to the philosophy that the best way to learn is through experience. If students are to learn the value of community and how to develop community in the practice of human service, they have to experience it within the college community first. An outsider to the college, Esther Lloyd-Jones of Columbia University, comments on the George Williams College experiment in community building. The Community of Living and Learning involves curriculum, extracurricular activities, and faculty-student governance.

"The Community of Living and Learning"
Charles Hendry, professor, 1939

> Think of the college itself as "a community of learning" not "an institution of learning." No college need merely be an institution of learning. The traditional college, to be sure, has been little more. Too often it has been chiefly a device to divorce the actual from the academic and to substitute ritual for reality. . . . The conventional college, as an institution of learning, has drawn a sharp differentiation between the curriculum and the extracurriculum. That which has been formal, scheduled, and fixed has had absolute right of way over that which has been informal, spontaneous, and free. An arbitrary and artificial dualism has separated clubs and classes into watertight administrative compartments. The integration of college life and college studies has been largely ignored.
>
>   It is not enough to teach youth to think the thoughts of great thinkers after them. Youth somehow must be taught to think thoughts worthy of great thinkers. . . . If college education is to have genuine functional value it must be concerned with the functions which persons perform in their day-by-day living . . . making homes, keeping healthy, orienting to life changes, participating in opportunities and obligations of good citizenship, using one's leisure, and developing a dynamic philosophy of life. Curriculum development is based on "functions of living," not "fields of knowledge." . . .

> Much occurs outside the classroom . . . more crucial as determinative influences in shaping personality and character than experiences related to formal curriculum. Certain experiences are "growing points," or points at which students are facing real problems, points at which education might well "plug in."
>
> Student self-government was deliberately avoided. It was felt most forms of self-government schemes . . . are artificial, based on the assumption that student concerns and needs differ from the rest of the community, that students are unready emotionally and inadequate intellectually to share responsibility about "really important decisions" and that one does not engage in "democratic citizenship" until "the magic age of twenty-one."

Hendry does not anticipate this "community" will always be a natural bonding of like-minded human service professionals. "Conflict is inevitable when there is freedom of expression." Hendry remembers his former colleague Eduard Lindeman, who himself struggled with conflict and differences with his colleagues when he was on the faculty at George Williams College in 1918. He takes a line from Lindeman's notable book on social education, concluding,

> A college education must prepare for a democratic life, given three inevitable things—the fact of change, the fact of difference, and the fact of conflict. . . . This kind of community building takes intention and hard work, but colleges can, if they will, become communities in which American youth can get experience with and develop confidence in the democratic way of life.[11]

Esther Lloyd-Jones, professor, Columbia University

> Behind the concept of George Williams College as a community of cooperative living were two basic ideas: First, the central objective of the college, instead of being subject-matter achievement, was conceived to be the development of persons who would be effective in personal and social living. Second is the classroom and formal curriculum.[12]

Karl Zerfoss, professor, GWC

> GWC is attempting to evolve [into] a community of living and learning which includes students, members of faculty, and house staff. Every phase of life is considered of importance to the growth of its members. "Looking at the individual as a whole" is an important mental health principle, and the program is a good program of mental hygiene.

Zerfoss describes orientation in Lake Geneva going hand in hand with this education and governance model.

> Students and faculty are involved, including students already in the program. It continues three days. Then each new student is assigned to a member of the faculty as counselor. Students and faculty look together at things like workload stress generated from trying to balance field work and course work. Also, at the end of the year members of the graduating class and faculty go to College Camp for a weekend of discussion, interview, and fellowship.[13]

The Community of Living and Learning idea took firm hold in the culture of the college and was put to the test some thirty years later, when dealing with racial conflict and confrontation within the lifespace of the college in the '60s.

Community Building Inside and Out: Chicago

The service challenge to build inclusive communities outside the college walls of ivy cannot be comprehended without taking a hard look at race and the role African Americans played in the history of Chicago, the city where the college evolved. Henry Louis Gates recently described the two "Great Migrations" of African Americans to Chicago's South Side in his book *America Behind the Color Line: Dialogues with African Americans*. The "First Great Migration" of African Americans from the American South to Chicago took place in the 1920s and 1930s, when the college was establishing itself in the community. The college was beginning to define itself professionally as a "group work" school, with a unique and relevant mission within Chicago's neighborhoods. The first group of migrants was highly motivated and optimistic, "with dreams of opportunity and hope" to be found on "the streets of heaven," the South Side of Chicago. For the most part, those who came as part of the First Great Migration were from urban areas in the South. They were able to find jobs because there was a need for cheap labor in the stockyards, steel mills, and manufacturing sites. Hope was centered not only on economic opportunity and faith in God, but on education as the door to opportunity for their children. They were also well connected. "It was community, and I mean that definitively in terms of the spirit and the feeling of the people toward one another, though we lived in the ghetto," says sociologist Timuel Black, who tells his own story in Henry Louis Gates' account of the Great Migrations in *America Behind the Color Line*. The South Side of Chicago was "a self-contained colored world," bound by restrictive covenants that no landlord or landowner would rent or sell to people of color. During the First Great Migration the "color line" was from "about 26th Street on the north to about 43rd Street on the south."[14] George Williams College was located on Fifty-third Street, just ten blocks on the other side of "the color line" in the '20s and '30s.

In the 1930s a spirited African American woman found her way to George Williams College, only a few years after the college opened enrollment to women in 1933. Her family was part of this First Great Migration, coming to Chicago from Hope, Arkansas, the home of President Bill Clinton. Verneta Hill ('39) tells us her story of how the college prepared her for a life of social activism, as a leader in the civil rights movement to integrate the South.

"You call it group work"

Verneta Hill, student, ('39)

I graduated from grade school and high school in Chicago, and then I went to a trade school where I majored in economics. Economics was not a subject for women, and black folks were not supposed to know anything about economics. I went on a scholarship to Bryn Mawr College and then Brooklyn Labor College in the East. I was a college tramp! While I was working and in school, I belonged to a club for industrial girls. It was there I learned from experience the value of organizing groups for women who were living in big cities trying to find their way to get an education and find jobs. After Brooklyn Labor College, I went back to Chicago to attend the University of Chicago. I wanted to teach workers labor history, and I wanted them to become better labor leaders. I took two courses at the University of Chicago.

While I went to school, I worked at the switchboard at the YMCA. One day I was in Hyde Park, on my way back from a class, I noticed this building that was George Williams College. . . . Someone came up to me, and asked if he could help me. When he asked, "What brings you here?" I said, "Curiosity," I told him I believed in the value of organizing clubs and groups, whether it was for labor relations or just making connections when you're a stranger. I thought that was an important part of working with people. He said, "You call it group work; that's the name for it." It sounded like he knew exactly what I was after. I left the University of Chicago and enrolled in the program in administration of group work.

I was born to organize; whether it was setting up committees, clubs, social groups, or you name it. Soon after I graduated from GWC, [World War II] was beginning, and my first assignment was to work for the USO. They drafted anybody, but when it came to assignments, blacks were more highly trained for their assignments than whites. My assignment was to train USO workers. The YMCA and the Salvation Army were the two organizations assigned to the task. I had the title "program director." The men could call themselves "executive director" or "secretary," but it was the program director that did the work—driving trucks, cleaning sewers, the works. I stayed with the USO until 1947. By the way, years later I was given recognition as a full-fledged "secretary" of the Y.

After the USO, I went to Battle Creek, Michigan, to work for the YMCA. It was there that it became clear to me [that] my mission [was] to include all people in service. For example, the Y there would not allow women who they thought were engaging in prostitution to use the services of the YMCA. I could not understand why the Y existed if it wasn't to provide access to services for everyone.

I returned to the South in the '50s, working for the YWCA. I was serving as field director for the School of Social Work at Tulane and working for a YWCA in New Orleans. Students were sent to me to work with the YWCA to desegregate the Ys in New Orleans. I trained both white and black social work students. I remember when working at the Y, there were times I had to wait in the car, when the white folks attended meetings or went to lunch, because I was black. In 1951 staff meetings were not integrated. Blacks and whites were not allowed to sit down in meetings together. The YWCA president where I worked broke all the rules. She would go out to buy a carton of Coke, and we would all sit down together and drink Coke while we were having a meeting. . . .

In the late '50s I was asked to represent my community in Washington, D.C., for government hearings on regional segregation in the South. At that time Whitney Young asked me to come to Atlanta to work. I got a degree in community organization from Clark Atlanta School of Social Work. In Atlanta I worked with Whitney Young to form block clubs through the Department of Housing and Urban Development (HUD). I felt I was using my group-work skills one more time in forming block clubs and facilitating groups in conflict to come to a point of collaboration.

The relationship building skills worked toward desegregating churches in my community. I wanted to work with a minister in town. I found out the minister liked flowers. I brought him flowers every day. I attended his church, though I belonged to another church. You know, you have to stoop to conquer. You have to give up something in order to get something. In the end, I was able to win over not only the minister but the whole congregation, who listened to what I had to say.

At the age of 96, Verneta had a few pointers for the students and teachers at George Williams College today:

First: When you supervise, you "train up," you don't "train down." You reverse [the hierarchy]; you listen to the experiences of the people you train. You let them do the talking, and you use their experiences for them to learn. You don't do all the talking. You listen to their problems. Only bad managers say, "If you complain, you get fired." Second: Staff development means just that—development! You need to build on the unique and individual differences of everyone if you are going to be an effective group worker. You need to know the psychology of individual differences. Third: You need patience. You may be mad at someone, to the point where you would like to fire them, but take the time to learn about their situation. You'll become more tolerant. Fourth: You need to detrain before you can retrain—to help people to let go of old assumptions about other groups and people before they can learn new things about people. Finally, you need to network with people to form alliances based on commonalities in every way possible.

For teachers of George Williams College, she had this to say—something she learned at the group-work college:

I'd have to know each student: their likes, their dislikes, their life stories. In group work, you have to understand every individual who makes up a group in order to understand how they learn, and that is a very individual thing. . . . And just as individuals in groups are different, all communities are different. The genius of a group worker is to try to enter into the cultural experience of each community and understand and appreciate the differences. When I was in Tulane, I ate a lot of crabs. When I was in San Francisco, I learned a lot about wines. You need to know the whole individual person in their unique community.[15]

In Verneta Hill's era, another student, Howard Winebrenner, tells us his story of coming to George Williams College in the '30s, and finding himself in the same struggle to build inclusive community. In Howard's case, it was right in his own backyard of Chicago and within the very YMCA institution that gave him the opportunity to complete his high school education so that he could attend George Williams College.

"A man who stood up for what was right"

Howard Winebrenner, student, ('32)

In late September of 2003 Roberta Winebrenner invited me to her home for her trademark homemade beef-barley soup and some conversation with her 99-year-old husband, Howard, graduate of George Williams College, class of 1932. Though bright, witty, and congenial, Howard admitted his memory of specific details about GWC was getting a bit foggy. But certain specifics stand out in his memory. He remembered how hard it was to be working and going to school at the same time. He had to work at the YMCA downtown to pay for his tuition. On cold winter nights when he wearily returned to Hyde Park from his job downtown, there was always hot chocolate and a sandwich at the information desk to welcome him and warm him up. He remembers one night he was caught in a snowstorm trying to make it back to the college in time to carry out a major leadership responsibility he had on campus. He was in charge of "gym night." Gym night was a celebrated tradition. It was the college's opportunity to show off to the community its gymnastic prowess, with formations, drills, and various physical feats.

Though memory may fade, Howard had no trouble recalling his lifelong friends who were his classmates at George Williams College. He and Roberta could track every one: Don Steward ('30), Nick Lattof ('28), Alex Coutts ('30), Ray Booz ('32), Harleigh Trecker ('34). Howard and Roberta were proud of their colleagues' leadership in human services in the Chicago area and beyond. Nick started the Jerusalem YMCA and the Des Plaines and Arlington Heights YMCAs. Alex worked for the Chicago Area Project. Ray lived and worked in a settlement house in Chicago. Harleigh became a nationally prominent social work educator. Howard's daughter, Susan Johnson, joined us for soup as Howard and Roberta were reminiscing. She also chimed in, revealing her lifelong familiarity with her parents' friends.

Howard was a high school dropout when his family moved to Chicago after his sophomore year. He returned to school at the Chicago YMCA to get his high school diploma. He then entered George Williams College and graduated in 1932. His degree was in group work administration. GWC was not accredited at the time, so Howard transferred what credits the University of Chicago would accept and got a degree from the University of Chicago in 1934. Upon graduation, Howard returned to the place where he worked as a student, the YMCA College downtown, an educational institution administered by the Chicago Metropolitan YMCA, a separate entity from George Williams College. (The terminology "YMCA College" must have been confusing in the city of Chicago. George Williams College did not adopt that name until 1933. Until that time, it was also called the "YMCA College.") Howard took on a full-time position as registrar. However, he and the faculty and staff of the YMCA College were disturbed that the YMCA was categorizing enrollments according to whether students were Jewish, black, or Caucasion. There was also a history there of Jews and blacks not being able to use the swimming pool, a practice that was not held at the GWC pool at Hyde Park. The faculty and staff resigned en masse, creating the temporary demise of the Chicago Metropolitan YMCA College. Those who left, found a building on Wells Street, which eventually became Roosevelt University. Howard was a member of the founding faculty and staff of Roosevelt University, serving as director of admissions and foreign student advisor.

A few days after my visit with Howard and Roberta, Howard had a bad fall, and his health declined steadily. Two months later, on December 15, 2003, I was attending Howard's funeral, a joyous memorial celebration. His children and grandchildren were inspired to say, "He was a man who stood up for what was right [when he walked out of the YMCA College]. Bear in mind that this was 1945, when it was less-than-heroic to stand up for racial equality and fight discrimination by race or creed!"[16]

"I am more a part of the College": Lake Geneva Orientation

Students, ('49)

In the '40s and '50s at GWC, students describe how the Community of Living and Learning had taken hold as a strong root within the college, showing itself in student governance, and how its personal regard for the development of the student as a whole person who is "welcomed, involved, and valued" was evident both inside the college and in service to the neighboring community. Community-building rituals continued to foster the process: the last lap ceremony in twos was an ending ritual; the orientation program at Lake Geneva was a beginning ritual to build community. By 1949, orientation was a well-established tradition.

In 1949, when 150 students got on the bus at the Hyde Park campus for orientation at Lake Geneva, the students who had been through the program had this to say to newcomers:

> The time and effort given to orientation of new students at George Williams College creates a program unique in college circles, and it is felt that the results achieved more than merit the time and effort involved. Orientation marks the first step in getting acquainted with the college, its faculty, and returning students. It provides, through sharing of experiences, for intelligent adjustment of new and varied situations and demands, for assistance in achieving one's goals in the personal, social, spiritual, and vocational realms. Orientation joins new students, old students, and faculty in their efforts to make the most of the opportunities available. Probably the best indication of results achieved are the remarks of a transfer student, "I feel after four days that I know more about and am more a part of George Williams College than I did after a year in my former college."[17]

Welcome, involved, and valued"

Mary Stowe, student, ('51) and Ned Stowe, student, ('52)

The ritual of orientation at Lake Geneva produced a myriad of stories attesting to the same experience. As students in the late '40s and early '50s, Ned and Mary Stowe tell their story of how the Community of Living and Learning worked inside and outside the college. Mary explained:

I considered going to GWC because I was good in gym, and my guidance counselor said I could go to George Williams College and major in P.E. That's why I came. When I got there, we would have to go to orientation. We became acquainted with faculty on a first-name basis. It was funny, when we returned to campus, faculty would have to take off their plaid shirts for something less casual, but we got to know them with their plaid shirts on.

The students pretty much ran the place. [There was a personnel committee, publication committee, athletics committee, social committee, religion committee. There was even an eligibility committee of students who decided whether a student was too overloaded to take on the responsibility of another committee![18]] And we did have responsibility. We took our committee work very seriously. When I came to GWC, my life was GWC; it was a total life commitment. . . . I felt I belonged there. . . . I felt welcomed, involved, and valued. I got a degree from another college [where she completed academic work]. I got educated at George Williams College.

I learned it's not just the task or getting the job done; it's how you go about getting the job done. . . . You can become knowledgeable on any subject, but you can't be an effective teacher unless you value students and build relationships. I remember I didn't like the course that Professor Karl Zerfoss taught, but he wouldn't give up on me. When I wrote a paper, he would call me in, and say, "That's an interesting thought you had there. Tell me more." He could spot somebody who had potential, and I got to believe in myself.

Ned Stowe says:

I was at loose ends when I considered going to GWC. I knew I did not want to be an accountant, something I already tried at another university. But I enjoyed church youth work, and thought group work would be a good major to support that interest. I felt, when I entered George Williams College, that I was not college material. But faculty and students believed in my potential. I was elected by students to different positions, like being president of the College Association. I felt personally valued and responsible for that trust. Dr. Ursula Stone believed in me and recruited me to work with her on the Southeast Chicago Commission, along with University of Chicago and government officials who were involved in urban planning and renewal. Dr. Stone taught economics at George Williams College, and her husband was a professor at the University of Chicago. Eventually I taught courses in group work and community organization after doing graduate work. I became an assistant professor of social sciences, worked as an admission officer, and eventually became the financial aid officer of the college.

Accoring to both Mary and Ned:

| What really bound us together was this spirit of service.[19]

"It's about spirit, not buildings and programs"

Sam Chollar, student, ('50) and Mary Chollar, student, ('80)

Student Sam Chollar speaks of "spirit," not buildings or programs, that characterize the college where he went in the late '40s and '50s, and his wife, Mary Chollar, speaks to the persistence of that spirit some thirty years later when she finally became a student at George Williams College in the '80s. Sam begins:

The Y was a part of me. My father was with the Armed Services YMCA. I came a long ways, from Bremerton, Washington, to come to the YMCA school because I intended to follow in my dad's footsteps and become a Y worker. I started at the "old shoe factory" in 1947. I found and married Mary when I was at George Williams.

Mary continues:

We're partners in a way of life. It's not a job; it's a way of life. Sharing my life with Sam, I feel as much a partner in this way of life. When I met Sam, I didn't know anything about the YMCA. I was more familiar with Boy Scouts, but I learned from Sam to see that all this work with kids was not about getting awards, pins, and badges. It was something unseen, yet something kids could begin to recognize within themselves, their own development in spirit, mind, and body.

According to Sam:

It's about the people at George Williams. My classmates—Bob Taylor, Dick Hamlin, Earl and Connie Iverson. My teachers—John Fuhrer, a stiff-collared YMCA guy who had a lot to say about the Y experience; Helen Westerberg; Hedley Dimock. Hedley would draw chalk circles on his desk while talking, then sit on it and walk away with chalk circles on the seat of his pants. It's about being a group worker, using ping pong balls and paddles at the Hyde Park YMCA to reach kids.

I began my career in the YMCA in Alameda County, California. I met with a group of young men in my home. They would say, "There's no Y here yet, no buildings, no programs, no triangle signs." I would say, "That's the point. It's not a sign; it's reaching out for people. Don't look for the triangle sign, look for what it stands for!"

It's the spiritual, the values that hold it all together. When I went to George Williams, I graduated from a program called "group work education," Mary graduated from a program called "applied behavioral science." It was an evolution of the same program, yet you could trace those constant values through time.

Mary explains her experience:

About 30 years after Sam, I decided it was my turn and enrolled in the applied behavioral science program. When I graduated [in 1980], I gave a little commencement speech. I talked about "my love affair with George." I talked about meeting "him" through Sam and loving "him" right away. A long time ago I had to leave "him," but never could get "him" out of my mind. Thirty years later I found "him" in a different place, and it started up all over. Now it was time to leave "him" again, but I will never stop loving "him." And, oh yes, I even plan on sneaking in another little time with "him" this summer (maybe a continuing education course or two).[20]

When I said goodbye to Sam and Mary, I said, "The Y seems to be like a family to you. I mean, I've gone to the Y at points in my life, but I don't think of myself as being 'in the family.' Sam responded emphatically, "Oh, yes you are!" I walked away pondering. When people tell their stories of their George Williams experience, they mostly speak of things unseen, a spirit or energy that drives the programs located in buildings, the thing that holds it all together. Sam and Mary gave me a new way of thinking about "the Y family," and how that spirit was reflected in George Williams College.

Fred Lickerman was another student of the '50s. Fred speaks of a personal "tap root experience" that motivated him to find a college that would prepare him for building inclusive communities in Chicago's neighborhoods. He finds, from his personal network of college friends who share the same mission, an opportunity to form a partnership that had a profound influence for good on Chicago's youth in the '60s: "something we could never have done alone." Fred and two colleagues from George Williams College created a strong agency partnership after graduation. Fred was director of Chicago Boys and Girls Club; John Root ('46) was director of the Chicago Metropolitan YMCA; and Russ Hogrefe ('41) was director of Chicago Youth Centers, all power-wielding positions for youth services in the city. Chicago was strongly influenced by these three men at a time when the word "partnership" was not the commonly used term it is today. Their visionary collaboration had far-reaching effects. They shared a common mission to build community in the toughest neighborhoods, where youth were growing up with limited options and social support.

"A tap root experience"

Fred Lickerman, student, ('51)

The spirit of George Williams College for me was not related to the roles I played as a student, alumnus, or board member. It was how I used its network and resources to drive my mission. Where we connected on mission, we achieved something we could not have done alone. This passion-driven mission springs from what I call a "tap root experience." In 1949 I transferred from a college in Wisconsin. I was looking to go into youth social work. That's because I had this tap root experience. It goes back to my childhood. We lived in the town of Sheboygan, Wisconsin, a German town. One day in the schoolyard, I saw a group of kids beating up on my sister, calling her "a dirty Jew." My family name [is] Lickerman, with one "n." . . . My father was Jewish, but converted to the faith of my mother who was Lutheran. Until that time, we were never told that half our family was Jewish. My mother's family members were German Lutheran farmers. This experience came at a time when Hitler was on the move in Germany. . . . Someone like me—half Jew—would have been shipped to Auschwitz. But for the grace of God, I was here, and not in Munich. . . .

This tap root experience struck me like a big crescendo. I began to look at anti-Semitism, and found that it was very much alive in Sheboygan. I wanted to be a part of changing that; I wanted America to be what they taught me it was in grade school, [that it was open to all]. I didn't want to be a teacher. I wanted to work with young people [who] were having difficulty even staying in school. . . . My high school counselor suggested, "What you want to do is youth work." I had never been part of any youth group. A friend worked part time in a Y. He encouraged me to transfer to George Williams College. I visited George Williams and found that "the shoe fit." It targeted preparation for youth work. It was community based. It was in one of the greatest laboratories in the world, the city of Chicago.

There were two people who helped me to understand a tap root experience. One was John Fuhrer, a man of the field; what he taught he lived. The other was Dr. Karl Menninger. Clement Stone brought Menninger to Chicago for a community mental health project. The tap root experience is the inner motivation that drives what you do. With a strong tap root experience, be it negative as mine was or positive, it makes you willing to put more on the line when confronting an opposing force. It could be your life. That "spirit" or "tap root experience" tells you why you're willing to go that far, because you understand the goal. When a goal becomes so large that you're not able to accomplish it without giving yourself totally to it, it becomes a mission. My evolution became mission-driven. And to have a mission is to have a gift. It was this spirit that I tapped into when the West Side was burning in the '60s, and I was doing community work.[21]

When he was a student in the '50s, Paul Staudenmaier found at the college "people who are interested in me as a whole person," and he gave that back in a career of service to youth in Boys and Girls Clubs.

"Someone interested in me as a whole person"
Paul Staudenmaier, student, ('55)

I chose to come to GWC because of the size of the student body. I did not want to be an anonymous number. I wanted students and faculty who were interested in me. When I came to GWC I was a nerd. I was feeling unconfident about my place and standing with my peer group, and about what contributed to my lack of confidence. Faculty took an interest in me, giving feedback about something I could change to improve the way I was coming across to others. . . . That made a difference. I am forever grateful for that kind of faculty interest and investment in my development and relational skills. When we would get into mischief, faculty and administrators had understanding and faith that when we owned up to making a mistake, we were given another chance. I appreciate human-service helpers who empathize out of their own human experience. The helping relationship is not a completely detached "scientific" relationship. It's something you feel passionate about, because you bring into it your experience.[22]

While the spirit of community within the college was palpable, the surrounding neighborhood of the campus was changing. The Second Great Migration of African Americans from the American South to Chicago took place in the '40s and '50s. Henry Louis Gates describes it in his book *America Behind the Color Line*. They came from the rural agricultural South to Chicago after World War II, bringing with them country blues more than city jazz, which characterized the First Great Migration. Unskilled and semi-skilled jobs soon dissipated. They settled in declining, overcrowded housing conditions, which the city eventually sought to alleviate through public housing high-rises. They had lots of children, which had been an asset in the rural South. They did not experience urban job skills training or value education like their forerunners. They did not vote or have civic input. They came out of rural isolation in plantation-like settings in the South, and they did not have connecting social support networks when they arrived in the North. They did not have the mentoring of blacks from the First Great Migration who were moving out of the ghetto to the suburbs as fast as the lift of housing restrictions allowed them to do so. Sociologist Timuel Black concludes, "Hope was on the decline. The new black migrants of the 1940s and 1950s plummeted almost immediately."[23]

Justice for Emmet Till

The College Association's letter to the U.S. Attorney General, 1955

The ghetto now surrounded the campus of the college in Hyde Park. The South Side of Chicago was overcrowded, opportunity and hope were on the decline, and social support was absent. By the late 1950s anger bubbled to the surface. In 1955 a 14-year-old from the college neighborhood was lynched in the Deep South. A few months later Rosa Parks refused to obey a bus driver's order to give up her seat. We now mark that event as the trigger of the civil rights movement. Though both events happened in the Deep South, Rosa Parks said she was thinking of the young boy from the South Side of Chicago when she refused to move. His name was Emmett Till. In August 1955, his mother, Mamie, said goodbye to him at Chicago's Sixty-third Street station. When Till's brutally disfigured body was returned from Mississippi, his mother insisted on an open-casket funeral for her son. Fifty thousand mourners lined up to view the open casket, not far from where George Williams College was located. The wounds of racism would no longer be hidden from view and buried in a closed casket.[24] When the perpetrators were acquitted by an all-white jury and the case was closed, students and faculty of the College Association protested the injustice in a notice to the attorney general of the United States.

> We, the student body of George Williams College, would like to express our great concern regarding the questionable state of justice in some of our southern states. . . . Our college has enjoyed a rich history of close and fruitful relationships between all races. The College Association, speaking on behalf of the student body, disapproves of the judiciary action practiced on numerous occasions, and specifically, the much discussed case of Chicagoan Emmett Till. It seems almost inconceivable that this case has been allowed to be closed, especially at the expense of public faith in the entire judicial organization of our country.
>
> It is our feeling that it is time for the federal government to take action necessary to remedy this disregard for the established democratic principles of our country. In considering the general welfare of the citizenry of our country, and in view of the adverse reactions abroad when advocating the democratic way of life, we ask that your department exercise its full powers in alleviating this disgraceful situation in our country.[25]

There was no response from the attorney general, William P. Rogers.

The decade of the '60s was a trying time for the college, whose core belief was to be proactive in building community both within the college and in the surrounding neighborhoods and communities where students engaged in work and field internships. African Americans from the surrounding communities enrolled in George Williams

College as commuter students and found community within its walls. However, the surrounding neighborhood was difficult to traverse for white students, who continued to come from all parts of the country to George Williams College. Tom Scott, Judy Sutherland Dawson, Mary Wiseman Walter, and LaVerne Duncan tell of their experiences in the 1960s.

"A far cry from the Canadian Rockies"

Tom Scott, student, ('61, '63)

> I came from Didsbury, Alberta, Canada, a town of fifteen hundred people. I grew up in a cabin; the people I grew up with, my community, were mostly farmers and ranchers. I had very limited exposure to people who were different from me, be it race, religion, or social class. When I think now on what George Williams College means to me, I would say it was the full range of my experiences living and working in the diverse city of Chicago.
>
> When I came to Hyde Park from Canada to become a student at George Williams College, I left a family back home full of doubts and fears about my decision. As I said goodbye and got on the train, trunk and suitcase in hand, my parents warned me about the trunk, "It'll never get there. They take everything in Chicago," they said. When I arrived in the big city and was not in eyeshot of my trunk, their words echoed in his mind. It turned out the trunk was only being held for customs examination. When I arrived at the college in late August and entered my room, the window had been left open to bring in air. But the incoming air caked the room with soot, a far cry from the fresh air of the Canadian Rockies. I looked out on to the neighborhood below and saw a sea of black faces. Feeling hungry, I asked the switchboard operator, a part-time student from Germany, where I might go to get a bite to eat. She suggested Sam's, down the street. While chowing down, observing the cockroaches marching along the window sill, I began to have my own doubts about the decision I made.

But that was before Tom met the people at George Williams College. Soon he was feeling connected to others, having spent an orientation at the Williams Bay campus with other students and faculty.

> Herb Mullen assigned me to a Boys Club on the South Side for my internship experience. I was the crafts instructor, drawing on my experience as a volunteer in the Canadian YMCA where I spent ten years in "so-ed" [social education] before I came to Chicago, Within a few weeks, Al Cook contacted me and asked him if I would come to work as the Central YMCA as director of adult activities. In exchange, they

would pay for my tuition, room, and board. Before long, Merrill Oleson ['60] was calling me. "We need help at the Woodlawn Boys Club. Can you give us a hand?" he said. I was happy to get involved. I taught kids how to make healthy snacks for after school. As I was working, I became aware that I was the only white person there, working with the boys. In Canada, it was just the opposite. I was in an all-white community where I knew of only one black person.

I had another experience like that. I had a second internship experience at the Wabash YMCA, to lead groups. The internship was part of the requirement for majoring in social group work. Once more, I had this experience of being the only white, male minority in a black community.[26]

By this time, Tom lost his self-consciousness about being different and found himself open to learning from his new experiences. Once Tom was connected to a personal community and got involved in collaborative activities with a shared purpose, he was able to confidently reach out to and make connections with people who once seemed very different to him.

"Why am I here?"

Mary Wiseman Walter, student, ('66)

I transferred to George Williams College from a state school. I did poorly. I was unfocused and drifting. I didn't know what to do with my life. I was the daughter of a YMCA director. When my dad died, I decided to try George Williams College. I grew up in the YMCA, and besides that, I would get free tuition if I went there. When my mother drove me to school and saw the place, she said, "I do not want to leave you here. I am so worried." I had a field assignment at the Boys Brotherhood Republic (BBR), [one of the Chicago Youth Centers on the city's West Side], an agency where I was the only white person.

Mary did not feel prepared or open for this experience. Her fear of being in a tense, hostile neighborhood was fanned up a notch up by Officer Baker, a Chicago policeman who covered the George Williams College neighborhood. Officer Baker counseled, "When you get off the bus [two blocks from campus], just run down the middle of the street to the college. We had people who were attacked this year. That's the safest way to get home."

Once when I was leaving the agency to catch the bus, I yelled, "Run!" to my friend Bill, who was working with me. At that moment someone threw a bottle towards us. It hit the cement and broke. By the sound, I thought Bill got shot. There was one kid at BBR who showed me his wound from a broken bottle. I couldn't believe, when I said he needs to go to the doctor to get a stitch for it, he said, "No man, I'm proud of it!"

Duane Robinson was my professor of group work. He required that students journal [about] their experiences in their field assignment. I wrote in my journal, "Why me? Why did I get picked to go out there? It's frightening. People get killed in the neighborhood where I am!" Duane Robinson's response was brief, "Why not you?" That comment gave me pause. I had some reflecting to do. Soon after, I was sitting in a meeting at BBR, when in walks Martin Luther King! That summer [of '65], he had an apartment right next door. He came in to get a basketball to shoot some hoops and unwind. As he was chatting with us, he asked us a question, "Why are you here?" I'm sitting there watching him, and I'm thinking, "This is a piece of history and I'm in it!"

George Williams College gave me my focus. After my dad died, I went where life took me. I was a failure at Ball State [University]. I didn't know what to do with my life. I was really floundering. From personnel and guidance, to group work, to everybody—the girl behind the front desk, admissions, my teachers—everyone cared about you as a person. I thrived on that. I found myself and I found Harry [Walter '64, '69]! Everything was about developing the whole person. You're here to serve others, but to do that you have to be a whole person yourself.[27]

"A humanitarian place where each person was important"

Judy Sutherland Dawson, student, ('67)

When I was in high school in Detroit, I was involved in Y activities. Once, a Y bus was going to Chicago for a weekend visit to George Williams College. I got on board with great enthusiasm. From that visit, George Williams College was the only college I applied to. That's where I was going. I was excited about this great multicultural neighborhood. . . . I loved the city. However, when my mom and dad arrived on campus from Detroit to bring their daughter to college, that was something else. My mother looked around and said, "You are not staying here." I protested, "Yes!" She said, "No!" My father turned around to my mom and said, "Gertrude!" And that was it.

I jumped right in, loved the group work program and my internship experience at the Salvation Army. For me, George Williams College was working in a humanitarian environment where each person was important.

Dave Dawson, student, ('69)

Dave Dawson (Judy's husband, also a GWC graduate) confirmed, "Yes! It was the closeness of community in a small school with such a variety of students."[28]

"A place that brought people together"

LaVerne Siemsen Duncan, student, ('68)

I transferred from another university because I thought George Williams College had what I was looking for. I didn't have a YMCA background; maybe I've been in a YMCA two times in my life. I wasn't influenced by any graduate to come. I wasn't particularly interested in urban work or working with youth, for that matter. I knew I wanted a recreation degree, or some people-serving kind of thing. My background was 4-H. I wanted to do something like that, something that brought people together. Rural people need the experience of community. I thought of using groups and recreation with seniors, if not working with youth.

People warmly remember the Hyde Park campus. For a person coming from my background it was an eye-opening experience. I lived in housing a few blocks away from the campus. We were doing fieldwork in places where they were having riots. I'm very close to my family, and they were concerned for me, so I moved back home and commuted to school.

But I still felt a part of a community. All my classroom experiences were in small group[s], and everyone was involved in a group-work setting in the field. It's not like we were all best friends, but we shared this importance of the value of relationship. There was this respect for each other . . . respect for the individual, and we learned from each other. When I was on campus, I went with my roommate Reggie Singleton ['69] to her church in the city. It was very different from my experience. Coming from my background, there was not a lot of emotional expression. I learned from that.

I did my field placement in the Hyde Park Home for the Aged. It was a wonderful experience. I really enjoyed [Professor] Don Clayton. I worked for him. He was so spontaneous. He had "a party class." We had to plan a party for group work. We planned a traveling party on a bus. I thought, "This is different!"

George Williams had heart! Everyone was striving for a sense of community. They were energized by a mission that they could change the world—not through greatness, like the president of the United States, but by respect, by putting yourself in the other person's shoes. How do you help people, but don't change their lives if they don't want to? I guess you could call that a democratic spirit, respect for the individual. It works in the field of geriatrics. I learned the basics on how to approach people, the development of self, the exposure to diversity. I work with independent elderly who want to continue to be in control of their lives. All around them, people are telling [them] what [they] have to do. At George Williams the teacher was a facilitator, not an authority figure. I sometimes felt like an outsider when sharing experiences, but to feel comfortable and familiar when sharing experiences was kind of cool. It was not an authoritative relationship. Teachers were not standing up front teaching at you. They involved you in problems and had a true respect of you.

Without the GW experience, my life would have been very different. I would have had a regular 9-to-5 job. Now I have a sense of passion about what I'm doing. I'm doing what I was meant to do all along, to look to the needs of others. This sense of passion was instilled by people who share their experiences and have a common mission. There was something about the student population there that kept pulling me in. It certainly was a nontraditional education.

LaVerne married Bill Duncan ('68), and throughout a good part of the Downers Grove era they lived on the College Camp grounds, where Bill managed the Williams Bay campus. They raised their family there.

The experience up here [at the Williams Bay campus] has been great. We raised four kids here. This is where our home is. . . . Being up here brings us back to some of the feelings we had. People come back year after year because there's something here they want their kids and grandkids to experience. They have come here for fifty years. They feel part of a family. When the college closed, people were able to come back here, to that caring place. . . . We used to have graduate students from campus [who] came to our house on Friday night for dinner. They were outdoor education students like David Bast ['71], David Hughes ['69], Lee Bay ['73], and George Graham ['81]. My kids remember them. They would babysit. These students were all family. Our own family was out of the area, and it was very good for us on a personal level.[29]

Building Community Inside and Out: Downers Grove

On the south side of Hyde Park, Chicago, where these students attended college, the spirit of community and hope in the surrounding neighborhood was not the only thing in decline. Even the college building, architecturally designed for the YMCA College in 1915, the building for which students felt "an obligation to the brotherhood" for its grandeur, was in decline. It was now commonly referred to as the "old shoe factory." Yet, buoyed by a spirit of community within, students continued to work to build the same kind of inclusive community without, and they did that with a sense of hope and passion.

In the '60s, with the assassinations of President John F. Kennedy in '63, Malcolm X in '65, Martin Luther King Jr. in '68, and Robert Kennedy in '68, the mood of optimism was changing. There were riots in Chicago in the summer of '66 and '68. Within these same tumultuous years, George Williams College did what many urban residents were doing: it moved to the newly developing suburbs. The city of Chicago denied a badly-needed expansion plan in 1962 and in 1966, the college relocated to Downers Grove. Commuter rail and bus services were limited, and car transportation became a mandate. It was not the typical "white flight" of the times, because the 772 students were not all white. The suburbs were mostly white, and whites were suspicious and hostile to the appearance of so many black college-age students in their neighborhood. The tables were turned. Black students who enrolled in GWC would have to travel to the all-white suburbs. At first, according to a college newspaper editorial, the George Williams College student "seems satisfied."

"The GWC student seems satisfied"

Student reporter, 1968

Students in our college are oriented toward community service, the "helping professions," identified with moral values, principals, and cooperation, as opposed to selfishness or ideals of selfish success in the materialistic sense of the word. This orientation seems to be understood and accepted by the students of our college. . . . Up to this point I confess, we are doing well. We are secure and, perhaps, very comfortable. . . .

It seems to me that in our school there is no controversy, no discontent, appetites seem to be fulfilled, and stability of a sort reigns. All of us seem to be adjusted to the system. Most of us see our future in a secured organization "somewhere" performing the role of a professional. Many of us see little reason to bother with talks or useless discussions.

The college administration and faculty, by practice and policy, permit an open campus in our community, a campus where ideological controversies are permitted and sometimes encouraged. College, by its nature, is not a safe refuge from the "terrifying confrontation" with the contemporary world. We should be a microcosm, a small world in which events and ideas from the big world are reproduced, challenged, or at least questioned, even at the risk of losing comfort and stability.[30]

Eager student applicant

Ellen Goldberg, student, ('72, '86)

I grew up in Hyde Park, on the east side of the railroad tracks. The railroad tracks divided the Hyde Park neighborhood, with predominantly low-income African Americans living west of the tracks and predominantly middle-income whites living east of the tracks. George Williams College was on the west side of the tracks. I found my home base for after-school activities to be the Hyde Park YMCA, located on Fifty-third and Blackstone, six or seven blocks east of George Williams College. From the age of nine or ten, I swam at the Y regularly, and later I was in the Y Leaders Club. In the summer I went to Morton Johnson Camp in Iron, Michigan, for a leadership camping experience. I remember [singer] Natalie Cole attending the camp with me on the strong encouragement of her father, Nat King Cole, who was living in California.

So many of the Y leaders were student interns or graduates from George Williams College. As a Y leader, I worked with them in community activism to deal with the racial tension and gangs in the neighborhood and provide after-school recreation and youth development programs. I remember going with my leadership group to the George Williams College campus in Hyde Park for first aid lectures in the anatomy lab. My Y leaders told me of their favorite faculty heroes at George Williams College. . . . A highlight experience for me in high school was when one of my Y leaders took me to George Williams College to meet Dr. Arthur Steinhaus. I also remember getting a little preview of the new Downers Grove campus when it first opened. I was attending a midstate meeting of Y leaders who met on the new campus.

Ellen feels a strong sense of belonging to the Y family. "You have people coming from all over the U.S. and the world because they have been involved with the Y. It's a solid common thread that most of us have experienced. It makes us a community." This "family" being a Christian association, I wondered what it was like for Ellen growing up Jewish in the YMCA.

I had heard the stories of the Chicago Metro Y in the 1940s, but that was not my experience in the '50s and '60s. Phil Brin ['49, '52], the executive director of my synagogue congregation, was a graduate of George Williams College, and his daughter Deborah Pruitt ['72] also was a graduate. I did not have difficulty with the Christian overtone with prayers and the like at YMCA events. When it was time for me to pick a college, it was a no-brainer; it was GWC. I was happy the college moved to Downers Grove. Like any new freshman, I was excited about an experience away from home.[31]

"Just the opposite of the Hyde Park experience"

Reuben Davis, student, ('67, '69)

I came to George Williams College from a suburb of New Jersey, Montclair. While in high school, I got involved in the YMCA and worked in what was historically known as the "black branch" of the Montclair association. I was hired as a part-time group-work secretary to work in Hi Y and college clubs, while I went to Bloomfield Technical School. Eventually I was recruited to work as a volunteer in the YMCA of another New Jersey area, East and West Orange. It was there that I met Bob Slater ['58], a graduate of George Williams College in group work. Following Slater's example, I decided to go full time into Y work and transfer to George Williams College for a group work degree. Through scholarships from the Y Men's Club and my church, I was able to scrape together barely enough money to get to GWC in 1963, when they were in Hyde Park. I was very involved in the College Association while there. . . . I was only one of three black residential students at the Hyde Park campus, and one was from Africa: Desta Girma ['66]. All the other African American students were commuters and lived in Chicago. When the college moved to the suburbs, they recruited lots of African American students who had to live together for the first time in an isolated, hostile environment. It was just the opposite of the Hyde Park experience. In Hyde Park, the Black Muslims were around the corner. Elijah Muhammed lived in Kenwood nearby. Once, a male black student and a female white student from the college were walking in the neighborhood a few blocks from campus, and a Muslim brother stopped them and slapped him in the face.[32]

Now, in the first three years of suburban relocation, incidents and indignities accumulated, raising tension to a height in one week of racial confrontation. It was the new test for the Community of Living and Learning. This radical change in community context precipitated one of the most trying moments in the history of George Williams College. Racial tension cut to core values the college held dear, values about community building, managing conflict and differences through dialogue, and trust-building processes centered around a shared human service mission. All these would be put to the test in what has been called the Spring Festival of '69. We now hear voices of students, faculty, and the president of George Williams College on Spring Festival and tensions leading up to it.

LEFT: Portrait of Sir George Williams, painted in England by artist John Collier, given to the college by the class of 1923. The son of Sir George Williams wrote from London, "I have the pleasure in advising you that the painting of my late father by the Hon. John Collier has been shipped to 5315 Drexel Ave. . . . Members of the YMCA who knew my father consider it to be lifelike portrait, in fact so good that a copy of it is to be presented to our Corporation Gallery, the chief Gallery of the city of London." (*George Williams College Archives*)

BELOW, LEFT TO RIGHT: "The Founders": William E. Lewis (1839–1890), I. E. Brown (1849–1917), and the visionary for a permanent training school for YMCA workers, Robert Weidensall (1836–1922). (*George Williams College Archives*)

ABOVE: Dr. Henry Kallenberg, athletic director of George Williams College (1897–1917) with Dr. Luther Gulick and child, leaning against hammock at Lake Geneva Summer Training Institute. Gulick founded and instructed the Western Summer Training School for Physical Directors from 1890–1902. (*George Williams College Archives*)

BELOW: "Lake Geneva Men" (ca. 1890). Men of the Western Secretarial Institute and Training School, seated outside the dining hall. Named people include Kallenberg, I. E. Brown, and President John Hansel. (*George Williams College Archives*)

LEFT: Four-fold symbol of the cross stamped on the Articles of Incorporation By-Laws of George Williams College indicating the social dimension was just as integral to human development as the body-mind-spirit dimensions symbolizing the YMCA mission today. George Williams College strongly focused on the social-relational situations of people in their human service mission. (*YMCA of the USA and Kautz Family YMCA Archives, University of Minnesota Libraries*)

ABOVE: "Wand Class Lake Geneva, 1890." "The wands were made by the students from bushes and small trees. We had no other gym equipment." Henry Kallenberg is on the right. (*George Williams College Archives*)

LEFT: "1890 Cornerstone Reunion" (ca. 1900). People reportedly present at the first "dedicatory campfire" of the college in 1886. (*George Williams College Archives*)

BELOW: "1897: Lake Geneva Summer School." The man on the top right has the symbol of the four-fold purpose of the YMCA on his sweater. The cross predated the YMCA triangle. (*George Williams College Archives*)

LEFT: Women played a significant role in the history of the Williams Bay campus. In August 1886, the state YWCA united at Camp Collie at Williams Bay, Wisconsin, where the Western Secretarial Institute of the YMCA was holding a summer conference attended by families of many leaders. Subsequent YWCA National Conventions were held at the YMCA Camp, including this one showing members and staff of the International Committee of the YWCA, 1893. (*George Williams College Archives*)

RIGHT: "City YWCA Conference" (1906). The Toledo YWCA group. (*George Williams College Archives*)

BELOW: "Watching a Stunt. 1910" Women had their own Student Conferences, with the same aim as the men's—foreign service. Though they dressed in white gown during the day, they slept in tents on the ground at night in the college camp. (*George Williams College Archives*)

LEFT: "Kite Flying Contest." According to the 1916 *Crucible*: "to keep the boys engaged in a character building enterprise, instead of being engaged in mischief." (*Private collection of Jean Bilstrom*)

BELOW: "Experiment in Blood Pressure" (ca. 1920s). The college was one of the first educational institutions engaging in exercise physiology research. (*YMCA of the USA and Kautz Family YMCA Archives, University of Minnesota Libraries*)

OPPOSITE PAGE, LOWER LEFT:
Sherwood Eddy, sitting on a bench on the Williams Bay campus. Eddy was a guest speaker at the Student Conferences at Lake Geneva and part of the Student Volunteer Movement, where college students vounteered for foreign service. An advocate of the Social Gospel, Eddy returned from foreign service to serve in the United States for social justice. (*George Williams College Archives*)

OPPOSITE PAGE, LOWER RIGHT:
John R. Mott, sitting on a bench on the Williams Bay campus. Mott led or visited the Student Conferences at Lake Geneva from 1888–1922. He was the general secretary of the YMCA from 1915–1928 and the Nobel Peace Prize winner in 1946 for his YMCA leadership in foreign service, particularly serving war refugees. (*George Williams College Archives*)

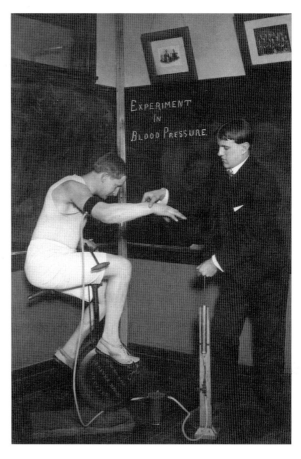

ABOVE: Dr. Arthur Steinhaus was a world-renowned researcher in the physiology of the human body. He is shown here working in the college laboratory. (*George Williams College Archives*)

LEFT: Many international students came to George Williams College to study under Arthur Steinhaus. (*George Williams College Archives*)

LEFT: "GWC Drexel Gymnastics." Demonstrations of physical acumen were commonly displayed for the public, as in "Gymnite," a popular public event each year at the Hyde Park campus. (*YMCA of the USA and Kautz Family YMCA Archives, University of Minnesota Libraries*)

BELOW: Group of students gathered in a learning circle on the dock of the Williams Bay campus (ca. 1950s). Informal settings for small groups was the preferred learning mode. (*George Williams College Archives*)

ABOVE: "Foreign Delegation. Lake Geneva Student Conference. 1922" (*George Williams College Archives*)

ABOVE: "Reception to Foreign Students by Mr. and Mrs. Stearns, Lake Geneva, 1925." (*George Williams College Archives*)

ABOVE: The size of Student Conferences increased in the 1930s and 40s. This is a Midwest Conference of students at Williams Bay. (*George Williams College Archives*)

LEFT: Student Martin Msseemmaa (2000) returns to Tanzania where he grew up and started a YMCA before coming to George Williams College. When he returned, the Maasai gave him a welcoming ceremony and a gift of a goat to his wife, Pat Hammond, also a student of GWC. (*Private collection of Martin Msseemmaa*)

RIGHT: Brad Burger ('01) found a passion for internationl service by taking a student service learning trip to South Africa, where he learned the power of human compassion during home visits to those suffering from HIV/AIDS. After graduation Brad returned to South Africa. (*Aurora University Archives*)

LEFT: Chris Blackburn ('01) also went on the student service learning trip to South Africa and is pictured here with new friends from that trip. After graduation, Chris went to a remote region of Alaska to become a school social worker.
(*Aurora University Archives*)

Racial tension rises: 1969

Dan Logan, student reporter, ('69); Reuben Davis, student, ('67, '69); Harry Walter, student and coach, ('64, '69); Yevette Newton, student, ('69, '74); Ellen Goldberg, student, ('72, '86)

A grad student reporter Dan Logan explains:

> Many persons familiar with George Williams College have noted its decades-old philosophy of including black students in phases of campus life to a degree much greater than most colleges. When the college moved to white suburban Downers Grove, further efforts were made to assure that blacks would continue to attend. As a result, the proportion of black students increased so that by 1968–1969, there were about 150 black students of a total of 850 students, with more than 20 percent of the new students being black. . . . Many of the new black students had been recruited from neighborhoods where educational preparation and financial support did not provide an adequate starting base for success in college.[33]

Reuben Davis adds:

> I completed my undergraduate work in group work at the Hyde Park campus, but then I decided to continue on to get my master's in counseling psychology. That brought me to Downers Grove for my graduate work. When the college came to Downers Grove, I was given a role of assistant director of housing and head dorm advisor. I worked to see that the black students who were new on campus would be forming good academic habits.

Coach Harry Walter offers the following perspective:

> In the first few years at Downers Grove, the gym was not yet completed, and I would have to take the basketball team to Downers Grove North High School to practice and play. Onlookers were not used to seeing so many black students in the gymnasium. Black students were refused service at local barbers, who claimed they did not know how to cut their hair. Some said they got hostile glares when going to restaurants in the area. Black and white students were having difficulty rooming together in the dormitories.[34]

Yevette Newton reported:

> In the dorms, a white student tried to pay black students to launder her clothes.[35]

Ellen Goldberg continues:

Early in my freshman year I noticed white students and black students were not talking to each other very much. It was not my experience in Hyde Park, where I lived. One student, who called himself "Kubla Khan," walked around campus decked in African garb with a turban, carrying an unsheathed spear. In the dorm black students were turning cans upside down and drumming. I didn't think it sounded any different from the drumming that went on down by the lakefront in Hyde Park [and no different from the drumming that goes on up and down Michigan Avenue today], but it stirred up fear with some of the white students. In light of what was going on in the country, it seemed to be a "between" year . . . a year between racial tension on campuses after the death of Martin Luther King and a year before Kent State and protests over the Vietnam War.

Whenever I joined my African American friends for a trip to the [newly opened] Yorktown Shopping Mall, we were met with stares. If I would join some [racially mixed] friends in an open convertible driving down Meyers Road, we were stared down. The Black Student Association (BSA) planned a series of events throughout the year for students, faculty, and people in the community to openly talk about racism.

Again Dan Logan reports:

It could not be said that the discontent of black students was not a matter of concern to the campus community. . . . The Black Student Association sponsored . . . a conference on black awareness attended by several hundred area high school students and very few GWC students and faculty. . . . Amid apprehensions by segments of the staff and student body, Fred Hampton of the Black Panthers appeared on the campus. For this event, classes were cancelled at the last minute. His speech was well attended by both blacks and whites and was followed by vigorous discussion by both blacks and whites in separate meetings.

Reuben Davis offers:

I was instrumental in bringing Fred Hampton on campus to hear an alternative view of what the Black Panthers were about. Though some people feared the Black Panthers, they did some social good. They had social programs like after-school programs for neighborhood kids. However, I have to add, I didn't appreciate that I had a full body search done on me when I went to their headquarters to invite them to come!

Dan Logan:

> In spring quarter two episodes of student assertion occurred [that] were in marked contrast to the usual pattern of campus decision making. . . . A group of students called The April Committee (TAC) began to take action. [They] staged a sit-in for several hours in the office of the president to underscore TAC's insistence that the college cease to entertain at a downtown club [that] had restrictive practices on black persons. [Also], an educational psychology class was entered by a group of Black Student Association members who took over the class and presented material [that] they felt the instructor was overlooking.

According to Dan Logan's report, several faculty members responded in kind to this incident, further eroding a well-established tradition of the college to engage in inclusive dialogue over conflict. They drafted a policy statement, specifying the rights of a "special purpose institution" to express themselves and warned that "outside forces may be called in if necessary if there were violations of the policy." Now it was the students' turn to complain that "there was no public discussion of the document" and "the usual pattern of discussions which characterizes the GWC atmosphere had been avoided at this time."

Spring Festival: Two weeks of 1969

Richard Hamlin, student, ('49), and GWC president; Ellen Goldberg, student, ('72, '86); Dan Logan, student reporter, ('69); and Reuben Davis, student, ('67, '69)

President Richard Hamlin:

> The way it all started was like this: I had a call at about two in the morning. I recognized a male voice on the other end. It was [an African American student]. I had known him as one of the Larry Hawkins kids. Larry brought him to Lake Geneva for college prep on one of those government grants. He was a very personable guy.
>
> He said, "Is this Prez? Prez, could I meet you some place?"
>
> "At two in the morning?" I said.
>
> "Yeah. Two other students and I would like you to meet with us. We got something really important to tell you."
>
> "Okay," I said. "I'll do it. Where do we meet?"
>
> "Turn a certain corner on campus, there's a clump of birches there; we'll be in there," he said.
>
> I went right away, picked up these three students, and brought them to our house.

"We want to give you some advanced notice that the Black Student Association is going to have some real tough things coming down. Man, they're really gonna come down."

The way these guys described it, it sounded pretty scary.

"When will it happen?' I asked.

"In the next day or two."

"Okay, I appreciate it," I said.

The next day I got together with Cliff Holmes, [and] Charlie Rhee, and I pulled in Nelson Wieters. I wanted Nelson, because I always admired Nelson's ability to work in tough situations. He was always levelheaded, always came out with a creative idea. We decided to put together the idea of what we called an "adult education" model for the college in the next few weeks. The idea was to continue having classes, but have them under an entirely different organization, not the academic calendar type, but seminar type things, things that would deal with the issues. We decided [to] stop the usual curriculum. Let's make this situation a learning experience.[36]

Monday: Vandalism, and verbal and physical assault

Ellen Goldberg:

I had just come back from Lake Geneva with my freshman class for a weekend with faculty. I was having fun, enjoying getting to know the faculty as real people. Bob Steiger was doing his rope tricks for us. I can remember the scent of cherry pipe tobacco coming from Charles Rhee's quarters. When I came back, I saw the windows to the bookstore had been broken. I heard rumors of other damage, like fires and floods in the dorms.

Dan Logan:

By early morning on Monday significant vandalism occurred on campus, including fires in two dorms. Several hoses were cut on washing machines in the dorms apparently in an attempt to cause flooding in the dorms. . . . Two black students were suspended. As tension and finger-pointing increased, Professor Nelson Wieters called for a special faculty meeting to find ways to resolve the conflict and relieve tensions. . . .

That evening two hundred black and white students and about fifteen faculty gathered in the dorm to discuss what was going on. Tensions ran high. . . . In the heated confrontation a black student attacked a white girl, and the situation threatened to get out of control as tempers rose. Direct restraint by friends of the black student, and firm and decisive intervention by Director of Graduate Studies Tom Bennett, provided enough stability . . . so that anger and frustration could be expressed verbally rather than physically.

Ellen Goldberg:

> There were verbal attacks, and then it got physical. I never heard of fighting at George Williams College. Some of the fighting was between black students. I don't know if some of the fights had to do with what was going on back in their neighborhoods in the city.

Tuesday: Group dynamics gone awry

President Richard Hamlin:

> We decided that one of the important things to do was to keep the communication going. So we appointed a steering committee to oversee this process. We asked Nelson to chair the steering committee. I knew that Nelson had a high acceptance among the students, including the black students. We solicited student input [from any group of students] on the issues that they had. The Black Student Association had thirteen points. They called them "demands," but they were really issues they were concerned about.
>
> All student groups were to present their concerns, which would be processed with faculty-student groups to work on them. We were to get recommendations, then it would go to the steering committee, then adopted or not. To keep communication clear, a newsletter went out from steering committee just about every day . . . to check rumors. If you did not it hear from them, it was not official.

Dan Logan:

> There was a mass meeting, with fifty faculty, seventy-five black students, and two hundred to three hundred white students. . . . The meeting was characterized by low trust and high anxiety, with such contradictory comments shouted by students to faculty as "Do something to get us moving" and "Shut up, I'm telling you." In frustration, black students withdrew, returning later with demands to reinstate . . . two suspended students and [to] recognize the BSA as the official group for handling matters pertaining to black students.

According to Logan's report, President Hamlin, while making a public announcement of the communication process the college would use to hear student concerns, also noted that he did not observe white students supporting black students in their standpoint, and he called on them to be more supportive. A response came quickly. That evening students organized the "Core Committee of Concerned White Students" to rally support for black students. Working late into the night they published a set of demands that they thought reflected the grievances of the black students, though black students were not involved in their deliberation. Black students were busily engaged in their own activity of articulating what was to be called "the thirteen demands." Dan Logan said "it appeared that the BSA was conveying the message that their thirteen points, while of sufficient urgency to be termed 'demands,' were also to be considered negotiable."

In the days to follow, other dysfunctional intergroup dynamics heated up. There was evident strength of white student support for the concerns of black students, but two separate groups of white students emerged with very divergent styles of advocacy. The first group, called the Core Committee, became a small group of white undergraduate male students who modeled their advocacy style on confrontation and assertion of power and control, much as was the style of student activism at the time. The second was a coalition of white students who organized themselves in reaction to the Core Committee. They advocated for a discussion and consensus approach congruent with the tradition of the college, and opposed the use of pressure upon administration. They called themselves the Action Committee.

Ellen Goldberg:

> I kept thinking, we came to George Williams to better ourselves and go back into our neighborhoods and work. Why are we doing things this way? I represented the Action group of students.

Wednesday: Working separately

Dan Logan:

> Core threatened a student strike if their demands were not met within four hours. The Black Student Association withdrew from any plans of strike. The Action Committee continued to react to Core.

President Richard Hamlin:

> The Black Student Association was working on one list. But we got another list from a group of white students [Core] who were acting like the SDS [Students for a Democratic Society]. They had taken up issues that they thought were the black student issues without talking to the black students. They were presenting things at the same time BSA was submitting demands.

Thursday: Student strike

Dan Logan:

> The campus was dotted with strike signs, and white students stationed themselves at entrances to urge support of a boycott of classes. . . . A *Chicago Tribune* reporter

arrived on the scene. She was told by Core students, "We don't want violence. We don't want any police."

Ellen Goldberg:

Everyone was glad they did not have to call in the Downers Grove police. I feared they would exacerbate the conflict. So many students had directly witnessed unfriendly, racist attitudes from the local police at that time.

Dan Logan:

By the afternoon a curious change had occurred. The Core leadership repudiated the strike it had organized as racist since it had been planned without the black students for whom it was intended to show support. They drafted a statement [saying] support of BSA demands was a top priority.

President Richard Hamlin:

When it came time for this group of white students to present, [Professor] Tom Bennett looked around the room and said, "We've got to tell you, your demands are out of bounds. They're not legitimate. You're acting like you don't believe me." Tom invited two African American students to come in. He said, "Here are the demands from this student group. What do you think of them?" They looked them over and said, "Man, what are you white students doing here telling us what we need? We know what we need. We think they're illegitimate, because you're the wrong color, presenting these things!" They had worked up these demands without even talking to the black students. The white students then withdrew their demands and began to work with and support the black student agenda.

The president met with a group of black students from BSA and established a three-part approach consisting of appointed negotiation teams of faculty and students, workshops on the African American experience, and a steering committee clearinghouse to assign proposals to appropriate committees for consideration.

Dan Logan:

Classes were canceled by the administration, and the next three days were announced to be devoted to negotiation followed by several days of the following week devoted to an all-campus workshop for faculty and students on racial awareness. The Reverend John Porter, who taught African American history at GWC, noted that a "de-honkification process" was beginning, and he expressed the hope that the college could lead the way in racial progress.

Friday: A shift in tone

Dan Logan:

> With Core, a significant shift in tone had taken place, with the leadership more actively soliciting new input from the audience. There was a noticeable increase in the humor and laughter. The situation was much more stabilized. On this day, all three student groups met to work towards consolidation of their proposals. Dean Cliff Holmes presented their proposal to the faculty, indicating that the black students were "acting in an open manner, appreciative of the complexity of their proposals." . . . [He] pointed out some of the deep concerns felt by the black students [that] they were trying to deal with through these proposals and acknowledged their diligence in preparing and revising their document, and negotiating the points in up to five committees simultaneously.

Saturday: Holiday goes on hold

This intense process involving faculty negotiation was going on during a Memorial Day holiday weekend, though little mention is made of it.

Dan Logan:

> The two groups, Core and Action, "began independent moves to consolidate their strength around matters other than demands" and began to coalesce under the leadership of the Black Student Association. . . . The meeting ran well past the dinner hour, and food was brought over from the dining hall by student volunteers. . . . A great amount of goods and services [including clerical and maintenance services] were made available in support of this whole extraordinary process. . . . The strains of long hours of negotiation and planning were becoming evident. . . . The president became ill in his office Saturday morning and was not seen in public again until eight days later at graduation.

President Richard Hamlin:

> I was sitting in my office on a Saturday, trying to get caught up. In walked [professor] Keith Hoover, reporting on some of the developments. All of a sudden I felt so weak and collapsed. Keith called [my wife,] Joan. She got the doctor to come. The doctor said I didn't have heart attack, but something close to it. He said, "We need to put you to bed." I said, "I can't do that now." He said, "Okay, I'm going to give you some pills. Go to bed, and if you feel like can go to these things, go ahead." Well, they knocked me out for three days. Joan was the communication link for me.

Sunday: "A working trust level"

Dan Logan:

> The mood was that of a team working toward similar goals, with both students and faculty members making suggestions and questioning certain steps. The black students seemed more attentive to the intent of the faculty to implement than to insist on specific dates or quantitative responses. This would suggest a working trust level. Students showed respect and consideration for matters of faculty academic freedom in curriculum and administrative authority in personnel decisions. Also, Core and Action took down their separate shingles to present a united front to involve returning students.

Ellen Goldberg:

> We worked around the clock on Memorial Day weekend to come to some resolution about the specific concerns raised by the black students. If you're interested in survival of what you think is important, you've got to make an investment. We were fighting for the survival of our college!

Monday: Tenuous resolution

Dan Logan:

> At an official convocation of seven hundred students and faculty, the BSA distributed a statement, which read in part, "The thirteen proposals of the Black Student Association were accepted." They had reached consensus on the intent of the points, without arriving at agreement on specifics. It appeared the meeting was a natural turning point of resolution, but more followed.

Tuesday and Wednesday: Outside group disruption

No one expected what was to happen next. An outside group disrupted the fragile indigenous process that was coming together. There was one more agreement that had been made early in the week's negotiation. Faculty, administrators, and white student leaders were to participate in a workshop on white racism.

Dan Logan:

> An arrangement was hastily contracted with an outside group. The group had a theatrical element to their presentation, at times with members bursting into the room accusing and insulting those in attendance. Separate sessions were held with black students and faculty, with a leader unfamiliar with the amount of work that had

gone into the thirteen proposals, [who] insisted that dates and numerical quotas were needed "because black students don't believe you've got one ounce of good will." The group used "a classic means of developing distrust between groups" by separating the students from the faculty. This did not go over with faculty. "[They] should have been warned about the inadvisability of attempting to use group dynamics techniques on a group of professionals in group work," faculty commented.

The BSA was now calling the thirteen proposals "demands" again. Faculty member Tom Bennett said, "This has all the earmarks of starting over." A fragile trust appeared to be fracturing, with more confrontations and threats hurled out in disagreements over dates of implementation, numbers, and even new "demands" from the BSA.

Thursday: "I remembered all the things I had learned"

Reuben Davis was appointed the BSA representative to negotiate the thirteen points. He moved the process along constructively by assessing and summarizing points of agreement, openly confronting points of concern, and moving the agenda forward.

Reuben Davis:

> I remembered all the things I had learned in group work. Group work was about conflict management and making sure all voices would be heard. I went through each point, one by one, allowing each side to speak. In the middle of point one, I could see the students were upset with me that I let [faculty member] Tom Bennett speak. But I wouldn't go to the next point until all voices were heard. Then I moved on. By the third point, I established the ground rule for negotiation: Everyone would be heard. I give Del Kinney, [group work faculty member and program director], the credit. It took time. We went back and forth. But my authority as gatekeeper became established. When it was all over, I got phone calls from students to let me know they felt they had been heard and treated fairly.

Dan Logan:

> By the end of the week, some good faith had been restored as the details of the proposal were worked out, taking into consideration faculty and administrative concerns about academic freedom and the financial limitations of the college.

President Richard Hamlin:

> A lot of good group work stuff was going on.

Dan Logan:

> [The president] could have used [one university] response and cancelled classes, enforced by police if necessary, or [another university] response to essentially do nothing, neither resist nor negotiate, waiting for the students to call off the protest. . . . [Instead] the president chose a course that accurately reflected the real balance of power between students and faculty, and the constructive feelings that dissenting students held for the college.

President Richard Hamlin:

> I remember the words Roy Sorenson said to me one time, "What we are working for is not for an institution; we're working for human values."

One week later: "Open and amiable"

One week later the George Williams College commencement ceremony continued on schedule. Reuben Davis was one of the graduates in that ceremony.

President Richard Hamlin:

> The final week of the quarter was perhaps one of the most open and amiable of the year, coming as it did out of an intensive encounter.

Reuben Davis:

> I accepted a job with the YMCA in Los Angeles. I decided to drive from Chicago to Los Angeles. It took me fifteen days. I felt beaten down by lack of sleep and the tension of the experience. I needed time to reflect, so the time was good. I thought about how the college handled this. I thought about my first experience with the college. It was Orientation Practicum. I remembered how impressed I was that all the experienced students . . . planned and directed the whole orientation from beginning to end. The role and responsibility of students was real at George Williams. Where it broke down in Spring Festival is that the college administration had to deal with a kind of student they had never had on campus before. The college was not prepared for them, and these students were not prepared for the college. [However, the outside consulting group] just thought they could move in on what they saw on campus, damn the administration, tear open the place, and push their agenda. . . . They truly did not believe in the students. . . . They thought they were too stupid to have their own opinions, too dumb to take their own actions. They were going to mold this in the direction they wanted it to go, and they used the students to do that.

President Richard Hamlin (later, reporting to all college stakeholders):

> Specific measures the college was taking to follow through on the agreements have been accepted by the Black Student Association representatives with mutual consensus to move ahead in good faith. . . . Work continued virtually around the clock for eight days and nights, including Memorial Day weekend. The investment of time, emotion, and energy by faculty, staff, and students was remarkable. . . . Basic agreements were reached, though "clarified and modified [in ways that were] educationally respectable, institutionally compatible, and financially feasible."

The resolution included ongoing library acquisitions, available course outlines, a black studies program, monitoring black relevance in existing courses, and in-service training in black studies. Faculty would monitor curriculum and accept transfer from accredited schools. Personnel decisions regarding faculty were left to teaching and administrative faculty, with an agreement to hire more black faculty in four position vacancies and to hire additional black counselors. The hiring of higher level administrative positions and "cooperation with 'racist' organizations" were left for presidential review and action. As icing on the cake, an additional proposal point was approved: to improve food service.

President Hamlin concluded:

> I view the events of late spring as a very difficult portion of the process of change through which the college and our society are going. This process is not concluded. . . . Hopefully, the most tumultuous part is behind us. The extent to which we can continue to act on our agreements in good faith—together—will determine the extent to which we can sustain the openness and rejuvenation of trust that was apparent the final week of the spring quarter.

He then reported the following endorsement from the Board of Trustees:

> Resolved, That this Board of Trustees stands in support the present posture of the faculty, administration, operating staff, and students regarding the recent activities on the college campus . . . and commends them for their selfless devotion to the task.[37]

Looking back on Spring Festival

Yevette Newton, student, ('69, '74); Peter Sorensen, professor; Gregg Robinson, student, ('77) and son of professor Duane Robinson; Dick Wyman, professor; Dick Hamlin, student, ('49) and GWC president

Though Spring Festival happened almost forty years ago, it is still regarded as a critical incident in the life of the college, imbued with meaning as to what the college was all about.

Yevette Newton:

> I followed George Williams College to the Downers Grove campus when the college moved out of Hyde Park. I wanted to be a student at George Williams College like so many of my African American mentors who were in the Wabash YMCA where I spent all my time growing up. I wanted to prepare for human service through physical education, like them.

The details of Spring Festival are fading for Yevette. Her lasting impression is that the overall inclusion of African American content in education with more inclusive representation of faculty and staff as mentors had to happen. "I learned much of my African American heritage in my family. But some of the students did not have that kind of educational background or identity. For a college that truly believed in educating the whole person, that would be important."

However, Yevette thinks the community bond was not broken through the strain, and that the shared commitment to human service was that bond. "George Williams College can be summed up in one word: *service*. That's the steady stream throughout history. You cannot serve anybody unless you have learned the value of service, and we learned that at George Williams College. Whatever field you are in, you are involved in service."

I asked Yevette if she knew of the whereabouts of a student known as "Kubla Khan," the student white students found threatening as he walked across campus during Spring Festival, dressed in African garb and carrying a spear. "Kubla Khan? Yes, I've seen him," she exclaimed. "I don't know of his whereabouts now, but the last time I talked with him, he was working as a youth worker with the toughest kids in the toughest sections of Chicago. He said he wants them to have more opportunities than he had growing up."

Professor Peter Sorensen:

> I was starting my first year on the faculty of George Williams College when Spring Festival occurred. I thought it was a great experience. I felt I was able to effectively dialogue with my students who sought me out to meet in small groups to talk. . . . There is no question about it, the college was driven [by] humanistic values to create better places for people. I believe these same values that were strong at GWC underlie effective organizational development, values related to involvement, ownership, and commitment.

Peter is now the director of a thriving doctoral program in organizational development at a nearby university. The program was a pioneer in the field of organizational development, evolving from George Williams College's courses on group work administration. He further reflects on the college's values, thinking of his Danish family origins. He was the son of Peter Sorensen Sr., a YMCA secretary at the Duncan Y in Chicago, and his father taught Danish gymnastics at George Williams College.

> My Danish family held to core Danish values that were congruent with the philosophy of GWC, values like tolerance for ambiguity and egalitarianism. These values undoubtedly got a workout during the Spring Festival![38]

Gregg Robinson:

> I was only a high school teenager at the time of Spring Festival. I remember my father [social work Professor Dr. Duane Robinson] had what we called "rap groups" in our home with black students at this time to listen to their concerns. I was young but very interested. I thought it was cool. My personal impression as a kid was that the students were very respectful, more angry about what was going on in the country than [at] George Williams College.[39]

Dick Wyman:

> It was hard to explain what was happening. You would walk across campus, and some student would make a comment because he thought you slighted him. Yet you could never meet a more democratic faculty. I took it as my responsibility to do my part. I would mount plays oriented to the black experience. I found that black students were strongly involved in theater on campus. It was a way to make connections, by investing in a common activity.[40]

Richard Hamlin recalls,

> I would get phone calls at home from people in the town. They'd say, "Why don't you kick the bastards out?" That was also true of some people inside the college. [faculty member] Clint Oleson did not think we were conducting ourselves according to his understanding of what a college should do, and he was vocal about it. About one or two years after Spring Festival, Clint asked if he could talk with me. He said, "I've really been hurting for the last few months. I've been wanting to talk with you. What I want to tell you is, the way you handled the Spring Festival, your point of view has been vindicated. You were so right." It took guts to say that to me.[41]

Storytelling, not confrontation:
A different way to build community

Manny Jackson, professor, 1972

The next years were fairly quiet, with ongoing processes to further the "good faith" agreements made through the thirteen points of Spring Festival. By 1971 stories of Spring Festival were already fading. Now the pendulum swung from confrontation to turning inward. Small groups were still used, not for caucuses or negotiation but for self-awareness and sensitivity training. If confrontation was used, it was for interpersonal "encounters" related to group dynamics and self-discovery.

Out of the college's agreement to hire more black faculty members, Manny Jackson came to George Williams College in 1972 to teach in the social work program. Manny grew up in Lawrence, Kansas. He would tell stories of white student researchers from the University of Kansas who interviewed his "poor, black" family. "We knew we were black, but we never thought of ourselves as poor; that was someone else's idea," he would say.

Every week students listened to Manny weave his personal stories about his life and experiences into every lesson he taught in social work. Students felt privileged that he would let them in on his private experiences of what it was like to be an African American in a white America. Manny's openness and active listening to students inspired them to share their stories, each so unique. Some delicately explored stories laden with assumptions and reactions that, they now wondered, could be racist. Together they shared what it was like to be defined as a member of a group without being known for your personal uniqueness. As stories were shared, inductions and concepts were generated. It was only then that students were assigned reading from the three hundred or so books about the African American experience that were added to the library as part of the thirteen points negotiated in Spring Festival. A different kind of knowledge building was taking place. But more was going on also. A community building process unfolded. As each person told his or her story, an understanding of each other as unique and whole persons grew in a way that could best be defined as "caring." In time, a classroom of students in an educational institution became a learning community.

As the decade of the '70s drew to a close, Manny died suddenly. Grief-stricken students who cared greatly for him as a teacher and a person urged me to make sure the Manny Jackson tradition continued on at George Williams College. Student Barb Schuppe ('77, '79) begged, "Please keep the storytelling tradition alive. That was Manny Jackson's gift to us. That's how we truly learned."

In that same year, on another part of campus, storytelling was going on as a way to advocate for a position where the stakes were high. This one was about preserving the Williams Bay campus, the soul of community. We hear President Hamlin's story of how students demonstrated social capital once more, "giving back for what you have been given," by working to save the Williams Bay campus from being sold.

Storytelling to save the Williams Bay campus

Richard Hamlin, student, ('49) and GWC president; Yevette Newton, student, ('69, '74)

President Richard Hamlin:

> On his deathbed, board member Frank Meyer told his son Dick Meyer, also on the board, "Don't ever let them ever sell the Lake Geneva campus." Frank and Dick knew of a board member's interest in selling the Lake Geneva campus. He disliked the place and would say, "It looks like a rundown motel." He was fearful of the college's incurring debt. He scurried around and found a party that he thought was a satisfactory purchaser of the Lake Geneva campus. I dragged my feet on this. [Board members] Dick Meyer and Elliot Frank got three or four students and three or four faculty members together and we told them what was up, asking them what [they could] do to help us out. Of course, students were, "Man, we can't let them do that." So together we cooked up this deal. There was to be an annual June board meeting in Lake Geneva. We invited students up. Yevette [Newton] led the charge. She mobilized the students.[42]

Yevette Newton:

> I tried to get students to commit themselves to definite action. I purposely sought a cross section of students, all classes, various nationalities, black and white, to go to Lake Geneva when the trustees met there. We invited trustees to an informal singing and rapping session in Coffman Lodge.[43]

President Richard Hamlin:

> Yevette saw that they got up to Lake Geneva. The students had dinner with the trustees. . . . During dinner students went around one by one, inviting them up to Coffman Lodge. . . . There were two or three students who had guitars, they were singing songs, then they would stop and somebody would tell a story about an experience they had up there as a student: Practicum Orientation; I was up here for a seminar; I came up for Nelson Wieters' September Camp; I was an intern in the Outdoor Education Program. They would intersperse that with singing and the guitar. About a quarter to midnight, [board members] John Root and Elliot Frank tapped me on the shoulder and asked me to come outside. They had gathered four or five trustees around in a little circle there. Elliot Frank said, "Look guys, no way

can we sell this place." They all looked at each other and said, "You're right." The next day at our board meeting, the first item on the agenda was introduced. The college had all this indebtedness, and probably our leading financial assets were the Lake Geneva campus and the Downers Grove campus. In no way could we dispose of the Downers Grove campus, but the Lake Geneva campus was dispensable. The board member gave an impassioned speech that we should accept this developer's offer for a million dollars and change. It called for possession of all the land, all the buildings, all the equipment. Then he said, "I will make the motion, and I'd like to hear a second." Dead silence. Elliot Frank stood up and said. "Mr. Chairman, if you don't have a second, I would like to make another motion." His motion was, in effect, that we do not sell the Lake Geneva campus. We engage in a campaign that would retire our indebtedness. . . . John Root got up and seconded it. With his second, John told his story of his own experience at Lake Geneva as a student. When it was put to a vote, it was unanimous that we would not sell.[44]

Winning the decision to save the Williams Bay campus was not enough for students. The board of trustees encouraged them to help with the financial situation by assisting to recruit new applicants to the college. During the summer, Yevette Newton, a physical education major, headed a committee of students who wrote to every GW student urging them to submit names of qualified applicants. The students, who knew the Chicago public school systems well, were effective in drawing student applicants and enhancing the reputation of George Williams College as the place to prepare for physical education in the Chicago public school system.

But working on recruitment was not enough for Yevette. She wanted to engage students in something concrete and symbolic, to demonstrate their care for the Williams Bay campus. So in the fall a group of students volunteered to go to the Williams Bay campus to rake leaves. When faculty arrived for the fall faculty retreat and observed what the students were doing, Yevette said, "The most rewarding thing for me to see . . . was the expression on the faces of faculty who realized that [we] had done something without relying on faculty help. 'You do care,' they seemed to say!"[45]

This demonstration of social capital is reminiscent of the first student activity in 1886 at the campus in the Lake Geneva area. The student "became a woodsman, using the axe that was given him to engage in the Clearing Bee, the first clearing of woods for the Lake Geneva campus."

Restoring social capital: Faculty memoirs ('70s and '80s)

**Don Morrison, professor; Dee Wyman, librarian;
Don Clayton, professor; Dick Wyman, professor**

The students and board members knew the cost of losing the Williams Bay campus, because it was always the place to generate social capital. Spring Festival was a test where social capital was spent within the Community of Living and Learning, and, as always, it has to be regenerated. Throughout the decades of the '70s and '80s, we hear from faculty of their experience in Williams Bay. At a reunion in 2002, faculty from the years of the Downers Grove campus shared their favorite memories. For the most part, they took place at Williams Bay during faculty retreats: "faculty singing in the silo room at Stevenson's"; "bridge games into all hours of the morning"; sitting on the dock with faculty late at night at Geneva Lake; "lots of laughter"; "Lake Geneva in the early morning"; "water-skiing at fall faculty retreats"; "the tennis at fall faculty conferences"; "playing golf at fall faculty retreats"; "drinking beer at night at local pubs at Lake Geneva and sharing ideas with colleagues"; "the evening cruise on the lake." These favorite memories led to this: "faculty retreats at Lake Geneva created a family of friends and colleagues and people who cared about the condition of our world"; "the fellowship among interesting students and faculty—always wishing to create the greatest good for the greatest number"; "I could not have asked for a more supportive group of friends and coworkers"; "every day feeling I had a big family"; "very real collegiality"; "working with wonderful teaching colleagues who had a commitment and passion for teaching and students"; staff felt "included, respected, supported, and treated as an equal by faculty and top administrators." Yet "the good fellowship that was fostered here was so difficult to keep up when we all got back to our silos on campus." Other experiences at Williams Bay included these: "for 53 years College Camp has continuously provided fond memories for our entire family"; "social work orientation at Lake Geneva and the wonderful sense of community we shared"; "language immersion weekends and September Camp"; "staff getaway days"; "Freshman Experience."

All these experiences and feelings of community came from times at Williams Bay. However, the Downers Grove campus also was a place for fond memories. Playfulness and spontaneity are good indicators of the strength of community in other memories shared.

For professor Don Morrison, a "most embarrassing" moment:

> Don and a group of student singers were waiting in the gym for a photographer who was to photograph the group in conjunction with a story about the chorus. Some gymnast rings were hanging down over the bleachers, and Don, dressed in academic robe, grabbed the rings and lifted his feet up until he was completely up-

side down, with his robe hanging down. The students suddenly became quiet. Don looked out to see President Hamlin standing in the doorway. Hamlin said only, "Morrison, I'm impressed."[46]

Librarian Dee Wyman:

> Trying to convince [chief librarian] Marilyn Thompson, over a glass or two of wine and some Greek food, that we librarians should be allowed to wear pants to work.[47]

After a June commencement ceremony, the faculty were returning to Steinhaus Hall to discard their caps and gowns, when Professor Don Clayton broke out in a "snake dance." One by one, faculty followed Don as we paraded our way through the halls of Steinhaus lower level, to the first floor, past the lab with the cadavers, up to the second floor, singing, laughing, picking up more faculty as we passed by, all the way led by our pied piper Don.

Other memories were of respect and appreciation for colleagues.

Dick Wyman:

> What was unique about George Williams College was . . . where students were when they started, and where they were when they ended. We were about developing the whole person—students came in needing so much help in their personal and academic development. Caring faculty like Chris Barabas and Mary Ryba [Knepper] took the long, hard road to help students develop reading and writing skills, so they could succeed in college.[48]

At times, the community bonds naturally, through a shared mission of service. At other times, it takes intentional bridging to bond together people with differences. Sometimes student-generated friendships bridge differences and make the glue that holds the community together. Clelia Guastavino tells her story of the friendship of "the Cee Gees": an international student, an African American from the rural South, and an urban savvy Chicago student.

"The Cee Gees": A friendship chain connects diverse worlds

Clelia Guastavino Giles, student, ('78, '79); Calvin Giles, student, ('80); and Celeste Gambino Peña, ('79)

Clelia:

> I came to George Williams College from Aruba. My dad was a YMCA worker there. He was originally from Chile, and my mom was from Uruguay. I came to the

college when it was in Downers Grove in 1974. I'm glad it wasn't located in Chicago. The city was too big and intimidating to me. I was very shy when I came. Before I came, I knew Phyllis Gilhuys ['76], who also was from the Aruba Y; we were both junior leaders and camp counselors in high school in Aruba. When I arrived, I already had a friend I could go to with things I might not understand. . . . Then, one wonderful discovery was meeting Marcel Neumann ['78], a Peruvian student who was the son of good friends of my parents. . . . When we got homesick, Marcel and I got together to drink maté, an herbal tea sipped through a silver straw from a gourd.

As I got involved in classes and clubs, I became friends with some American students who were very different from myself. I found that I not only fit in; I had this sense that, even though we were so different in so many ways, we really liked each other. Some had a very different lifestyle than I, or they had very different views on many issues. I think of Charlie Pittman ['78], or even Marcel, or Paul Atkins ['78]. Our family has remained very close to Paul Atkins and his family over the years. We could have really heated discussions, yet our respect for each other and the friendships have continued through the years. . . . It was a wonderful time of growing up. . . .

I met Celeste Gambino at a Christian fellowship group. In this group, different individuals and groups had very different ways of worship. Just as today we know that worship in white churches, African American churches, and Hispanic churches takes very different forms and styles, it was the same when we were students at GWC. But Celeste was able to lead this group . . . allowing us all to worship God and feel welcome. Celeste grew up in the city of Chicago and went to a high school with a lot of diversity. She was comfortable with students from all different cultures. She could be playful and joke with them. She had a personality that was like a magnet. She moved across all kinds of groups on campus and crossed barriers so easily. She could be gregarious and cheerful, greeting people clear across the cafeteria. She could also be quiet and serious when something was close to the heart.

When I arrived at GWC in the fall of 1974 the cafeteria was clearly divided by race at mealtimes. People were friendly to each other, but there wasn't much across-the-board mixing. With an occasional exception, the white students sat on one side of the dining hall, the black students at the other place. . . . Celeste sat anywhere. And wherever she sat, she invited any other friend she saw enter the cafeteria to join her at the table, black, white, Latino, whatever. . . . She was so good at bringing people together! I would say it was because of her natural personality, her spiritual faith and beliefs, and her experience, being raised in the city with people different from herself.

Soon I came to realize that, other than my friends who were foreign students, all my other friends were white. I never thought about racial mixing very much when

I was in Aruba. There, there was an easy mixing of blacks of West Indian descent, Chinese, Latin American, Dutch, and East Indians. The island of Aruba is small, and its history was very different from the racial history here in the U.S. When I came to GWC I assumed that the civil rights era had taken care of all the racial problems and that everything was okay now. I was very naïve and didn't pick up subtleties on differences in cultural or racial experiences or expressions. Besides, being a foreigner, all Americans were American to me, and it was hard to distinguish the differences. It was even hard to hear the difference between a southern and a northern accent! I began trying to make friends with some of the black students. It took me awhile and didn't come as easily to me. I thought it helped if I started by identifying myself as a foreigner. It opened up doors to conversations, and, as often happens, conversations lead to friendships.

I learned from watching Celeste personally connect to others. Also, she was always busy connecting people to each other. In my senior year of college, she connected me to my roommate, Barb Hall ['81]. Barb married Kevin Merritt ['80]. We are still very close friends and consider each other practically family.

Celeste was also good friends with Calvin Giles. One time she arranged for Calvin and me to go together to the Alpha Psi Kappa fraternity's dinner dance. Another time, she arranged for Calvin and me to come back from Lake Geneva to attend her graduation. Calvin was working at Lake Geneva in the summer and I was ending spring quarter with the outdoor education program. She never pushed it, but I think she knew us both well enough to know that we were very compatible.[49]

Calvin Giles ('80) came from Canton, a small town in Mississippi. His school, segregated and poorly funded, was not able to give him the kind of educational foundation he needed to go to a good college. But then he was selected to be a part of a national program called "A Better Chance" (ABC), a nonprofit organization offering opportunities to disadvantaged students who have shown academic potential. They move to a city in another part of the country and live in an area with a good public or boarding school program, in order to better prepare for higher education. Calvin attended a public high school in Edina, Minnesota, completing his junior and senior years there. Another GWC alum, Kevin Merritt ('80), was in the same Edina ABC program, and he and Calvin met there. Kevin was from Cleveland, Ohio. Calvin and Kevin were two of about ten black students at the Edina high school at the time, and most of them were from the ABC program.

Calvin's lack of academic preparation showed when, in his junior year of high school at Edina, his teacher asked him to write a term paper. Calvin did not know what a term paper was. Showing the initiative that ultimately made him successful, he went to the local library to research "term paper." While in Edina, Sharon Thomas, an admissions counselor, came there to recruit Calvin and Kevin to George Williams

College. They were offered a good financial aid package, and both decided to attend GWC in 1976.[50]

Calvin Giles:

> When I came, I was most impressed that this college really was about human service. I learned that not only from my professors but from my friends. Everybody was doing different things, but they were all interested in service. I majored in therapeutic recreation. I learned the value of human service, along with its theoretical underpinnings and its practical applications, from my studies at George Williams College. The many classes and various practicum experiences that allowed one to actually "practice what was preached" was such a helpful and solidifying approach. It allowed me to firm up my commitment to the basic mission of human service that I believe GWC stood for.
>
> Celeste Gambino was not only a friend but a mentor for me of what human service was all about, particularly in tough, urban neighborhoods. She was the perfect big sister for me. I saw in her the realization of GWC's professional vision for its students. . . . I would occasionally accompany her to various locations in the inner city of Chicago. It caused me fear and apprehension at times. She worked in the heart of gang territory and was well known and respected by all of the people in the neighborhoods where she worked. I saw in her a fearlessness and single-mindedness about the mission of human service that I would only hope to emulate in my own life. I felt she stayed true to the mission until the end.

Having completed their programs at different times, the "Cee Gees" went their separate ways. Celeste graduated first and stayed in Chicago developing a human service career that started with neighborhood youth work. Calvin stayed in the Chicago area and worked for the handicapped as a recreation therapist. Clelia went on to get her master's degree in LERA (Leisure and Environmental Resources Administration) and then returned to Aruba, honoring her commitment to serve in the YMCA when she completed her degree. But then Celeste's talent and timeliness for linking people together resurfaced. When Celeste was to marry Julian Peña, she reunited her old GWC friends to celebrate. Clelia and Calvin, whose relationship had grown through a three-year period of letter writing, came to Celeste's wedding.

Clelia Guastavino:

> When Celeste got married, Calvin and I decided to "take the jump" right away also, instead of waiting another two years. With the help and love of several GWC friends, Felipe Chavarria ['81], Barb Hall Merritt ['81], and Arthur Brown ['83], we were able to pull off a wedding ceremony within three days! The same pastor who married Celeste and Julian married us in the same church, in his office, a week later. . . .

We waited for Celeste and Julian to return from their one-week honeymoon, and Celeste and Julian joined Arthur Brown as witnesses in our ceremony. . . .

Calvin and I eventually moved back to Minnesota to be tutors in the same ABC program that had made such a huge difference in Calvin's life years earlier. . . . We have been married now for almost 23 years. Calvin eventually got his law degree; he has been working with the Hennepin County Attorney's Office in Minneapolis for about fifteen years.

Though there were occasional visits to Chicago to reunite with lifelong GWC friends and their families, the final gathering of friends around Celeste came on the occasion of her funeral in 1998. "The word of her death spread quickly. . . . Many GWC friends came from all over the country: from Virginia, Florida, Minnesota, Missouri. . . . And the racial mixture was an expression of who she was. There were white friends, black friends, Puerto Ricans, Colombians, Mexicans, Chileans. She made a difference in all our lives."[51]

Clelia's story of Celeste becomes my story some twenty years after the "Cee Gees" graduated and were married. I was present at Celeste Gambino Peña's wake. I came to honor her life out of a different context. She was now known as Celeste Peña, a name that would be recognized in public child welfare service for years to come. In 1994 the director of the Illinois Department of Children and Family Services, Jess McDonald, convened the deans from the major schools of social work in the state to put a challenge before them, one that would require close collaboration, or it would fail. The challenge was to move Illinois from one of the lowest achievers of child welfare permanency planning standards in the nation to one of the best, and this had to happen in record time. Getting all of the deans to come to the table to work together was like herding cats.

Celeste was now Director McDonald's assistant. She was being called on to harness those community-building skills, some natural, some well honed within the GWC environment, to meet the challenge. She worked tirelessly, listening to our concerns, humoring us, spreading a contagious upbeat expectation that we could do this. She lapsed into speaking in Spanish or English, as the situation demanded. Most people thought Celeste was Hispanic. Fueled by federal funding, each school of social work prepared a three-year master's in social work degree program, well coordinated in standards and outcomes, to meet the requirements of the state for child welfare education. The George Williams College program was well over a $1.5-million program in just the first three years. In the years to follow, over two hundred students would come from the Department of Children and Family Services to the George Williams College program. In five years all DCFS employees who did not have the MSW degree were returning to schools of social work to attain it. One by one, local child welfare offices were meeting national accreditation standards for child welfare. Within five years, the Illinois partnership was becoming a model for child welfare training partnerships all across the nation.

At times when it was just the two of us, Celeste would look at me, pat her hand on her heart, and say, "George Williams College—I loved that place. I love the people who I found there. They are my true friends."

Celeste worked nonstop forging this partnership, though she was told to slow down. She could not hide the ravaging signs of cancer and aggressive chemotherapy. By the end of the fourth year of the experimental project, Celeste died. I attended her wake, where Clelia and all her George Williams friends gathered, along with Director Jess McDonald and all the friends she made in child welfare, youth work, and other human service fields along the way. By June it was her husband, Julian, who stepped to the platform at the Aurora University graduation ceremony to receive, posthumously, the George Williams College Award for Lifetime Achievement in Human Service. At the same time, the Illinois Department of Children and Family Service designated its child welfare education scholarship fund as the Celeste Peña Scholarship Fund. Each year students across the state apply for Peña Scholarships to prepare for child welfare work through social work education.

"The last graduation"

Helen Scoggins, student, ('82, '86)

Though the college's social capital ran high, economic capital was threateningly low. In 1985 the drama ended and began when notions of social capital and economic capital collided. On Friday the 13th of December, the college was constrained to close its doors due to financial difficulty. The news was devastating. Students and faculty dispersed to other programs and colleges. Some from the graduating class were privy to arrangements to complete their degree from George Williams College by June of 1986, and one last graduation ceremony was held. Student Helen Scoggins, spoke for all students, at the last graduation ceremony of George Williams College.

> Today is not the end of George Williams, but a beginning, the start of a new era, with new challenges, new goals, and new desires. The class of '86 is a special one, because we have been entrusted to carry on the mission and purpose of George Williams.
>
> There is not another generation following behind us, so it is vital that we carry forward the mission. I would like everyone who is graduating today, to take a moment and reflect on some of the reasons that brought you to George Williams. There were many schools out there that you could have chosen, but you came here. Those thoughts and desires cannot end today, but must grow and be nurtured and kept alive. Just because classes are not being taught at the Downers Grove campus does

not mean an end to George Williams. What we leave here are our buildings, and that does not make a school. What we take with us are friendships, memories, knowledge, and special moments—people—that is what makes up a school and that is what we are—people who are George Williams, and we are far from gone! We are still intact, a little bruised perhaps, but a lot stronger and more determined than ever. We are going to go forward and keep the name and purpose of this school alive! . . . I would like to leave you with a thought that was recently shared with me by a friend, "Keep the fire burning in your heart!"[52]

Though economic capital failed, social capital survived. The spirit of "community" kept some core elements of the educational process functioning, even after the announcement that the college closed.

When the college announced its closing in December of '85, of course there was shock and anger. Mostly the anger was about the college losing faith in itself. The college was always hard-pressed economically, but rich in spirit that expressed itself in the attitude, "We're in this together"; "We can make it work"; "We give back for what we've been given." Students and alumni were angry that the dire economic nature of the situation was not openly shared in time for them to do something about it. They would have mobilized to action. When the announcement was out, faculty attempted a massive fund-raising effort, but the plan was abandoned. They were told it was too late.

I never really believed it was all over. That may have looked like denial, or naïveté, but hindsight reveals hidden truths. At the time we were just behaving instinctually. The college was built on the value of mobilizing community to face and solve its own problems, to survive and even thrive in adversity. Social work faculty did not accept the pronouncement to "provide no further service to the college," as if this was all about an economic contract that was terminated. Students did not accept the notion that they would have to continue their education elsewhere.

So, with that behind us, we were busy. In the final weeks several town meetings were held to gather information about our options. Other accredited social work programs opened their doors to all GWC social work students for immediate transfer. Students concluded, "If we individually transfer to another program, it will all be over. There will no longer be a George Williams College. And if the whole program transfers, we'll be something else. We'll no longer be George Williams College." At one of those meetings, a spontaneous cheer rang out with the declaration, "One thing is clear. We will not disband. We will continue to have classes together, if it means we have to meet in our homes or public meeting spaces." That cheer sealed it. We were on our way down a different path.

Several academic programs of the college were "given permission" by the board of trustees to negotiate with other colleges and universities for transfer. The LERA (recreation) program was on its way to Aurora University. At this point, the social work program had only agreed we would continue together to the end of the academic year, hoping we could protect the professionally accredited status of the program for the students and alumni until the end of the year. A program loss of accreditation would affect both students and alumni. The "where" and "how" of any continuation plan needed to be worked out. No plans were made to transfer the program to Aurora University, nor at this point was it given serious consideration.

Social work alumni got involved. They created telephone trees to pass along information coming out of social work student town meetings. They took over faculty offices to make telephone calls to other alumni. As I welcomed them in, I was aware the administration feared looting in the midst of the chaos and anger. I had a petty cash drawer inside my desk. I never moved the money. Each day I checked, and not a cent was missing. Students and alumni were respectful, polite, focused, efficient, and organized.

As word got out about a "critical mass" of over 125 students attempting to negotiate their future, several options were generated. As least two schools of social work and other universities wanted to explore and negotiate possibilities for taking over the program, or at least taking in the students. I recall social work Dean Don Brieland's words, when he came to campus from the University of Illinois to negotiate options. He confessed he was surprised there were no high-level administrators present to discuss proposals in the back room. There he was in a room full of students who had questions about their future. I'll never forget his comment: "Oh yes, I forgot that's how you do things around here. You're the group work school."

The last days on the Downers Grove campus were not pretty. Security guards were stationed outside abandoned offices to protect from looting and vandalism. Offices and halls were littered with discarded books, term papers, furniture, and blue dittoed meeting minutes. Appointments were scheduled with the guards to retrieve personal belongings from offices. In the middle of the chaos, Jean Fritz ('75), a social work faculty member, called her colleagues together to form one last "GWC circle." Though the program would be moving on, she wanted a proper good-bye to her college and colleagues. She handed each one a carnation, along with a personal message to each, affirming their unique contribution to the program and the college. It was a single moment of focused, peaceful beauty.

Loyola University School of Social Work agreed to a plan that would work for us. They would support faculty and support the provision of space for faculty and students. Both Bethany Seminary and Northern Baptist Seminary, just across the tollway from George Williams College, agreed to provide space on their campus for 125 students and twelve faculty. Within twenty-four hours, they entered into an agreement, explaining the three institutions had always helped each other out in the past (for example, the seminary students used the swimming pool at the college). Why not now, in George Williams College's most dire moment? The students voted on this agreement for continuation at one of their town meetings. The plan would carry us to the end of the year and it was hoped give some umbrella protection for our accredited status, which was in jeopardy. The best part of the Loyola plan was that we could continue on as a separate, distinct body. We could call ourselves George Williams College, and students who completed their work could graduate with a George Williams College degree at the end of the year in June 1986.

From January to June, students did not skip a beat, carrying on with their classes, field internships, and—an important element—their parties. There were fund-raising parties to raise money for students who lost financial aid. Students raised seven thousand dollars in a few weeks. A student rock band bellowed out some Beatles favorites for dancing. Chicago Bears football lineman Keith Van Horne joined the party. His sister, Alison Van Horne ('85), just graduated from the social work program. Keith Van Horne was a hero in Chicago; he was fresh from a January Chicago Bears Super Bowl championship. The whole city of Chicago was still giddy with celebration. He congratulated the students on something he knew something about—teamwork. He encouraged them to carry on.

By June the social work students were completing their academic year from what they called "the George Williams College Traveling School of Social Work." Some of the students were graduating from the final class of George Williams College. It was not until late spring that students and faculty decided to continue on and move the program to Aurora University. It was time for a "moving on" party. Aurora President Alan Stone came to the party. At the end of the evening, students gathered in a circle, putting three candles in the center. One candle was burning for George Williams College, a second was burning for Aurora University, and the third unlit candle was "the unity candle." Students took the two burning candles, lit the third candle with the flames, and extinguished the other two. Student Ellin Bressler Snow ('80) sang "What We Did For Love."

The president of Aurora University stood to address the students. He gave them the ultimate reassurance. "I've been watching you, and I like what I see," he said. "When you come to Aurora University, don't be afraid of losing who you are. Be yourselves. . . . Be George Williams College. In fact, I invite you to transform us. I would like our university to become what you are."

The word that George Williams College had closed reached the accrediting body, the Council on Social Work Education in Washington, D.C. Problems about maintaining accreditation had to be worked out. Within a year of the transfer to Aurora University, the social work program had an accreditation site visit in its new home. The chair of the site team visitors concluded his report to the council with a statement that the program had passed through an "amazing transition" and "the faculty have provided strength of character and steadfastness to students."[53] He invited me to "tell the story" at the next commission meeting in Washington, D.C. Storytelling was not in their tradition, but I did what I was told. Afterwards several commissioners, who were also deans of schools of social work throughout the country, came to me and mused, "I've been wondering if that ever happened to us, how would we respond?" It's a good thing to wonder about before a worst-possible scenario, which was our fate. All I could think about was the old adage, "Crises don't really make or break you, they reveal you."

Community Building Inside and Out: Aurora, Illinois

From 1986 on into the 21st century, George Williams College eventually was fully merged with Aurora University in Illinois. The history, spirit, and meaning of the college, which revealed itself in crisis, was articulated and lived out in a new environment. Two faculty members who were involved in the transition of the social work program to Aurora University after George Williams College closed in Downers Grove, tell their stories. Professors Sally Bonkowski and Janet Yanos tell why they did not leave their students in 1985, when the college closed, and they were told they were no longer employed and were advised to "provide no further service to the college."

"Held in trust": 1985

Sara ("Sally") Bonkowski, professor, GWC and AU

I responded to an ad when I interviewed for a faculty position at George Williams College in the late '70s in Downers Grove. At the time I had no idea what this college was about. It certainly was different from all my experiences in higher education, which were always in large universities. At first, I was very quiet; I needed to listen to understand the system. One of my first experiences was at Lake Geneva with a group of social work students. I remember there was a group of African American students from the city who had never been away from the city, and they were afraid. This one guy went out to the bar, and he shared in a small group that he was wary, worried about how white men at the bar would react to him being a black man hanging out with white women. Nothing happened. But I was impressed, first, that that's what they were thinking; secondly, that they felt safe enough to say these things in a small group; and finally, that they were supported. That kind of learning has staying power in a person's life; it carries over to practice. Across the whole program, the time that people spent away in community at Lake Geneva was one of the defining, powerful parts of the whole college. Look how it affected me, talking about this some thirty years later. One of the things I love most about teaching is learning from students. They learn from you, but you learn from them. And they learn from each other. If it's done right, it really is a learning community.

Why didn't I leave when the college closed and we were told to provide no further service to the college because you would no longer be paid? Hmmm. Why didn't I leave? [Pause] One time an attorney said to me, "Dr. Bonkowski, you've been seeing this person for a year, and they're not paying you anymore. Why are you still seeing them?" I said, "It's my fiduciary responsibility." I thought lawyers might understand that.

Social work Orientation Practicum continued in Williams Bay when the program came to Aurora University. Sally addressed each new class of students, speaking of the "covenant" of human service: when you've been given much, you give back. "Covenant," "fiduciary responsibility," "holding something in trust,"—these were familiar words from Dr. Bonkowski. She continued to explain her response, when the college closed,

We were in this together as a program! All these students were in field placements. We're going to leave them? Once we met together and decided we're going to pull this through and stay together, I never thought of leaving. . . . Also, I didn't want to lose this community. The interactive energy that came from that process was great. We could try to find a place where we could continue to be who we are!

"Getting to know the whole person." It's good modeling for practice. A core issue in practice is to understand that a person needs to be known as a whole person in their environment. I do custody evaluations now, and I don't know of any custody evaluators who do home visits. Why? I don't do home visits to investigate to find something wrong. I do home visits to get a picture of the whole child in that environment. I don't think we totally knew how powerful it was when we were doing it (at George Williams). People would tell others [to] go to that George Williams program. I think it was because of the community idea.

You have to experience community for it to become a part of who you are. It becomes an internal thing. It's the core of social work; not "look at these three theories and five ways of measuring them." The best way to learn how to do it out there is to experience it here. Also, the college modeled flexibility, to go with the flow, to tolerate uncertainty. And those relationships at George Williams College last a long, long time. . . . They become the core of strong professional networks.[54]

"We had this thing about developing the whole person": 1985

Janet Yanos, professor, GWC and AU

George Williams College was a humanitarian enterprise through and through. It was the kind of place where there was a sense that the most important thing about the education was service to others. It was true across campus, not just in social work.

At GWC in Downers Grove my office was at the end of the corridor. It was kitty-corner with a faculty member who taught religion. Across from him was another faculty member. He was involved in an ongoing struggle of ideas with another teacher. Sometimes they were yelling at each other. The walls were wee thin. I sat in my office thinking, I love it! I loved the freedom of it. I loved the sense of people's expansion of ideas, playing with interests and values and speaking them. It was wonderful! At the same time, I did not encounter people being mean to each other. It was an environment that was not competitive, but collaborative. There was this focus on groups, group process, and collaboration. It was a kind atmosphere, where people were pretty sensitive to issues affecting youth, families, and old people. We were probably the poorest paid faculty in Chicago, but students and faculty all came with this idea of serving other people.

Our program was about community-based service. We were dealing with kids in groups, kids in the Y, community-based agencies. The context was mainly suburban, but the suburbs were really in need of services. A lot of the western suburbs had new services that were not very professional. Our students were prepared to serve in the community. It was a very organic process, working on connection within a college community, and serving in the community.

Another thing that was really different was the teaching model. The students were adults, and we were adults. We had an adult learning model. Not that there wasn't a formal hierarchy between teachers and students. There was, and there should be. But this model was based on the student's ability to think, problem solve, have their point of view heard. It's not a dummying down at all. I like to regard people as equals. It's a good model, to be with students on same level.

[At other college and universities I attended] we were not treated as equal to the professors. I didn't think teaching promoted holistic growth, no room for the whole person in all of their experience. Just get the material, write the paper. I found that George Williams was exactly in line with what education and human service should be about. I never chose to go anywhere else, because it was the right fit.

When the college announced it was closing in 1985, I remember being told, "Please provide no further service to the college" and being given directions to the nearest office of unemployment. But it never occurred to me to leave. We [students and faculty] were tight with each other. Everyone was personally connected because we had this thing about development of the whole person. The students were personally meaningful to us, and we were to them. The idea of "You're dismissed"— What do you mean we're dismissed? When we got the idea we were not going to walk away, we had a going enterprise, an organic group. Okay, so you can't pay us, but the idea we were going on was natural. We wanted the program to move on, not just the students. We promised we were not going to leave them. We made that promise. It was a holding environment.

A big part of staying together was that we wanted to be George Williams College. I recall in our second meeting, our students were talking to [administrators from other schools]. The administrators said they were surprised. They were struck by all of these students saying we want our program, not just a degree.

When we got to Northern Baptist Seminary [for classroom space], teaching was tough. We had no audiovisuals, we had nothing. It was also a tough, tough winter, weather-wise. . . . We had no offices. We had one little shared apartment. We were clearly camping out. I taught, but I was looking straight ahead, not to the right or left. It was tough, but I think I did okay. . . . We had the same syllabi, the same books. We tried hard to maintain the illusion that nothing was changed, but it had changed. I think programs that went elsewhere did the same things we did to keep things going, like George Williams.

I was really grateful that we were allowed to survive at Aurora University. We had our differences in culture, but Aurora allowed us to run our program, maybe too independently, but we were allowed to survive. Programs going elsewhere were expected to absorb. It may have been inappropriate at first, to call ourselves the George Williams Social Work Program when we weren't anymore, but we did. We continued doing Orientation Practicum at Lake Geneva. If we weren't doing Practicum, we would not have had that cohesion.

Students still just want to be serving in local communities and families. . . . Students are still committed to the development of the whole person. They are also committed to their own lives in community, making things better wherever they are.

On the Aurora University campus, I love to take students to the Schingoethe Center. It's about the Native American experience. The Native American experience is more holistic, connected to community, connected to nature. It's about integration of body, mind, and spirit. It seems a more congruent model with George Williams College. You are part of a whole, a member of community. The whole person is totally integrated into community.[55]

"Doing things the Ubuntu way"

John Morrison, professor, 1987–present

When I came to Aurora University from the University of Pennsylvania, there were two things I knew about George Williams College: it was a group-work school, and it had some connection with the YMCA. I came just after the program came to Aurora, and I frankly didn't know where Aurora was. I had to take out a map to find out.

My first experience with the school after being interviewed was going up to Orientation Practicum [at Williams Bay, Wisconsin]. It struck me as a different way of doing business, a refreshing model that I had not experienced elsewhere. Students seemed to be having a good time; the pace was much more laid back. At Penn, professors were known as "Doctor" or "Professor." Though not clearly stated, at Practicum, you could pick up the underlying value system right away. It reflected the settlement house movement. In those settings, six- or seven-year-old kids were on a first-name basis with you. They were very comfortable with me, and I with them. Where students were involved, it was much less hierarchical than most schools and institutions. I really liked faculty and students being addressed on a first-name basis.

Student leadership at Orientation Practicum sent a message. We really did trust students with a lot of responsibility for planning and delivery of Practicum. This was intentional, preparing them for social work leadership roles with incoming students. They were learning in the process. They were learning who they were, how groups work, the limitations and strengths of their role as social workers.

In recent years alumni would request to come back as volunteers to play a role in Practicum. Most of the time it meant taking vacation time off from work to assist in planning and sharing leadership. Practicum was personally powerful to them. They knew the importance of this activity in the future of school, and they could make a contribution. They need to feel they have a valued role, and it fulfills a need to give back. Alumni would say, "I've been given so much. It's my way of giving back." We know in youth work that the best way for kids to grow and develop is to give back. Kids need to be seen not as a problem, but as essential contributors. They need to know "I'm valued, I'm needed, I should be giving back." Reciprocity is one of the valuable contributions of group/community-oriented social work. It's a self-help model. When you get something you're expected to give back.

A "community-building model" is a radically different notion from the "the student-as-consumer model" prevalent in higher education today. The student-consumer model goes like this, "I paid my money. You haven't entertained me; you haven't given me enough. I expect more, but I don't expect to be inconvenienced in any way, to really have to work very hard. Your job is to provide me." The consumer model is very limited. It doesn't require much. It's not very fulfilling.

When you came back on campus from Orientation Practicum, you could be a real person in a classroom situation. This was about knowing people for who they really are. People related as "neighbors" in a way. The relationship philosophy has allowed people to ask questions, raise issues and problems that they may not have felt comfortable sharing in more hierarchical settings. Here, you are educating or developing the whole person. We're not just developing your mind, without caring about the whole person.

The group approach, to me, is the process of building on the strengths not just within but between people. People have strengths to be called upon through their affiliation with each other. Students see faculty as being whole persons also. Students say this is very different from other experiences they have had. Faculty weren't playing faculty roles; they were being "people," enjoying themselves, not having to put a show on; they could have fun. Consequently students were less guarded and took risks to ask questions back in the classroom.

Community building is not very familiar in our society. It's hard to value if you haven't experienced it yourself. Living in community within the classroom results in student commitment to improve the social structures in which they live in their daily lives. They become committed to doing things that are not required of them in their human service job descriptions. They say, "I'm inspired to do this, in my church, community, agency, wherever I can make a difference."

In Africa [where I spent a sabbatical, teaching], they call it the Ubuntu way, an African way to say, "We're in this together." Africans will talk about the Western model, which is, "I think therefore I am." The Ubuntu way is "I am because we are." You are always a part of a group. The Ubuntu way is "What do we need to do as part of the community covenant? How do I relate to the whole?"[56]

"Neighborhoods in Partnership": 1994

Joy Howard, student, ('97); Beth Plachetka, student, ('76, '97, '99); John Morrison, professor

Finally, social work students of George Williams College of Aurora University Joy Howard and Beth Plachetka speak of a passionate commitment to build neighborhood community, coming out of their life experience. For Beth, the murder of a community youth triggers her call to social action as it mobilizes the Aurora community to fight gang violence and build community. It is a new age, reminiscent of another time, when Emmett Till was murdered, another youth from the old college neighborhood of Chicago's South Side.

Joy Howard:

I came into the social work program in 1994. Ten years earlier, I checked into the program when it was in Downers Grove, but I wasn't ready. I heard the program at GWC was about group and community work, and I knew I wanted to do that kind of social work more than clinical work.

Since I was 17, I was interested in working in the human service field. My dad was a minister, and I would say he was a closet social worker also. In the '60s and '70s he was a social activist. He marched with Martin Luther King and was involved in the civil rights movement in Indiana and southern Illinois. He also was an activist opposing the Vietnam War. When he worked in the Presbyterian Church in Oak Park, Illinois, he was involved in community development in the Austin area. He developed a health care facility for the community and was involved in developing opportunities for youth in the community.

I didn't have the calling to be a minister, but I did think I could do social work, and I worked in different areas. I was interested in geriatrics; I worked in a nursing home. Then I also worked in child welfare. It was when I was employed with the Department of Children and Family Services [DCFS] that I had my second opportunity to attend George Williams College, and this time I was ready. I was part of the first group of DCFS workers that returned to school to get our MSWs with the encouragement of DCFS. [As a participant in the program coordinated through Celeste Peña, Joy becomes a part of the story of Celeste Peña, told here.] I also had a Manny Jackson Scholarship to do community work. [Manny Jackson's story is told here also.] I was ready to learn, open to new ideas.

My first experience was Orientation Practicum, going up to Lake Geneva. It was such a beautiful campus. I enjoyed the community-building experience so much I went three times [as a three-year, part-time student]. The first time I was a new student, the second year a Practicum leader, and the third year again a Practicum leader. People in the program were friendly and helpful. I felt like I was at home.

Back in Aurora, the east side of Aurora had problems. Gang activity was prevalent, and in some years gang-related homicides were higher than the city of Chicago. In 1994 there were fifteen homicides, twelve gang related; and in 1995, when I was ready to go to work, there were twenty-five homicides, twelve gang related. Nine were younger than age twenty.[57]

Student Beth Plachetka:

My family were residents of the Aurora community for generations, and for generations my family was concerned about community. My family worked with neighborhood kids and taught us you always give back to the community for what you've been given. We watched our neighborhood change, when it came to safety. I received my undergraduate degree from Aurora University and was a religion teacher in grade school at Central Catholic. In that role, I got to know Moshe Rogers. Moshe was a typical, nice, likeable grade-school kid. As he grew up, he went on to excel in track and basketball in high school. He stayed away from gang involvement in the neighborhood. One day he was coming home from a basketball game, and he stopped to pick up a friend in his car. In that split second, a gunshot rang out. It fatally wounded Moshe. The shots came from some kids walking down the street drunk. They were shooting indiscriminately, just because they had the guns. Moshe's car reeled into a house. I remember hearing on a radio scanner at my home the report of a car striking a house outside Aurora Central Catholic. I thought it was an accident. The next morning I learned it was Moshe.

One year later I was enrolled in the master's program in social work. I heard the social work program was engaging in partnerships with the community—not just any community, my community, the Aurora community. I was ready, ready for action, ready to do, ready to learn, to make my community safer. I wonder if Moshe Roger's death ignited something in the community also? While Moshe is no longer with us in body, he's definitely with us in spirit, and that spirit motivates many people.[58]

The mayor's office of the city of Aurora established a contract with the School of Social Work to support a faculty member who would provide supervision to students doing community development in the toughest areas of the east side of Aurora. Elizabeth Cervantes ('82, '89), an alum who was director of field instruction, was a resident of the Aurora community, and she laid the groundwork for this contract. Denise Hayworth was hired to be that faculty member, and Joy and Beth were the first students to try out this new community building project.

Beth was assigned to community policing, a new approach they were just beginning to test out in the neighborhoods. She worked the beats of some of the most high-risk neighborhoods.

Beth Plachetka:

I found out that, because I grew up with many of the people in this partnership, it came easy. I went to school with Alderman Chuck Nelson's brothers. Police Captain Mike Nila went to school with me. These men became key players supporting the partnership [and advocating for a School of Social Work contract with the mayor's office].

Beth and Joy worked side by side with police officers. The police department targeted blocks in high-risk neighborhoods.

Joy Howard:

> We wanted to establish a strong linkage to neighbors in certain designated blocks . . . to find out what they thought about their neighborhood, what they needed. We structured a needs assessment survey. We went door to door. It helped that I could speak Spanish, since most of the residents spoke only Spanish. We learned a lot from the neighbors. They wanted more community police presence; they wanted to establish a neighborhood watch program; they were interested in forming block clubs. They did not know who their alderpersons were—they wanted to meet and talk with them. We set up community meetings in a local school to speak to their alderpersons. People from the fire department, department of economic development, police department, the community resource center, and local school administrators showed up to communicate and plan together to meet the needs of their neighbors. Then, we organized a "family night" in the local school to link parents with the school.

The police were impressed that these student interns helped them to uncover two drug houses on the blocks, due to their door-to-door survey of residents. The police were able to intervene and shut down the drug traffic. One year later a follow-up survey was conducted by the interns on the same neighborhood blocks where they started working on community policing.

Joy Howard: "Residents felt more unified because of block party activities; most participated in the neighborhood watch program; they knew their block captains; and they felt more of a police presence in their area. They all felt that their community was a safer place to live."

In the middle of the year, Joy Howard's assignment shifted to another initiative that was brewing in the Aurora community. Her eyes light up when she talks about this project:

> I worked with Dr. Morrison, and Dr. Morrison worked with me. [Though Joy Howard and her professor John Morrison are friends, Joy prefers to call John "Dr. Morrison." "It's a sign of respect, as an African American; that's how I was raised," she said.] Now that was fun! I enjoyed that a lot! A middle school asked for help in the community with the problems they were facing. In that year, 256 of 550 students were suspended for a total of 868 days. The rate of graduation was projected at only 36 percent. There were increasing incidents of violence, child abuse and neglect, and student depression. I was given significant responsibility. I was charged to work with Dr. Morrison to pull community agencies together to meet at [the middle school] and discuss the issues. I was amazed at the response! Most of the key players in the community responded. We aimed to set up a "partner school"—among the middle school, university, and families at the center. Twelve community-based

social service agencies were set up to provide services on site at the school. Services were comprehensive, including tutoring, homework clubs, anger management groups, family counseling, food and clothing services, and parent-to-parent support.

After school kids could stay there and see a counselor. They were not dependent on transportation. . . . Services surrounded the students and their families instead of being provided at a distance. Services were not only accessible but free. The community, agencies, and the middle school worked together to raise thirty-five thousand dollars for the first year of operation. By summer, resulting from a parent survey, a family resource center, parent advisory board, and parent volunteer network were developed.

The results were supported by data. More kids were going to high school. Expulsions had gone down the following year. Staff built trusting relationships with the youths and their families. In a few years, a full-time staff person was hired to direct the middle school project.

The students named the East Aurora project "Neighborhoods in Partnership." The police department demonstrated their faith in the university-neighborhood partnership by designating a student internship office in the new community center that also housed the East Aurora Police Department, a gymnasium, an alternative school, and other community-based agencies. The center became a modern-day model of a settlement house, with students from the School of Social Work a vital partner in community development.

Captain Mike Nila of the Aurora Police Department joined students and John Morrison in a national social work conference to present their Neighborhoods in Partnership project as a good example of "town-gown" collaboration to meet human service needs. Both students and faculty saw their work as demonstration of the historic mission and vision of George Williams College.

Student Joy Howard:

The main thing is networking. Tied to that, I learned the value of positive relationship building. It's how you know them! I also learned that this concept of community building that I learned in the classroom really can work. I was surprised at how willing people were to jump in and join in a partnership. They understood a school problem is also a city problem.

Also, Dr. Ponquinette, [then Superintendant of Schools in East Aurora and member of the Board of Trustees of Aurora University], was phenomenal. He was able to wield his influential power to pull everything together. The community organizing idea can work as long as you have stakeholders or people in power who are willing to act. It does work!

Being turned loose in a community as a student to help resolve real social problems satisfied my need for creativity. . . . Looking back, I can see more clearly what was valuable about my professional development at GWC.

I am grateful to Gerri Outlaw, my research professor, who helped me fine-tune what to look for, to have a critical eye when we were conducting surveys and community interviews. Also, I felt I was becoming a responsible contributor to the academic community of social work through a journal publication.

Joy was aware that her faculty mentor, Dr. John Morrison, could have authored the journal article himself, with perhaps a brief footnote of acknowledgment to the students who participated; but instead she and other students were recognized authors in a social work text that was a seminal book on community building.[59] The students were also co-presenters at a national social work education conference where traditionally only faculty presented. . . . Captain Mike Nila of the Aurora Police Department participated, witnessing to the effective work students had done in the East Aurora community.

Professor John Morrison:

When individual achievement and hierarchy is the value faculty play by, you don't hear a lot of "we's" when it comes to professional recognition for success. Student empowerment involves a giving over of exclusive power entrusted to the professor to the student, along with trust and some risk taking, lest they should fall on their face. But there has hardly been a time falling on their face ever happened.[60]

Students learn community building inside. They exercise its power in institutional crises, like Spring Festival of 1969, and the closing of the college in 1985. They take their experience outside, to build community and hope in neighborhoods of Chicago and Aurora that were impoverished economically and socially. The college and community create partnerships. The strong root takes hold and will not die—community building, inside and out.

Chapter 4
Learning-by-Doing

*"Think of the college itself not as an institution of **learning,** but as a **community of living** and learning."*

(Professor Charles "Chick" Hendry, 1939)

*H*ow did education become a hallmark of the YMCA? How did George Williams College, a training institute for YMCA workers, become an educational institution dedicated to principles of how people learn? How was the learning process itself a hallmark of the college?

Sir George Williams, the founder of the YMCA, set the stage when the YMCA movement ignited first in London, England, and then spread to the United States and worldwide. The genius of the movement was its fourfold purpose to develop the whole person in body, mind, spirit, and social dimensions. "Developing mind" was a part of developing the whole person, but it was never viewed as separate from developing the whole person. The educational mission of what was to become the YMCA College, or George Williams College, was always holistic. Motivation to learn, the learning process, and retention of learning had to touch the whole person, including his or her personal, particular life experience.

The focus of George Williams and his "band of brothers" was on the spiritual dimension as they conducted prayer groups for men before their workday.[1] As early as a year into it, George Williams envisioned the popular prayer groups as classes, where people could share their experiences and learn from each other, "something like a class meeting at which they might relate any particular trial . . . which beset them."[2] Their Christian faith was pragmatic; they were more interested in how Christian teachings would make a differ-ence in their everyday lives than in correct theology. The test of spiritual truth was how it worked in individual experience. Family members said that for the pragmatic George Williams, "truth was the wisest expediency."[3] These two contributions—the absorption of knowledge through the totality of personal experience and the process of testing out truth through learning-by-doing—became the legacy of George Williams College.

These early seeds of pragmatic thinking were nurtured by the location of the college, when it moved its summer institutes from the quiet, retreat-like shores of Geneva Lake in Williams Bay, Wisconsin to become a year-round Western Secretarial Institute in the burgeoning city of Chicago in 1890. In the Progressive Era, from the 1890s to the 1920s, Chicago became a center of thinking and doing, both in progressive education and progressive social reform. Just one year before the college opened in Chicago, Jane Addams opened Hull House in Chicago; it was to become a seminal model of the settlement house movement. John Dewey, one of the most recognized American pragmatists, was developing his "learning-by-doing" school of thought, lecturing at Hull House and interacting with the YMCA institute instructor, Eduard Lindeman. "Communities of inquiry," discussion groups, and dialogue abounded, focused on building community and democratic societies.[4] In 1894, just four years after self; learning through the direct experience of doing a group project; solving society's ills through experiential learning; creating democratic societies through dialogue; knowing things through learning about people's diverse and particular experiences; embracing ideas because they work in personal life experience; and learning through action and reflection, both of which are best done in group

"The learning process . . . had to touch the whole person."

George Williams College opened in Chicago and only two years after the University of Chicago was founded, John Dewey founded the Chicago School of Pragmatism at the University of Chicago.[5] Dewey's learning-by-doing approach became the hallmark of progressive education. From 1892 to 1918 the "Chicago School" of sociology was significant in the development of that academic discipline. George Herbert Mead, Charles Cooley, and Robert Park generated ideas about social interactions in the development of self and about the understanding of diverse, small social groups and ethnic societies within the larger scheme of things.[6]

Down the street from the University of Chicago, at George Williams College, an experiential learning approach was developing that included learning-by-doing in small groups to develop the individual

activity and process. Students were "doing" in the Hull House settlement, side by side with Jane Addams; they were "doing" in YMCAs, youth service agencies, churches, gymnasiums, and civic organizations. They returned to the campus classroom to reflect, share, and integrate with the conventional knowledge of the time. They postulated new ideas, challenged ways of thinking, until they "knew" something. From its beginnings George Williams College (commonly called the "Association Training School") embraced a pragmatic approach to learning.

Photograph, page 151: Children are guided to reflect on what they learned from group activities. Students do the same when they return to class from their fieldwork experience. (ca. 1940s)

Building Character, Practicing Democracy, Serving Community: The Chicago Years

"The Practical Side"

The Association Training School statement, circa 1913

In considering the desirability of school training for the employed officer of the YMCA, much emphasis has been laid upon the importance of making his training "practical." . . . The Institute and Training School believes in practical training, but its definition of this much abused term may differ from that of some. It believes that a practical possession is the power to think. . . . that culture of mind and heart is necessary. . . .

The danger, common to all schools, that instruction may become academic, that an unreal life and atmosphere may come to exist in the classroom, and that imaginary rather than actual conditions may be the basis of discussion, is recognized and constantly guarded against. . . . [Students] have ever before them, not a theoretical association, a creature of the classroom, but a living association in its everyday work. . . . [T]he student is required to become acquainted with institutions of the city other than the YMCA, including the University of Chicago, Hull House, Chicago Commons, the Armour Institute, the Lewis Institute, other institutions in field work in sociology, . . . public playgrounds, outdoor gymnasiums, public bath houses of Chicago. This . . . is, in all cases, done under supervision of the school, and reports are submitted in writing.

The school instructors . . . are, without exception, men who are not only theoretically acquainted with the YMCA . . . but are actively engaged in meeting the actual condition and directing the activities of the living association of the present day. Students not in employed association positions are assigned to specific volunteer positions. That gives a large range of . . . observation and study in the Chicago and neighboring associations. Reports as to efficiency are rendered to the school by the office under whom the work is done.

Good textbook work in sociology may, under the direction of a competent instructor, [be] obtain[ed] anywhere, but in modern educational life, the study not alone of the text but of living men is recognized as essential in sociological study. The opportunities in the city of Chicago for field work in sociology are unsurpassed by those of any city on the continent. Places visited are the County Jail, the Municipal Lodging House, the John Worthy School (for boys convicted of petty crimes and misdemeanors), the Parental School (for confirmed truants), the county institutions (for care of the poor and insane), the Chicago Commons (Social Settlement), Hull

House (Social Settlement), the County Hospital, the Juvenile Court. . . . In anatomy, the work . . . is not confined to the study of charts, manikins, or bones, but the students do actual dissection of the human body and just as thoroughly as is done in the medical schools.[7]

In the 1930s George Williams College was clearly articulating pragmatic views, including religion.

"Taught from the standpoint of their effect"

Arthur Steinhaus, professor, 1939

The spiritual purpose has changed. The college attempts to help the student develop the religious philosophy and high spiritual purpose [that] are the basis of all success in the field of human guidance. Religious subjects are taught from the standpoint of their effect upon the growing personality of the students.[8]

By the late 1930s, as world events led up to World War II, the YMCA College (now called George Williams College) extended its purpose of spiritual, physical, social, and mental development of individuals into a mission to "practice democracy" in every learning context. "Practicing democracy" included experiences in camping, small-group activity and discussion, physical education, and not-for-profit agency administration.

"The democratic ideal and camping"

Hedley Dimock, professor, 1936

The term "democratic method" has been widely used, greatly abused, but little understood. Under the impact of current happenings—national and international— the democratic ideal and its implications need to be thoroughly re-examined. . . . In recent years, many of us have found ourselves going back to Dewey's *Democracy and Education* and similar sources to study afresh the meaning of the democratic way of life. The depths of the democratic ideal are not easily plumbed. . . . The summer camp, perhaps better than any other social institution, with the possible exception of the family, can actualize the democratic ideal in practice. It can recognize the supreme worth and the integrity of each person and make everything else subordinate to this value. It can deliberately seek the growth and creative expression of persons in terms of their individual abilities, interest, and aptitudes. It can provide resources for the essential of life for all, according to need. It can give each person an opportunity to participate in the common social life and to have a sense of being an important member of a community.[9]

In 1939 the YMCA engaged in intensive discussions about democracy and how that should be practiced as experiential learning in YMCAs. The college followed suit. Learning about democracy by experiencing it was the primary objective of learning-by-doing approaches.

Definitions of Democracy

Alexander Stoddard, progressive educator, 1939; R. E. Davis, YMCA leader, 1939

Addressing a YMCA conference, Alexander Stoddard had the following to say:

> Democracy is an elusive term. . . . We often fail to distinguish between democracy as a philosophy of life and democracy as a way of government. . . . It is a way of thinking, living, and governing groups and relationships [that] is truly of the people, by the people, and for the people with the primary objective being the welfare of the individual.

R. E. Davis:

> What is democracy? Is it a form of government based on majority rule [or] a way of life that expresses itself in all relationships between people—in government, business, law, family life, administration of YMCA, and in all the multiform group life of our total programs? . . . Democracy as a way of life rests on three main assumptions: (1) A belief in the worth of persons—of all persons; (2) A belief in freedom and self direction as the essential conditions for the growth of personality; (3) Belief in the essential equality of [people], . . equal opportunity for the development of their capacity.[10]

At the same time, the educational process of learning-by-doing was woven into the entire fabric of the college curriculum, extracurricular activities, and college governance.

"Think of education more as a process, less as a program"
Charles Hendry, professor, 1939

Colleges can, if they will, become communities of a democratic way of life. . . .

The central objective of the college, instead of being subject matter achievement, was conceived to be the development of persons who would be effective in personal and social living; secondly, the classroom and formal curriculum. . . .

[The formal curriculum] was based on six broad areas of experience or life functions: the making of homes, keeping healthy, continuously orienting oneself to changes in life, participating in the opportunities and obligations of citizenship, using one's leisure, and developing a dynamic philosophy of life. Field internship work was considered a requirement for testing out ideas and learning. . . . There is no dualism separating the curricular from the extracurricular. . . . The College Association [the governing body of the college] is preparation for everyday life in the college community. . . . Some years ago, a study of student problems by the GWC faculty led to this conclusion: Activities in a college community are very closely related to activities in the larger outside community. The college community embraces homes, employment, medical care, recreation, news, regulations, and many other social characteristics. If the student played an intimate part in the management of the college community, it was found, he would be better fitted to take his place in the larger community after graduation. As a result, the College Association, made up of both student and faculty, was formed. By tradition, a student is president of the association. The College Association has sponsored activities such as the college health insurance plan, social affairs, assemblies, intramural athletics, music, glee club, dramatic club, spiritual services, government of the college community, and many other projects of practical benefit to the student body. . . . Think of education more as a process, less as a program.

Building on his former professor Eduard Lindeman's ideas, he concludes, "Real democratic living takes into account three realities of social education: There will always be change, there will always be differences, and there will always be conflict, and democracy must be made safe for differences.[11]

In the late 1930s, learning democratic process by experiencing it in small groups was becoming the foremost purpose of group work, superseding character building. The charismatic, authoritative leader modeling "character" was giving way to the leader as facilitator of the development and expression of each individual group member.

No more "stunt man" leader

Everett W. Du Vall, group work educator, 1943

> In the earlier periods of what is now called social group work, "social adjustment" meant that the members of the various agencies were provided with a program of activities that it was hoped would lead them to conform to norms of behavior [that] the workers thought of as "good character." With the advent of a democratic philosophy and the introduction into the leisure-time program of methods from the field of progressive education, there has been some modification in the concept of what constitutes "adjustment.". . . The primary objective is to help the individual to help himself; normative goals have given way to purposes for particular individuals stated in operational terms. . . . There has been a consequent change in the type of worker desired by the various types of agencies. The "stunt" man, the promoter and organizer of activities, is being replaced by educators capable of using progressive methods.

Du Vall cautioned against "group think," a dangerous outcome of group cohesion that was becoming manifest in German patriotism, as the United States entered the Second World War:

> Group members should be helped to redefine a social code at variance with that of the group when difficult situations grow out of culture conflicts and acquire the ability to stand alone in defense of convictions against opposition from the group as well as to make adjustments to majority decisions. . . . Group objectives should be designed to widen social consciousness such as to realize the significance of their present behavior for the future of mankind: that what each generation does makes a difference in the kind of a world the next generation will have to live in . . . to recognize the extent to which their own individual welfare is bound up in the welfare of other individuals, group, and society as a whole. . . . It is not enough to compare a pattern of behavior with the standards set by the group. Attitudes and behavior must be understood in the light of the total situation of a particular person. . . . An educational program, formal or informal, that attempts to change attitudes and behavior in the interest of social welfare must therefore be individualized. Democratic principles imply a proper balance between the demands of society, group standards imposed for the good of the whole, and needs of the individual for freedom and release of tensions.[12]

In the decade of the 1930s, Hedley Dimock and other faculty members held institutes on the camping experience at Williams Bay for the purpose of developing standards and sharing common goals and objectives. The institutes contributed a strong foundation to the American Camping Association. In the 1940s a student came to the college to learn more about using camping experiences for the development of self in relation to others.

Learning-by-camping

Armin "Whitey" Luehrs, student, ('46, '48)

I came from Sheboygan, Wisconsin, to George Williams College. In high school I was a member of a Hi Y club. There was no building called the YMCA in town. We had what was called a "Town and Country Worker." A Town and Country Worker was a Y leader who related to kids and developed programs in the community apart from a YMCA building, which usually did not exist. I started helping out doing things like refereeing basketball games for young kids. When it came time to go to college, I went to the University of Wisconsin. In the summer I began to get involved in the Y camping program. . . . It was through my camp counselor and the new director of the Sheboygan Y that I first heard of George Williams College. I decided to transfer there.

My first impression of the college was that it looked like a high school: one building with a quadrangle in front, a swimming pool, a gym. . . . It seemed a comfortable size for me, coming from a small town and a large university. The small college feeling was in sharp contrast to the vast, diverse neighborhood of Hyde Park, where the college was located.

The next thing that impressed me was the people. My classmates were all focused on similar fields of human service in Chicago, if not Y work. They were in settlement houses, like Hull House, Boys Clubs, and Chicago Youth Centers. Many of my classmates turned out to be leaders in Y work and related fields. There was John Root ['46, future CEO of Chicago Metropolitan Y], Dick Hamlin ['49, future president of George Williams College], and Frank Kiehne ['47, '51, future head of the International YMCA World Service]. I met my professor of group work, Harvie Boorman, at freshman orientation in Lake Geneva. He led the orientation. He immediately set me up with a job at the Lincoln-Belmont YMCA. The next year I worked in the Southtown YMCA doing group work with clubs of kids. Harvie was my supervisor. He was a guy who really "walked the talk." Boorman was qualified and inspiring; he was boy's work secretary of the Kenosha YMCA. I had great respect for John Fuhrer, who taught administration and how to organize groups for fundraising. He was the master at that.

A teacher I set my mind to take classes from was Hedley Dimock. He was a national leader in the creation of standards for group work and camping. When I stayed on at George Williams to do graduate work, I had to work in the Milwaukee Y. The only way I could take a graduate course from Dimock was to drive each day from Milwaukee to Chicago! A year after I graduated in 1949, I was attending a conference in St. Louis. Hedley Dimock was asked to chair the conference and to draft some standards for the American Camping Association. The whole idea of being accountable to standards for camping did not sit well with many, particularly those from private camps who were used to having complete autonomy on what they did in camps. It was a pretty rough meeting, and the proposal was not accepted at that St. Louis meeting. Now the idea of accepting common standards is considered par for the course.

Whitey spent a lifetime career in YMCA work, advocating for standards and good group work practice in the camping experience. The standards are part of his lifeblood, which he calls forth readily:

One is you have to get to know your campers as individuals. I have a standard of five campers to each camp counselor. When the group is small enough, no one in the group can hide. . . . Another is to find ways for each camper to develop themselves in the group and camping context. This is where leadership is developed. Everyone can't be a leader in every situation of life. But individuals discover what they're good at, explore and learn new skills and things about themselves, and then are encouraged to develop those strengths. Another is to develop an identity. Group members begin to see how they're seen by others, and that's connected to how you see yourself. . . . Another is concern for one another; a consideration for the welfare of others in all decisions and actions. Another is—words we heard over and over again in every course with Dimock and Boorman—"democratic process." This does not mean voting. It means listening to every person and taking all expressions into account, being open to conflicting ideas, and working toward consensus. When kids go out on canoe trips, they have two decisions they have to make as a group, where to go and what to eat. Both have consequences. For example, they have to carry everything they are going to eat. So they need to understand the consequences for their decisions.

George Williams College was the best there was in terms of its mission. Those were good years.[13]

The popularity of the college mission was so well recognized that it led President Frank Burt in 1938 to declare, "We have seven jobs in informal education for each student!"[14] "Informal education" was the term used by the college in the 1940s and 1950s to describe the learning-by-doing mission. In 1950 the *Chicago Daily Tribune* published an article describing how "theory (classroom) and technique (field)" were all directed toward experiential learning through leisure-time activities. The article was titled, "Play Is Work at this South Side College."[15]

"The idea stuck with you"

Richard Bowers, student, ('62)

I transferred to George Williams College from Jacksonville University in Florida. I was encouraged to come by Jim Leiby ['51], a YMCA director, and I received a YMCA scholarship. I majored in group work. Sylvanus Duvall, Arthur Steinhaus, David Misner, Don Clayton, Nelson Wieters, Ned Stowe, and Duane Robinson were my professors, and I'm grateful to them for giving direction to my learning.

When I came from Florida up to the South Side of Chicago, I was immediately struck by the extreme change in my learning environment. It wasn't the classrooms I'm talking about. It was the community, both inside and outside the building on Drexel [Street]. At first, I was naive about the neighborhood. I came from the South (with a southern accent), and all of my tuition was in my back pocket. It was 10:30 at night, and I asked where I could go to get something to eat. They told me to cut through Washington Park for a McDonald's. God looked after me for my innocence!

I was coming from a place where "diversity" meant black or white. Now I was meeting students who were from all different racial and ethnic backgrounds, including international students. I hung out with an integrated crowd. At the time, the college was very integrated though most of the African Americans weren't in residence. They were from the community, commuted to the college, and worked with us in the community. Some of my friends were Erwin France ['59], Bill Moore ['60], Bob Steinhaus ['61], Jesse Ary ['61], and Bob Anderson ['62]. The first year I brought home some friends to Jacksonville. Nobu Yonamine ['66] was with us, from Hawaii. Until recently Nobu held political office as a state representative in Hawaii. At that time, we had to drive through Atlanta, and we came into a [Ku Klux] Klan rally. Nobu couldn't believe it. He only heard of Klan activities. He couldn't believe he was personally witnessing a Klan rally.

I got involved in the culture and social activism of the community surrounding the college. You could hear Miles Davis perform at the Sullivan Hotel for two dollars. You could hear and see the Smothers Brothers and Joan Baez on Forty-seventh Street. On Fifty-fifth Street, I worked with University of Chicago students in the Student Peace Union.

The college was not academically strong. By that I mean the learning that you picked up was more experiential though it was in the classroom also. It was strong in tying experiences you had to a theoretical component and in sharing experiences. When I learned about Kurt Lewin's group dynamics concept of force field analysis in Ned Stowe's class, I had already tested them out in my internship experiences and the idea stuck with you. I remember experiences where I tried them out in the Duncan Y, Lincoln Boys Club, the YMCA hotel, and the Kenwood Community Council. My professor, Ned Stowe, directed me to the idea of force field analysis. . . . In any situational analysis, what are the driving forces? What are obstacles to overcome? How can you overcome the obstacles?

The "idea that stuck" was applied again, some twenty years later in 1980, when Richard was back in Florida.

I was deputy secretary of community affairs for the state of Florida. I was responsible for coordinating responses to major disasters in the state. This was the time of the Mariel boatlift off the Florida Keys, with refugees coming from Cuba to Florida. [Fidel] Castro released Cuban prisoners, allowing them to migrate to Florida, along with one hundred thousand people who were coming within a period of fourteen days. We had a problem. What could we do? What would prevent us from doing it? What were the driving forces? Restraints? How could we overcome that? We devised a master plan, using Kurt Lewin's force field analysis. We got systems set up. We were first on scene, working out of Tallahassee. There were four deaths and three births on the docks. The federal government was supposed to provide help, but simultaneously they had helicopters sent to release U.S. hostages, crashing in the Iranian desert. They couldn't respond fast enough. The slow emergency response of the federal government is reminiscent of Hurricane Katrina and its impact on New Orleans. That one took eleven days. This one was fourteen days.

Another big idea that stuck had to do with what Richard learned outside the classroom, "though it was in the classroom also." It had to do with race relations and lessons learned among student friends and colleagues and in fieldwork in the Chicago community.

After graduation, I got involved with student Ys in the South during the civil rights movement. I was involved when they were integrating Clemson [University]. When Harvey Gant was the first black student on campus, I helped to make a smooth transition for him, and it was. Harvey Gant went on to run for office as mayor of Charlotte; he then ran for senator against Jesse Helms and lost. At the Blue Ridge Assembly of the Y, I helped them to become integrated in the summer of 1963. We were integrating conferences when no one else was. . . . I was fired at the Fort Lauderdale Y for giving membership to a black person in 1967. I wasn't trying to be an activist. I was just starting my Y career. It's just that this was never an issue at GWC.

It laid the groundwork for how I looked at things. When I went to Louisville, I integrated Y camps there, both regular and fresh-air camps. They used to have separate camps. I turned the camping experience into a learning experience about race and class. I had a lot of parent support. The upper-class kids from Miami wanted to be involved. We stayed away from discussion; we let them work it out in relationships. I planned on going to law school, but instead I did a master's in community development. I worked in eastern Kentucky. From there, I was offered a job as director of community development for the mayor in Jacksonville, Florida. The Citizens' Council became a think tank on housing and economic development.

One more idea that stuck was related to what was once called informal education in the field of group work.

I helped to start the First Tee program, which was sponsored by the PGA Tour. Now there are 150 chapters of First Tee programs in the country. Kids learn lessons of character, while learning to play golf. For me, character building is helping people in the Great Society kind of way. I work with poor kids. I want them to feel they're worth something, they're capable of doing something. I want them to have good housing and to know where their next breakfast is. I want money to go to community development. I'm a political wonk. I want to do political work to make that happen. Do you call that "character building"? That's what I mean.

One thing about GWC . . . it had a strong idea of what "giving back" was. Anything you're given, you're expected to give back. . . . It was in the whole makeup of the college in Hyde Park. This is unusual . . . to have that kind of bond and feeling. You were doing something together that was bigger than yourself. I was amazed. It's not your typical school. I was inspired by the words of [President] John F. Kennedy, "Ask not what your country can do for you but what you can do for your country."

Tracy Strong was a visiting professor teaching the history of the YMCA. He was the general secretary of the International YMCA in Geneva. He brought Benjamin Mayes in from Morehouse College to speak at the college. In WWII, Strong worked with prisoner of war staff. He brought in Sir Frank Wallis from the British YMCA. His son Robin Strong became a high-ranking diplomat at the United Nations. His sister-in-law, Arma Robbins Strong, stayed in China with the Communist takeover, to become a moral compass point. . . . Then there were the "Crazy Canadians." Actually I learned they were Anglo-Saxon Scotch-Irish like us southerners. There were international students from Southeast Asia and Germany. There was Maddie Massasi, an Arab from Palestine. There were Polish, Puerto Rican, Lithuanian, and Mexican students. Most of them were first-generation college students, as I was.[16]

Learning by Looking Inward:
The Downers Grove Years

In the late 1960s, the college moved from the urban context of Hyde Park, Chicago's South Side, to the western suburbs of Downers Grove, Illinois. With the change in location came a change in experiential learning, a shift from a societal focus to an introspective, personal focus. It mirrored what was going on in society at large. The shift in experiential learning was evident in some academic areas more than others. The academic discipline of social work was one.

Juanita Copeland, an African American woman who grew up in the Chicago area, participated in George Williams College's informal education programs when she was a kid. When she was ready to come to college to gain these skills for herself, the college had moved to Downers Grove. She decided to follow it to the western suburbs.

"Learning how-to-get-along skills"
Juanita Copeland, student, ('73)

My role model was Edna Somerville Oates ['56], a graduate of George Williams. She was my leader at the Abraham Lincoln Center in Chicago. Since I was in junior high, I attended the Abraham Lincoln Center for ballet and piano. I got acquainted with Edna Oates and was impressed that Edna not only worked there but lived at the Abraham Lincoln Center . . . like a settlement house. Edna recruited me into a Leaders in Training program. Edna's programs and activities were designed to get mostly middle-class African Americans together with young people from the local housing projects. We had a lot of service projects—we did a lot of painting of buildings—followed by discussion groups. We learned from each other, learning how-to-get-along-with-each-other skills. There was also a church group that would spend weekends in the Abraham Lincoln Center. We would do projects together and then dialogue with each other. On weekends we would go camping, and sometimes Edna would arrange for city youth to meet with youth from farms in Wisconsin. Again, through activities and evening fireside chats, we would learn about each other's lives and build understanding of our differences and commonalities. Edna was indirect, working behind the scenes. She was low-key, not confrontational. She could reach the most difficult persons in this way. Once Edna gave a sports magazine to young man who kept to himself. Through references to topics from the sports magazine, she drew him out.

I had to be Edna Oates. When I was considering going to college, Edna encouraged me to go to George Williams College, which at that time [1961] was located in Hyde Park. However, I was not ready. . . . Eventually I got married. Six years later, I was divorced. Edna Oates came into the picture again. She was helpful to me in this difficult transition. Through some counseling, I was again encouraged to go to college. Now I was ready to go to Edna Oates' school, George Williams College.

The only problem was the college had moved from the Hyde Park campus to the Downers Grove campus. I wondered, Why did they move out of the city? Their service and impact was so strong in Chicago. The new campus was so removed from the city. But nevertheless I signed up. I lived in married student housing, that building nestled in the woods on the edge of the campus. I signed up for the applied behavioral science program, which eventually became the bachelor of social work program.

I immersed myself in the program, which had a heavy emphasis on relationship building. But it was different from Edna Oates' relationship building programs. We would spend weekends in what was called "lock-ins" as part of group dynamics and relationship building. Though the goals were the same, the group dynamics process was different. There was less shared activity as a means to get there—more talking. And the group discussions were more confrontational and direct, more "touchy-feely." I learned a lot about the mismatches between how I saw myself and how others saw me. It was helpful for my professional development. But there was a much greater emphasis on self-awareness as the goal of group dynamics, whereas in Edna's groups it was more on collaboration and team building. Edna focused on individual linkages to groups, and groups' linkages to each other to build bridges and create community. . . .

The George Williams spirit was an international spirit. Herbert Murerwa was a classmate from Zimbabwe. I saw the spirit of helping as something to improve the world situation. I also remember how George Williams was ahead of its time in promoting environmental education. They would plant trees on Arbor Day and read books like *Silent Spring,* and encourage recycling throughout campus long before it was common practice.[17]

"They thought we were a little too experimental"

Jim Collins, student, ('71)

I came to the college as a graduate student when the college was brand new on the Downers Grove campus. I enrolled in the social work program, which was not yet accredited by the Council on Social Work Education. [The council] had come to the college for a site visit. They thought we were a little too experimental. Don Lathrope was brought in as the director to ensure we would get accredited. The faculty were Eldon Montgomery and Duane Robinson.

For me, George Williams College means small numbers, . . . learning group work by being a member of a group. Experiential learning was a way to learn and feel comfortable in working with groups. . . . George Williams College grads were in demand for their expertise in working with groups. A lot of professionals are afraid of running groups. I did a lot of group work. After I graduated, I worked with Catholic Charities, doing parent groups. I ran outpatient psychiatric groups for the probation department, where I worked for twenty years. I led orientation groups for people on probation and employment-seeking groups for probationers.

I remember the first experience new students had in Lake Geneva when they started the social work program. It was an intense small-group experience. The length of time was seven to ten days. I thought it was too intense. People did not know what they were getting into when they came up to Lake Geneva for Practicum. A few people dropped out. I remember a friend dropped out who I thought would be good in social work. There were these experiential exercises, like being blindfolded and carrying out "trust walks," a trust-building exercise. The leaders I remember were Karen Johnson and Estella Benn. Not only in Practicum, but throughout the year, people learned skills of group dynamics well. Del Kinney led the way. Group dynamics in class were videotaped and critiqued. We would have to do journals or process recordings after every class.

Orientation Practicum was not the only time we had a retreat. In the second year of the program we had another retreat, this time to become oriented to skills we would need to do group work in Ys, settlement houses, and such. A lot of the focus was on activities. Activities included things like square dancing and canoe trips. I led the group activities. I remember being exhausted from a canoe trip, thinking I had just about had it, when Duane Robinson came in and announced we were going to have an "ecological day." We were going to clean up all the trash in the river. I was so exhausted, I didn't know where I was going to find the strength to engage in this new activity.[18]

Throughout the college, in liberal arts programs as well as professional programs, a philosophy of the learning was evident. Learning was relational, personal, particular, and experiential.

Ways of learning and knowing

Voice of professors in the 1970s

Nick Kokonis:

I came from Greece with a very strong conviction that the best idea of teaching was the Socratic . . . method, based on the concept that the student already knows; he already has that idea that you are going to communicate inherent in him; it is in potential form. All you do is bring it out like the midwife. . . . The [Socratic] method works, but it works . . . because there is a very important master, a teacher who has . . . an effect on the student. I don't believe there is a person who can teach you. There is a person who can help you learn what you want to learn. The teacher creates a better way of helping, of aiding that process of learning. And that way is by fostering the proper attitude in the student. Students will learn—will grow—if the teacher provides a significant human relationship. Real learning cannot, in my opinion, occur unless the student has a concrete sense of how he feels about the things he thinks. Human beings learn better . . . under those conditions of emotional arousal. They have felt good inside so, if they can identify with you, they can come closer to you; they can take from you. It is this climate that, I think, can account for a good deal of the learning that takes place in the classroom.

Jaslin Salmon:

Rapport is probably the most important thing in the whole scheme of education. We have repeatedly said there is a good relationship between student and faculty in this college. . . . If we can come closer to the students genuinely, the students respect that. Students aren't afraid to deal with you. I think students must also be made to realize that they have something to contribute to the class. I think if one approaches teaching from the point of view that I'm also learning something from my students while students are learning from me, it makes a much easier experience.

Gladys Robinson:

You can't stand there, look at students' faces, and talk above their heads! I have no difficulty in motivating students for biology courses. I just play on their natural biological urges and carry their imaginations with me through our lessons together. There's no text in the world that I'm going to follow verbatim. I give them the skeleton but they put some meat on it.

Gladys would take students out to the natural wetlands that were part of the landscape of the Downers Grove campus, on your left as you entered the campus. On any warm day, driving into campus, you could see Gladys's straw hat, with a body somewhere under it, covered from view by the protective wetland foliage. A group of curious students cautiously trailed behind her, wading through the wetlands.

Pete Healey:

It's a covenant-like commitment to give back to others what you have learned. My high school gymnastic coach would say, "Now this is your obligation—to teach others." . . . I know it's my obligation to try and pass it on and to keep trying until I can. . . . If a student can't multiply or can't add, I start there. . . . There's no point below which I won't go. My feeling is not that there is this bulk of material that we are going to cover. We would like to get to a certain point, but we're going to start back where we need to. . . . If there is no understanding, there is no sense in going on.

Jerry Perlmutter:

There are two things that I am interested in when I'm teaching: that the teaching not become obsolete, and that what a student learns he can use. I try to get students more actively involved in the learning process, to open them up to their own experience as highly relevant. The learning in the classroom has to somehow relate to the student's experience base and to help him value it, expand on it, and keep learning from it. That way he keeps on evolving [and] learning. In traditional learning, you get a theory from the teacher or from a book and then you experiment. But reality has been structure for you. In the experiential approach, you may get oriented as to what to expect, but you don't get told what to see. Then you became much more active in the conceptual part, which comes after the experience. You become actively engaged in looking at the theory and the concepts.

John Sims:

In Socratic dialogue, rather than lecture, the teacher engages the students in discussion so that the student discovers the points himself rather than the teacher telling him. Let us say I aim for this; it is accomplished only rarely. The dialogue doesn't require that the teacher and student like one another. They have mutual respect, which permits the student to allow himself to be vulnerable. The student remembers the attitudes, the ways of looking at things [that] he picks up from identifying with the teacher, rather than substantive knowledge primarily. The important thing is that he acquire a critical viewpoint that he can apply to anything. Through the Socratic method the student has to answer, and when he does, he is saying, "I am taking the responsibility for my learning."

Tom Bennett:

The most fundamental goal is helping people to develop the distinction between knowing something and being informed about something. Knowing means how do you go about inquiring and organizing both that information and your experience in a way that you can do something with it. It's saying that I'm using information as a way of shaping and guiding behavior.

David Misner:

Some system of involvement with the material . . . puts it into the permanent memory store. . . . We [the college] for a long time have believed that you learn by being out on the front line doing a job and learning by experience in part-time jobs and supervised field work. Students bring their real on-the-job experiences into the classroom. The international type of experience also opens students' eyes.

Helen Westerberg:

I help people get to a second wind. . . . They taste a freedom and creativity and joy from having pushed through to another new level. . . . In anatomy, I remember a C student who came by my office after he had studied the skeleton in relation to the muscles. He said "I really know that arm, like I've never known anything before." To me, that was a second wind. Enthusiasm comes from really knowing and also from having worked together. Just listening . . . doesn't do it for the students. It's got to be involvement, the giving of self, if one is going to reach this new level. To look something up, discuss it, synthesize the data into new understandings—that's something to get excited about.

Joe Nasvik:

The teacher creates "involvements" or "moments" that will help them get emotionally excited about a subject. Then students will learn on their own. The instructor can indicate sources where [information] can be found, or he can set up experiences to produce needed information. . . . The other thing is to try to hit those magic moments where we can all touch theory issues so that it can all fit together really nice and clean. This doesn't happen often enough for me.

Don Lathrope:

Knowledge about practice is a hypothesis. It should lay a foundation for a lifetime career of learning. [Teachers] create an investigative, open-minded stance. Obviously we don't have the knowledge to practice twenty-five years from now. [We teach] practice as hypotheses, not practice as tradition, nor practice as firmly established truth. . . . The practitioner always has to live with uncertainty. He doesn't know how firmly established his knowledge is, but he still has to act with conviction. This is the best the profession can do at that point.

Bill Duncan:

The courses I'm involved with are highly participatory. . . . There's high challenge to the students and also the opportunity to experiment a little bit, to try out new ideas. . . . I work with graduate students in the classrooms this quarter and then next quarter we spend at Lake Geneva in a living situation. We're working perhaps from 7 a.m. to midnight. I have the opportunity to see them in many different situations dealing with real-life problems. In the outdoor education program, elementary school pupils come with their teacher for a week at a time for environmental education; some high school students come as assistants. They're guided by GWC undergraduate and graduate students. The learning is multidisciplinary. You see a rock and learn about geology. . . . You see a rock in a quarry, its relationship to where it comes from. You see a quarry as an economic resource. George Williams students are evaluated more by the real-life situation than an instructor's judgment. They will find out if what they are doing is working.

Steve Van Matre:

I don't think one can teach. One helps people learn, by motivating, challenging, creating exciting learning situations. Students don't remain passive.[19]

"Let your imagination fly"

Lyle Johnson, professor, 1970s–1980s

Lyle Johnson was my mentor [in] experiential learning when I first came to George Williams College in 1971. In the big university where I came from, we learned about experiential learning through books and class lectures, and then were told to go out and do it in fieldwork. Theoretically it was a big part of practicing social group work. But I never saw it practiced within the walls of ivy. My introduction to Lyle's method of teaching and learning was through a series of courses we team taught on human development. The class met for four hours straight, starting at 8 a.m. There were between fifty and seventy students in the class. When I first saw the schedule, it was intimidating. . . . I pictured the ultimate passivity: . . . students coming in late without their morning coffee, requests for lots of breaks, and a push for early closure. How were we going to entertain them, to keep them in their seats for that long?

From the very first class, I was amazed. Everyone was on time and alert. My first class was on adolescence, and my first teaching assignment was to bring a group of adolescents that I knew well to class. The questions and dialogue that followed were penetrating. These young people who I thought I knew well, were sharing their experiences on a deeper level than what I knew of them. The time flew by. When the panel and dialogue in "large group" was over, the class broke up into small groups, and my youthful guests spread themselves out, attaching themselves to a small group. There was further dialogue. My guests were asked if there was anything they would like to know of any of the students in the class. They didn't want my guests to feel like laboratory objects; they were willing to reciprocate. After "small group," we moved back into a large-group reflection of what we individually heard and learned. At this point, the concepts and theories from the assigned reading came out and were tested against the experiences that had just heard. It was 12:15, and the class was still engaged. We had to break them up to go to lunch.

Class was not over for me. The teaching team met to plan the next session. What was the next learning goal, and how could we use an experiential exercise to learn the concepts inductively? The planning took hours. The exercises were not from books. We dreamed them up. Lyle said "Let your imagination fly!" At first it was difficult for me to be creative. I think I was too caught up in [the] "professor" role and what I thought that was all about, based on my observation of my own past professors. Yet planning activities to accomplish learning goals was exactly what group workers have to do "in the field."

In time, I was having lots of fun with it. When we had a session on the toddler or preschool stages in the child development course, I was borrowing my little children's toys and bringing them to class! We spread them out on the classroom floor and played with them like toddlers or preschoolers. Only parents who get down on the floor and enter into the play experience with their own kids know how much they learn from that experience. It's active learning. It defines questions you have. It may challenge the "truths" you read about child development. It makes you want to know more. I found that my classroom preparation time was intense, but it was not about preparing for a lecture performance. It was about preparing an exercise that would motivate and engage students in their own learning.

Recently I met with Lyle Johnson, over thirty-five years later. I wanted to thank him for what I learned from him about experiential learning. Lyle, in turn, was thankful to the college. "The college allowed us to do what we wanted to do in the classroom. We had the freedom to create. Creativity was encouraged. We could let our imagination fly!"[20]

The new look of experiential learning in the 1970s was derisively called "touchy-feely" by outsiders. Though it mirrored the societal times of the early 1970s (the "me" generation), it perhaps did not invade other academic institutions as strongly as it did at George Williams, because GWC had practiced and not just taught experiential learning since its founding. For about a decade the terms "experiential learning" and even "group work" were used simultaneously with terms like "encounter groups," "laboratory learning," and "sensitivity training." Many student stories refer to Orientation Practicum at Williams Bay as the introduction to intensive experiential learning. In 1979, social work students conducted research for their master's thesis on whether the Practicum experience was unique for any school of social work in the country and whether it was useful preparation for their professional experience in human service.

Social work Practicum: Unique and useful

Students Sandra Blumenshine ('79), Jack Lewandowski ('79), and Barbara Schuppe ('77, '79)

Orientation Practicum is unique for any school of social work in the country. All other orientation programs were held on the main campus, none lasted more than three days, none were residential, and no other graduate school reported the use of any type of experiential or laboratory approach to learning in their orientation program. . . . In the majority (three-fourths) of the cases, alumni support the notion that Practicum was helpful preparation for them as developing professionals. . . .

It [Practicum] is built on the lab learning method, providing incoming students with a special time and place to experience themselves individually, in groups, and in the community at large. The first contact with the graduate social work program at GWC is this learning-by-doing experience called "Practicum." It sets the stage for the learner as a student, and for the learner as a professional. Thus, Practicum initiates a philosophy utilizing an experiential approach to self-growth and trust in a supportive environment, which sets the standard for the educational experience of the social work student as well as for the profession of social work.

They summed up their research on experiential learning with a quote from Alfred Whitehead in a 1929 book on the aims of education: "Get your knowledge quickly, and then use it. If you can use it, you will retain it."[21]

Did all students buy into "encounter groups" as a valid direction for group work and professional social work in the '70s? Not by a long shot.

"GWC changed my life. . . . It wasn't the encounter"

Ray Lestina, student, ('77)

I came into the social work program in 1975. My first experience was going to Lake Geneva for Practicum. Quickly I picked up some pressure to "share your feelings" [and] "have an encounter" in the small groups and large groups. I did not sign up for that. I was looking for basic social work. I had no clue I was going to have to reveal my inner soul and we'd do therapy with each other. These were a bunch of strangers. I was not going to tell them my real problems. I wasn't going to do it. The way we picked groups in Lake Geneva was brutal. Maybe there were eighty of us in the Administration Building. Our job was to go around, introduce ourselves to people, and by our own selection, form our small groups. We'd meet people and then give them the bad news. "In my group? I don't think so," I remember telling someone, "You remind me of my mother." That was cruel. There were a lot of painful feelings created. Then we would "process" them. There was a lot of pressure to share feelings. When the heat was on, I decided I'd make something up.

Ray muddled through at Practicum, and actually enjoyed himself, mostly by creating playful relationships with others.

We weren't having encounters. We were having fun. We all went to this old barn to sing. It echoed all the way up. We sang all the old songs. . . . We made up a dictionary of words to use to make it through the program: "trust the process," "closure," "termination," "reentry," "be in touch with where you are." Maybe a sprinkling of these new words here and there would get us through the program. When we came back to school, some classes—not all, but some—were the same way. Get your feelings out. We would be assigned a short paper and we would spend the next two hours talking about our feelings about doing the paper. They were "anxious," "overwhelmed." We could have taken all that time to actually write the paper!

Thirty years later Ray still "did not like the encounter stuff." Since his graduation from George Williams, he has been a school social worker and eventually served as dean of professional programs at a nearby college. Did his education prepare him for those roles?

I have to say, my experience at George Williams really changed my life. It wasn't the encounter. It was the community we became. Starting off at Practicum was the best way to do that. By the time we got back to campus, it was almost a real community. Practicum was a whole week. There were all types of students. We had people my age: young, green; then there were people in their 50s: "old." We had blacks, Hispanics, women; we were from all over. Everyone had very different perspectives on things. Sitting out on the front porch at night overlooking Lake Geneva, we would play around, like "Let's open a restaurant." We'd serve some creative combination of the best foods from our ethnic background: ham hocks and greens with rice and beans, fish balls and dill with tomato and oregano, matzo ball soup with Polish sausage and cabbage. . . . When we got back on campus, we actually tried out something like that. Every Thursday at lunch, all students came back together again. . . . People brought their ethnic specialty food, and we had a community lunch. It was fun!

When I look back at it now, I got the basic knowledge and skills to do social work that I could get anywhere. But more than that, I learned how to relate. I learned leadership. I learned communication. I was gaining confidence. It was a great experience; not always pleasant—difficult at times, but I came out a better person. You were in learning situations where you get a lot of feedback from different people about you, how you are, your strengths, your weaknesses. I learned from my peers as well as the teachers. People would share, they would ask questions. What I learned from George

Williams was [that], you could feel confident if you had a different view of how things work. You felt supported to have a different view outside the classroom, because that's what was happening inside the classroom. Teachers didn't act like they had all the answers. That was a new experience for me. When I came in, I was pretty rough around the edges, blue collar, Melrose Park, greenish. I needed some polishing, and I got it.[22]

"The learning reached me on a personal level"

Jack Lewandowski, student, ('79)

"This paper was monumental in my life." After more than twenty-five years had passed, Jack Lewandowski hands me a paper he wrote for a graduate course in social work. The pages are yellowing, the edges torn and dog-eared. Not only the title page, but each of the pages that follow show the stress signs of having been fingered again and again. He holds it in his two hands like a precious artifact. The title reads "Autobiography: My Childhood and Adolescence as Affected by Culture, Ethnicity, and Family System. Social Work 632, Winter, 1978." The contents appear to be well written, sufficiently conceptualized, integrated, and documented with appropriate references to theorists. Along with some brief comments on each page, a big "A" appears on the last page, with the faculty name "Manny" scrawled beneath it.

> This paper was the hardest paper I ever wrote. And writing comes easy to me. This paper was the starting point of my whole experience. . . . I came to George Williams from the South Side of Chicago from an Old World Polish Catholic family. "Old World" meant a maternal grandfather who held a national office in the Polish National Alliance, a nationalistic organization [that] strongly opposed acculturation into the American melting pot way of life. Both my parents were therefore raised to believe that to differ with Polish tradition was wrong.

On the first page of his paper, Jack wrote, "In researching for this project, I have reached a greater understanding of where my parents are coming from that would explain their way of thinking and behaving, and as a result, have been able to work through some of my anger toward them about their inability to relate to me on a feeling level because of their strict cultural role expectations." Jack looks up from reading his paper to explain:

> I was a compliant child growing into young adulthood. In writing this paper, I was now breaking a strict family code. The assignment required at least a certain level of disclosure. Telling things about the family to outsiders was definitely frowned upon in my Polish family. I chose to do the assignment by facing it head on. I could have skirted all of it in an intellectual exercise, but I didn't want to kid myself.

I didn't know much about George Williams College when I applied. I applied because I wanted to do community work and help kids. My parents wanted me to be a lawyer. I started out on a track scholarship at Kansas State [University]. While I was there, I did youth work in the inner city in Kansas. A friend who was going to GWC invited me to apply there.

My first experience with the college was Social Work Orientation Practicum in Lake Geneva, Wisconsin. . . . When I got there, I thought it was kind of cool. But as it came morning, the next day, I was very anxious. We went into a "community" room. There were quite a few people, and in my mind everybody knew everybody. I didn't. I didn't open up in large group, but I did all the exercises, guided imagery, etc. I liked the small group. We had a good student facilitator. Eventually I got to talk out loud in the large group. That was a new experience.

Coming back to school, I felt connected. If I thought of an example of something we were learning, I would share it in class. If I disagreed, I would say so. . . . Well, at first I may have waited to see a professor after class, but eventually I did. I was the baby in the class. The majority of students were women. They were empty-nesters, first or second career, going through divorce. There was a lot of self-exploration as people's lives were in transition. . . . I was so hurting in adolescence. I needed an outlet where I felt I was okay. It's okay to disagree with my parents. It's okay to have my own career, and not be a lawyer. It's okay to be angry or sad. So many issues were going on inside. I needed a place where I could feel good about myself. Here's what made it important: it was the individual who was cared for. You were not swallowed up in a system. Everyone knew so much about the personal life of each other. We were a small group of people, about sixty in the class. You have meetings to work on a paper, you wind up sharing things. You have a support system you could call on twenty-four hours a day. Faculty were just as reachable. Nobody used titles, which is way different for graduate school even now. . . . No desks. We were sitting on pillows in a circle. Each class was like a group of friends getting together. . . .

We may have been presented with some of the same stuff [as other schools], but we had this additional experience of self that went beyond. I remember everything that was presented. There was no class that I could say, "Well, I don't remember what I learned in that class. It was nothing special." The learning was powerful, up close and up front in me. It all had personal meaning. It reached me at a personal level.

A year ago I was at a meeting in California, as president of the Illinois Association of School Social Workers. Someone asked where I got my [master's in social work], and I said, "George Williams College." She said, "George Williams? Isn't that the touchy-feely school?" I said, "Absolutely—and proud of it!" When I told her about my experience, she said, "Wow! In my school, we just came in, read the book, wrote the papers, and that was it. It sounds wonderful!"[23]

After college, Jack got a social work job in Dallas, Texas, as a therapist in a residential treatment center for adolescents. He became involved in another form of experiential learning, an outdoor wilderness education program as a treatment program for adolescents. In the program, boys built their own shelter, cooked their own meals, had to take responsibility for creating and sustaining their own lives as part of an inclusive treatment plan. He also worked with a well-known family therapist, Virginia Satir. Jack thought he had been prepared to do this kind of work by learning to disclose things about family before large groups.

"Someone please tell us what to think and do!"

Jim Sheffer, student, ('80)

Jim Sheffer was a student who didn't initially like what he saw of the '70s style experiential learning or "group dynamics," but then he began to see it differently. Over twenty years after graduating from George Williams College, Jim was battling cancer. Still a young man, he was thinking maybe he had only a few months to live. Struggling "to keep my spirits high," Jim wanted to tell a story of George Williams College. He also wanted to thank all his friends from the college—something he had not found the energy to do yet.

It's really important to tell the story of this college. George Williams College was a prime mover in my life. It started in Orientation Practicum. At the time the orientation consisted mostly of small-group dynamics, using material and approaches based on the NTL [National Training Laboratory]. It drove me crazy. I kept saying, Where's the leadership? What's going on? Where's the agenda? Someone please tell us what to think and do! There was racial conflict; there were power and control issues. It seemed like no one was in charge. But [faculty] kept hanging in there. You handled resistance, and you could also confront people pretty well. Later [Professor] Lyle Johnson talked a lot about creating a "social vacuum" to allow group dynamics to emerge. Lyle tried to give me a clue that my anger and anxiety could have to do with my own lack of participation. About a month later, in a group dynamics class with Lyle Johnson's help, the light bulb went on. I wasn't taking any risks. I wasn't putting my ideas out there. Instead I was withdrawn and attacking, like a snake in the grass. But once . . . I started participating and putting my thoughts out there, amazing things happened. I learned so much about myself and group dynamics.

Now I teach classes in group dynamics at Dale House. I have a training program in the spring for college graduates and seminary students. . . . People come locally and from throughout the country. It's a little more structured than those days, with exercises, scripts, and reflection on personal dynamics. But I think I lecture too much; I don't naturally listen very well. I learned that from my group dynamics class.

Shortly after this telephone conversation, Jim died, but not before he did what he learned to do at George Williams College. His lent his voice to something that was important to him, expecting that his voice would be heard.[24]

"Sensitivity training" held on for a little over a decade in the 1970s. In the 1980s, Orientation Practicum shifted to a "stress-social support model" to explore a life transition into a new role as a graduate student. Less emphasis was placed on expressing feelings. Confrontation or "encounter" shifted to "social support." Seasoned second-year students continued as leaders, sharing their experiences and coping strategies. The new approach mirrored changing paradigms in the field of group work, where "indigenous support groups" were rapidly growing and gaining popularity. The Alcoholics Anonymous self-help group model is an example. The support group movement came close to rejection of the helping professional role in the group entirely. Self-help came through mutual accountability, support, and sharing personal and particular coping strategies.

Other academic programs in the college continued learning-by-doing through camping, outdoor activities, and challenging experiential exercises. Another kind of experiential learning took place in Williams Bay. It was called "September Camp."

September Camp and Outdoor Education

Lee Bay, student, ('73)

September Camp was truly a camp. Of course it was a requirement for undergraduates in camping, recreation, leisure/environmental education, and physical education. They also got students from social work and organizational development. You went up to Lake Geneva, to College Camp, you slept in bunks, you worked from morning to night learning skills: . . . rock climbing, sailing, rowing, canoeing, motorboating, doing camp crafts, having nature experiences, tying knots. You were learning fundamental bread-and-butter skills that you could use as program activities. They were used for building self-confidence in learning new skills, starting where a person is and motivating them to move to another step, learning the skills you need to get you to where you want to go, learning about the structure and discipline needed to gain those skills. . . . It emphasized structure and discipline more than what they learned about in other outdoor education experiences. . . . There's a strong bond that develops in September Camp, through a similar philosophical bent, a similar value approach to things; you're learning these skills for a purpose. It can be said in one word: *service*.

To try to explain experiential learning for recreation and outdoor education, Lee repeatedly referred to his teacher and mentor, Nelson Wieters, not so much for what he said, but for what he did.

Once Nelson led a sailing adventure in the Caribbean, where he brought some high school kids on one of his "Man and His Land" adventures. Besides all the goals of September Camp, there were other goals—[including] cross-cultural awareness, discovery from new experiences, and listening and respecting each individual's ideas and intentions—which had consequences when planning activities for the day. Nelson used an experiential learning approach all the time. Nelson led a class on camping, where he wanted students to learn how everything has logical consequences for what we want.

"Everyone has a different idea of what camping is supposed to be," he would say. "All these are possible. . . . Maybe someone over here doesn't have the same as someone over there. Check out with others and see what theirs are. Then pick out your top priorities. Which do you want your camp to run on? Now develop objectives. Do you want a skill camp? If you do, you can't have lots of small-group interaction. Skills require a structured environment. Is the small group going to determine what to do? Are you going to take the time to get a group decision? You can't have them both at the same time. What happens if you're walking down to the beach to learn swimming, and you see a snake giving birth? Do you stop to watch? . . . Do you encourage small-group interaction with experiential things that come along? You may be sitting for a whole hour watching snake give birth, but you never got to swimming."[25]

On certain occasions, like fall faculty retreats at Williams Bay, the recreation program modeled their learning-by-doing approaches for other programs and faculty in the college.

Climbing the high ropes of life

Nelson Wieters, professor, 1984

It was early September of 1984. Another academic year was about to begin, jump-started as always with a fall faculty retreat at Geneva Lake. This year the program was planned and delivered by the LERA [Leisure and Environmental Resources Administration] department. Nelson Wieters was in charge. We knew we were in for a heavy dose of experiential learning. For me this was a treat. My colleagues led me through many experiential exercises since joining the faculty at GWC, and I always learned something. This time it was about high-challenge experiences. We had choices about the exercise that would suit us, but we were told to select one that would really stretch us beyond what we thought was our comfortable capacity to respond. As Nelson gave us our instructions, my mind drifted to what I left behind at home that morning. I had two high school sons who played football, and they were gearing up for another season. Their high school team had a long-standing tradition of success, not because it was a large high school oozing with natural talent in the sport, but because they were disciplined in learning skills and were always expected to give beyond their reach. High challenge. I left my son that morning wearing a shirt that said, "I give more than 100 percent." I thought to myself, if my son is learning what can happen when you reach beyond what you think is your limit, why can't I? At that moment, I decided I was going for the highest challenge. There were other options . . . sailing, climbing walls, for example, but I would go for the high ropes.

Along with some other faculty colleagues, I sauntered off to East Camp, where the high ropes were set up. The ropes extended from one tall oak tree to another, and I mean tall! A helmet was fitted snugly on my head. I was hooked to a repel. Then I was instructed to insert my feet into the mounts on the tree and climb high into the branches above, until I reached a tiny wood-framed balcony. It was a bit dizzying when I reached the balcony. Before me was a long stretch of rope. There were probably hand-support ropes, but they did not seem significant enough to boost my confidence. My heart pounded. It seemed impossibly risky. "I'm not sure this was a good idea," I thought. "Maybe I should turn back, like the faculty member in front of me." It was then that I heard Nelson's voice drifting up from below, very far below. "Come on, Sandy, you can do this." His words were punctuated by a chorus of faculty colleagues, way down there, echoing, "Yeah, you can do this, Sandy." I felt a rush of strength and trust from their calm, assuring guidance. I was ready. I took my first steps out on the ropes. Nelson's voice: "Just take one step at a time." I looked down. Oh boy. That's a long fall. Nelson's voice again: "Don't look down, Sandy. Look straight ahead. One step at a time. You can do it." And there I was, stepping onto the balcony on the other end! I did it! As I repelled down, exhilarated from a rush of adrenalin, I remember shouting, "Piece of cake!" That was not true. But I did it! With the support of Nelson and my colleagues, I did what I thought I could never do.

Fast forward to one year later, December of 1985. I was on the high ropes again. This time, it was no exercise. This one was for real. George Williams College announces it is closing. The faculty are told we have choices. We could go home, go to another college, get another job. I could play it safe. But instinctively I chose the high ropes. I'm boldly declaring to students we will not disband as a social work program, and we won't simply transfer the whole program to another college. What was I thinking? Was I too buoyed up by the enthusiasm of students and faculty who said, "We can do this"? Was I crazy to think we could continue on, as an independent pack, just so we could continue on together as George Williams students and faculty? I'm the leader, and I have no clear plan beyond the day. Once out on the high ropes, every day is an eternity of problem solving. It's a long way down if we fall. This time I bear the weight of students and faculty with me. But it seems right. Worth the risk. Nelson's voice comes back to me again and again. Every night, in my dreams, every waking hour, "You can do it, Sandy. One step at a time. Don't look down. Look straight ahead."

In the early years of the 1980s, before the college closed, something was changing. The clear, unified objective to educate the whole person, in body, mind, spirit, and social dimensions was showing cracks. The unexpressed found expression in a faculty commencement speech in 1980.

"Continue to hold us not in your hearts, but in your minds"

Faculty commencement speech, 1980

> Our wishes for your future are . . . somewhat abstracted. You are already removed and separated from the focus of our work, which must be always on perpetually changing those-who-are-here. . . . It is not the ties of affection that will continue to bind us . . . it is the life of the mind. Of course, a school wishes to nourish the spiritual and emotional life of the students, but such concerns must be tangential. For a school is not a church or a clinic or a family. Rather, the role of the teacher is to cherish and nurture the intellect. To promote reason, to develop logic, to convey knowledge, to insist upon rules of evidence, to identify values and reveal the workings of ideology, to train the mind, that is the goal of the teacher and the purpose of a college. . . . To accomplish this may indeed involve a teacher in the roles of holy man, healer, parent, friend, enemy, saint, and fool. But always and only as a means to the end of enjoining the student to think. I hope that we have done well by you . . . that you will continue to hold us, not in your hearts, but in your minds.[26]

This farewell address could have passed muster in most colleges for its eloquence alone. In this college, it invited a blink and a pause. Did he say the college was only about developing minds, not the whole person?

Learning by Living Through Crisis:
The College Closes, 1985

Five years later, the college closed, due to financial difficulty. The following are student voices on their experience of the crisis; they instinctively chose a path of social action to respond. When they did survive as a "community of living and learning," they were constantly encouraged by faculty to reflect on the experience and what they learned, as student Sally McCarthy recalls.

"Drawing on a foundation. . . . Write about this!"
Reflections of student leader, Sally McCarthy, 1985–1986

1884. Wow! The history of George Williams goes back that far! Well there it is, that foundation, a foundation of justice, of fairness, of speak your word in truth, of sharing, of being companions in the journey of life together. It was already embedded, though we didn't name it at the time [1985]. The values were modeled, and when we needed to draw on them, they surfaced. When the college closed, I don't think we were so good at creating a good outcome for ourselves, as we were drawing on a foundation. We saw that foundation in the professors who were there, who lived it, breathed it. It became a part of us when we needed it.

The student meetings started after the first rumblings that the college might have to close. As the first news leaked, there was an assumption that the college would work it out. When we met with students, we at least wanted be heard about the impact of that decision on our lives. I don't know if there was a debate as to whether financially it was a good move to shut down, as much as it was being heard. When you do something that is difficult, if you do it well . . . you keep people informed. It doesn't change the devastation of the final decision, but at least people feel they have been heard. We got to talk to the board of trustees. We said, "Whether you change your mind [about closure] is one thing, but the fact that we need to be heard is another." We weren't in a fight mode. We just wanted to know: How did this happen? How will you handle this? What needs to happen next? . . . You ask for meetings, you gather people together, you find out what people are thinking and feeling. You ask whether this is really covering what everybody is thinking and feeling. Then you represent the whole of opinions, not just individual opinions.

When I'd walk through the building at the college, I was consumed with students who wanted to give their opinion, wanted to be sure something was said about what they were thinking and feeling. We had meetings constantly: day, evening, up to midnight. Though we were from social work, we met with the entire college of students. It was natural for us to take a lead role, because we had the foundation to say, "Let's do this together." The students' issues with the administration were: Did they know that this could be a possibility? Did they know this when they opened the doors to this class that was going to graduate? The ones most [affected] were the ones who came into the program and were finishing up their final year. Would they have to take additional years to finish programs elsewhere? They had work, family, had made sacrifices to get to this place. Athletes were on scholarships that were at risk. Are they going to play or not play? We met with the board, pressing for honesty. At first we were trying to get answers about the past, about where and why they failed. . . . We went back to the students and said, "We're not going to get those answers." We've been putting energy into how did this happen versus what do we do now, how do we move forward? That was hardest thing, to bring the group out of that place. They wanted people held accountable. We said if you want to take that cause on, go ahead. We're not. We have to direct our energy toward what we do from here. As the reality sunk in that there was no turning back, the college was indeed closing, different plans for transfer began to emerge. The college community as a whole dispersed, by individuals or programs. It was good-bye, good luck, and the story continues with the social work program for me.

Social work had the numbers to work with well over 125 students committed to staying together. The power was in the numbers. At the time, we weren't realizing what we were doing. When I look back, this learning was so much better than the blackboard or what you can read. We picked up the undergrad students, the part-time evening students, others who were a little more out there. They knew there was some kind of energy, and it was going somewhere. There were lots of meetings to keep communication clear. We did have this very real sense of the loss the faculty experienced also. I know we were all adults, but it was like if you see parents devastated, and you were the kid, what prayer do you think you have? But the faculty encouraged us to stay with our own issues, and they would deal with theirs. In the middle of total chaos, there was somebody who had strength. I looked to faculty and if they looked worried, I was worried. There was no division between faculty and students. There was a sense of a united cause that just penetrated the place. There's a lot of power to that. Whenever we heard individual student stories, we were re-energized to work together.

The social work program opened up its winter term at Northern Baptist Seminary, just across the expressway from the old campus. The program was supported by the Loyola University School of Social Work, an accredited program that it was hoped would be a protective umbrella, if professional accreditation status was threatened. From January 1986 to June 1986, students could complete their academic year as George Williams College students through this transitional program arrangement with Loyola University.

When we got back to the books and the classroom, our papers were always [to] write about this. . . . You've been through this; what did you learn? Apply it. Our discussions were about what happened. There were times when people would say, "We need to move on. I'm tired of talking about this." Others would say, "We're talking about it because I'm still in it."

There was one other thing. I was also Sister Sally McCarthy. I was part of [a religious] order [of nuns], another community. The order had serious concerns about staying with George Williams. . . . They felt [social work] accreditation would be a long time coming, once it was gone, and I wouldn't be graduating from an accredited school. Losing accreditation was a huge risk. So I made the decision to transfer out of the George Williams College social work program and into the Loyola University social work program, [the same program that was supporting the George Williams program, though they were completely independent of each other]. It was a very difficult decision. Of all people, I was going to jump ship! At least people were going to interpret it that way, no matter what. People said, "I can't believe you're not staying." I thought, "How do I get them to understand my commitment without saying [my order is] making me do something." I really wanted us to maintain to the end a respect for individual student's choice. I didn't want to see something where the ones who were staying on were seen as better than the ones who decided to transfer. Some were saying, "I have to leave and go with a program that is accredited." Others were saying, "I have to stay with the group, because we have fought together, to stay together to the end." People were fighting hard to get that program going that landed up at Aurora. Let's not say, to any individual or group, "Are they crazy?" Let's, to the end, respect our individual decisions. There were even meetings about respecting peoples' decisions about why they were doing what they were doing. . . . Foundations, . . . things you don't talk about, come to the surface in crisis. Their greatest impact is in a time of crisis![27]

"I learned the power of community to achieve great things"

Carol Donegan, student, ('86)

It was about midway through the fall quarter when we, the part-time students, began hearing rumors that George Williams College was in a grave financial crisis and the doors of the college would possibly be closing. This was something nobody wanted to hear, let alone believe. In fact, many students and some staff were in disbelief, denial, and refused to discuss the "nasty rumor." I personally didn't like the thought of it, as I was hoping to finish and graduate from George Williams College the following June. But at the same time I had no reason to disbelieve that it was no more than a nasty rumor, and the likelihood of it happening caused me to reconsider my alternatives immediately. . . .

I wasn't involved in much of this campus activity [the student response to the news of the college closing], but did keep abreast as well as I could, as each new event surfaced. I knew the students were spending long hours meeting, discussing, canvassing, and attempting to raise funds. I attended all the part-time evening meetings for updates and signed petitions. . . . The biggest conflict was not wanting to abandon my alma mater, but at the same time, sensing the hopelessness and need to pursue some of the alternatives offered. I think most of the students felt this way and researched other schools while hanging onto the threads of hope that the right solution would come along if we hung together and supported the efforts of our leadership . . . [who were] available day and night . . . to gear and steer the student community, . . . gathering information about other schools, organizing student meetings, revamping, reviewing, reorganizing, researching, recalculating, listening, offering empathy, considering and supporting everyone. Staff and students drew closely together and worked diligently to reduce the overwhelming sense of powerlessness and doom. . . . [At first] it appeared our community was alive with fury, anger, and energy to fight back. . . . Then the fight was on to survive, and there was increased trust, belief, and hope seen on a daily basis. A ray of hope turned into terrific enthusiasm. I'm sure [people on the outside] viewed this as foolishness, a hopeless case. . . . Not so within the community of George Williams College. The public, in my mind, didn't see it as so important. Granted it made the TV news and newspapers, and there were minimal donations to the fundraising goal, but in most cases people would comment, "Oh, isn't that a shame," or "You don't hear of colleges closing up very often," and they would go about their business. . . . I'm sure some parties who wanted the land to develop for their own interests relished the idea of the college closing.

The students saw themselves as peers and copartners working together on the same goal. It didn't matter about one's age, undergraduate or graduate level. The main focus was to get the help needed for each and everyone, give them alternatives, and work together for what was best for the majority of the community. It was a painful, scary, and, to an extent, unbelievable situation. But in retrospect, it was a marvelous experience.

I think everyone learned something from it. I learned the power and ability of a small community working together for one another to achieve great things. I see how including every student in the process with staff support increases motivation, hope, and solution.

I've seen tears shed from a loss of "home." It's been a struggle for all concerned. I'm pleased with the outcome and hope to graduate in the last graduating class of

George Williams College, but it doesn't stop there. I have made some very close friends. Some will graduate with me, and some are going on at Aurora University. We plan on continuing our relationships, getting together periodically for updates in our life and how we're doing with our goals. We will always be a part of that greater community.[28]

"The learning was not apparent to me until January"

Pat Connelley, student, ('86)

The experience resulted in feelings of shock, denial, anger, sadness, fear, and confusion, to name a few. These feelings were experienced by individual students. However, the whole student body joined forces to share these feelings, forming an alliance. As disturbing as this situation was, it brought to light the safety and security that can be obtained with group support. It reinforced in me the concept that I try to reinforce in others: consolation is best achieved by forming an alliance with people who share the same problem and helping one another work through it. People in crisis can achieve this by sharing ideas, feelings, and taking some form of action. . . .

The college that had become a part of our identity was crumbling. Our security, our future . . . was suddenly very much threatened. This was something that could not be dealt with on an individual basis, but only as a group of people who needed to support each other. As part-time evening students, having to work during the day prevented us from being "on the scene," so to speak. We couldn't be a part of the group that waited in hallways and outside of boardrooms for decisions and new information. This was difficult and increased our confusion and frustration, to the point where many of us began to pull away and detach from the problem. I, for one, felt totally and completely powerless over what I perceived as a monumental reality that could not be resolved by signing petitions and/or carrying signs. Others felt disgust and anger at the administrators. . . . Some of us made the decision to transfer. Our subgroup began investigating this possibility and shared admission information as well as positive and negative aspects of transferring versus hanging on. We felt concern for ourselves and our futures, and, to be perfectly honest, we selfishly chose to take care of ourselves rather than believe that the school could remain open. We decided to cut the ties permanently. In spite of this decision, I did remain connected. My calm detachment, I realized, was my way of not dealing with the sadness and disappointment that I really felt. Although I felt that it was hopeless, I attended the meetings and anxiously awaited new information. As time went on, the subgroups were reunited with the larger group. The more active members of the student body and faculty emerged as advocates. They shared explanations and clarifications of issues and decisions. This information was then shared with others by way of a designed telephone tree. People became dependent upon each other. A cohesiveness began to develop, along with a renewed sense of our numerical strength. At this point, no one knew what the end result would be, but we decided to join forces to hold the program together. We realized we had to accept the reality that George Williams College would not open in winter quarter.

Plans were being made, alternatives were available, and the group made unanimous decisions based on realistic solutions to our problem. . . . We contacted schools in an attempt to allow us to keep our program together while completing our education. The unanimous decision to work through Loyola was rational, realistic, and very generous on their part. Loyola University was different, but not necessarily negative. They made their requests and expectations to comply with their standards. I'm very willing to do this and feel that it's worked out extremely well. . . .

This was a particularly stressful yet extremely beneficial learning experience for me as well as for others. The learning experience was not apparent to me until January. I was grateful for the opportunity to ventilate my feelings, both during the crisis and in processing it afterwards. I discovered the benefits of organizing and sticking together, maximizing our strength. I marveled at the sacrifice students and faculty made in order to arrive at solutions and alternatives. . . . Crisis often brings out the best in people, and it was interesting to see the leaders emerge. I learned some uncomfortable things about myself, such as my eagerness to detach and remain uninvolved. . . . Probably the best lesson I learned from this experience was the realization of how much my education, George Williams College, students and faculty, really mean to me. . . . I feel that the outcome has been positive for me. I hope I'll graduate in August with a George Williams College degree, which has always been my goal. Things have settled down, and the program is well organized, despite initial turmoil.

I remember the first day of winter quarter, when we entered the unfamiliar surroundings of Northern Baptist Seminary, wondering where to go and what to expect. After wandering the halls, we eventually wound up on the second floor. I saw many familiar faces. Among them was Sandy Alcorn and David Wright. Almost instantly I felt at home and I knew things would be all right.[29]

"It is my own personal belief . . . faith in community"

Laurie Munson, student, (AU '87)

Solving community problems is an activity performed by many [human service] professionals, [including] building the capacity of grassroots citizens groups to solve

them. . . . We banned together and made a pact that we would keep each other informed and would make every effort to stay together and continue on. We felt the
strength of numbers and felt we could be more effective together than each man for
himself. In December a meeting took place with the entire community of the social
work program, and a democratic vote was actually taken as to where the program
would go, . . . Loyola University.

We [our subgroup] agreed on a goal of "staying together, maintaining optimism
and mental health." Our basic strategy was "Let's all get together and talk this over;
every individual needed to be heard. . . . We encouraged group members to express
feelings and process the situation." We tried to focus on mutual goal agreement, although we did not ignore differing interests; we processed them. . . . There was a
unity of community life, a spirit of "we will get through this together, and only together can we get through it." There was a sense of the common good arrived at
through a deliberative process involving a cross section of interest groups within our
community. . . . Each member of our community was viewed as a person who pos-
sessed considerable strengths and inherent capabilities that could be released and
developed in this process. Communication and consensus happened through lots of
small-group discussion.

The closing of George Williams College was a difficult time for all involved and
took its toll on the entire community. However, it is my own personal belief that the
faith in the community and the desire for it to continue enabled us to find the
strength and resources to carry on.[30]

Carrying on the Tradition:
Aurora, Illinois, and Williams Bay, Wisconsin

The social work program successfully concluded its transitional program as George
Williams College up to the end of the academic year. In the fall of the new academic
year, 1986, they moved permanently to a welcoming and supportive Aurora University. There, the experiential learning philosophy continued. Though the location
changed, potential students followed the program for its recognized history. Some represented a new generation of African Americans who grew up in the South Side of
Chicago and connected to people from the college when it was in Hyde Park.

"Recognized for bringing experience to the table"

Glenda Blakemore, student, ('97)

The YMCA has been in my bones forever. In the late 1930s, early 1940s, my grandmother and my grandaunt came up from the South, Kentucky, to establish themselves in Chicago. They stayed at a YMCA downtown, because the Y had room and board. My grandmother and grandaunt both worked for the YMCA. The YMCA has always been there for them, a safe place, a main support system.

When I was in high school, I started to work for Neighborhood Youth Corps, run by the Y. I lived on the South Side, on Ninety-fifth Street. I always heard about George Williams College, but I didn't know anything about it. Besides the Neighborhood Youth Corps, I went to [the] Wabash Y for teen group year-round. I called it "the country club for poor people." We went on hayrides and dances at [the] Y. I did know that most of the staff from the Wabash Y were from George Williams. Then on Saturdays I would go to the University of Chicago for a science and math group. I didn't know Larry Hawkins ('56, '72) [director of the program and a George Williams College alumnus who tells his story in chapter 2, "Developing Body with Mind and Spirit"], but I'm sure it was his program. This was something educational. My mother was going around saying, "My daughter's going to the University of Chicago!" I said, "Mom, I'm in high school; I'm going there on Saturdays!" It was the first college I had ever been to. I was learning and having a good time.

My mother used to talk about George Williams College at Lake Geneva. She would go for conferences there. I remember once we went with her to College Camp. It was like a family vacation. It was like a foreign country for us. It seemed like such a long way, coming from the South Side. There were no expressways like the Dan Ryan at the time. . . . Light years later, in 1994, I enrolled in the MSW program at Aurora University. It was a George Williams College program, and I went up to Lake Geneva for Orientation Practicum. As soon as I saw the cottages, I said, "I know I've been here before." Then we heard the story about how the college started here with the YMCA. My mother was so excited about me going to GWC. She said it was a good thing; it was about people, about doing the right thing. I didn't enroll in this social work program because it was convenient. I could have gone across the city to get what I wanted. I heard good things about the program. I heard it was student-centered. I heard they had a heart and passion for true social work. They were doers. They worked with marginalized people. Up to the time I got my MSW, I had not been kind to social work. I didn't think much of the degree, because I saw people who had it, [but] that didn't make a difference. They talked a lot about it, they researched about it, but they didn't do anything.

I already had a master's degree in community mental health, and I already had an established career when I signed up for the MSW program. I had been the first female warden at the Illinois Youth [Correctional] Center in St. Charles from 1981–1991, and now I was warden at the youth center in Warrenville. I got to know Sally McCarthy [whose story is told in this chapter], working in the police department there. She was a doer.

I have to say this about my experience as a student: You spoiled me. I found the program very challenging. I worked harder in this program than for my other degree. I always challenged everyone. Where's the research on African Americans? Where are the women? In the class on adult development, if we were talking about Daniel Levinson's model for stages of adult development, I said, "What is this based on? Research on white males who went to Yale? No, no, not me. This does not work for my experience!" But it was okay for me to say that, and for us to discuss it. In Fred McKenzie's class on adolescence, he asked us to watch *Breakfast Club* for an exercise in class. I said, "That doesn't work for me." I asked Fred if I could write on *Boyz n the Hood.* He said, "Sure!" I was always allowed to bring up an alternative view. Now, that's learning. That's what I liked about the program. We were treated like the working adults we were, who brought our own experiences to the table. We had things to contribute. There was respect for strangers and their words in class.

My staff at Warrenville did not like when I was a student there. I'd learn something in class, then I'd run back and try it out to see it this was true, if it worked. They'd say, "When is she going to graduate?" It was a good experience. I needed to be recognized for bringing something to the table. Once I was, I was like a bad penny. I never went away. I became a field instructor after I graduated. Then I was a child welfare trainer for DCFS [Department of Children and Family Services, through a social work grant program] at Aurora University. Now I'm the coordinator of field instruction for the program. It's been hard for me to find a program to get my doctorate. I found here at George Williams people who care about me as a person and a student, and think that I have some experiences to bring to the table. I really have not found that recognition elsewhere. They say it, but I don't see it operationalized. I want to be treated like an adult.[31]

"You didn't say,
'Oh no, that's not the correct way of thinking'"

Melissa Sofia, student, ('01)

Becoming a social worker was not one of my lifelong plans. My dream was to become a professional dancer. Ballet was my forte. I was moving along that path, directing several dance companies after college. Since body movement was a big part of my interest and medium of expression, I started to prepare educationally to be a dancer. Then I moved into academic preparation in the field of therapeutic recreation. However, I was soon turned off by my formal education with the experience I had at another graduate school. One professor didn't share my view on things. He would belittle me. I quickly learned to shut down and not share with anyone my curiosity and inquiry about the world. Consequently I shut down from formal education. My degree became something I had to do, a credential. The last straw was when I called my professor on the telephone, and he put me on hold. That was a power thing. I don't remember his lectures, but I do remember being put on hold on the phone. I dropped out of school, and took up professional dancing again.

I came to George Williams on the recommendation of Linda Orange ['93], an alum who thought I would be good at social work. I noticed something different right away. Faculty related to me as a student. I could use words like *personable,* [or] *inviting,* but these words take on new meaning when I think of them because it goes so deep. For me, being personable means being accepted, one's views being understood. It goes back to the value of respect for others and their experience. For me, the word *experiential* means taking somebody from where they are and watching them choose to move a certain direction. If faculty wanted us to get to a certain place in learning, they helped us get there. They didn't pull us there, they didn't yell that we had to get there. They helped us get there.

I would ask professors if we could bring somebody in to talk about body movement. I was always curious about the integration of body and movement with human behavior. I was curious about dance therapy, though it was not in the curriculum. Dr. Mikal Rasheed invited people in from George Williams who were involved in body work. He was open to it, even though he had some other lesson plan. Faculty made room in the learning environment for me to pursue my interest and share it with others. Chris Ahlman was another professor like that. We would have an idea of what we wanted to learn about, and Chris made it happen. To bring people into a learning community and have that respected, to share your curiosity about the world of human behavior, to have your viewpoints respected—it started the learning process. You were helped to move beyond where you were.

For me, "What else can I learn?" always goes with "What can I do?" This kind of learning makes me want to give back. That's how I got involved with the mentoring program that [faculty member] Terri Dalton initiated. Terri asked if I might be interested in getting involved. A classmate, Raman Mace ['01], and I got to work. The goal was to link master's-level students in the social work program with professional mentors in the field. Students and professional mentors would voluntarily sign up, and we would link them to each other. The mentor would be in contact once a month. Students could visit their agencies, ask questions; mentors would respond in whatever way was needed to learn about the professional world students were entering. . . . Many of the linkages made remained in a continuing professional network long after graduation. Recently I talked with another student, Mike Brunetti ['01], who said he was still in touch with his mentor years after graduation. Students got what [they] needed; we didn't overplan, we just made the connection. The next year the mentoring program took a broader course. We started having meetings with incoming students to find out what they needed to learn. . . . The students indicated a need to know how to deal with the stressors of being a student . . . managing heavy course loads and assignments, working through difficult collegial relationships, faculty expectations, dealing with financial insecurity and need for aid, and preparing for licensure exams. Students also wanted a place to drop in and just hang. We created this sense of place in a lounge area outside the offices of faculty. I made curtains to make it homey, and I would bring muffins. People would just come; students met between classes, using each other as resources for guidance and support. We started having speakers come to talk about special topics the students wanted to learn about: . . . working with gifted students, ways of learning, drug abuse, domestic violence, infertility. The group began to meet on Saturdays. We all chipped in a few bucks for bagels. Terri started to put together seminars for students to prepare for their licensure exam. Faculty here are not saying, "Oh, no, that's not what you need to know," or "That's not the correct way of thinking about it." It wasn't just me on the receiving end of learning, it was giving back. I know the big lessons students learn are by doing things. It was all part of my education here. I don't see that in other schools.[32]

"We're from GWC also! . . . thinking the same way"

Ann Bergart, professor, 2004

When we moved to a semester system at Aurora University, we were invited to propose innovative courses for a single month term in May. Experiential courses were encouraged. Two other group-work teachers in social work and I decided to offer an experiential group-work course. We created an idea of a program for high school students for interracial dialogue. We thought, "Let's go to the George Williams College campus at Lake Geneva for a camping experience." Graduate students who enroll in this course will prepare a high school camp program. Faculty will give them resources to study content and programs on interracial dialogue. Then the students will develop their own model of what they think would work, using play activity and small-group talks for high school students. They, in turn, will be like camp counselors, passing the program of activities on to a camp of younger kids in the future. Faculty would be with them in camp to troubleshoot. After preparation and the camping experience, there would be a day of class afterward for evaluation. How did it go? What was the experience like? We had a wonderful experience! We as faculty played the games and shared our experiences in small groups along with everyone also. It was a life-changing experience for all of us. I felt like the spirit of George Williams College was present with us at camp. We learned some things we might do differently next time, and we definitely want a next time.

I was telling a friend of mine about this exciting experience, and she recommended I talk to Michael Terrien ['84] . . . who started an organization called Play for Peace. It uses play activities and dialogue to bring young people together from communities around the world that are in conflict. The young people, in turn, become leaders and play leadership roles in passing the program on to other younger kids. It was a very similar model, only he's using it on an international level. He's been asked to do the Play for Peace program in the Balkans, Israel, and Ireland; Queen Noor from Jordan invited him to bring the program there. He's had requests from the United Nations to do the program in all different parts of the world.

I invited Michael to class to broaden the students' perspectives on what you can do with models like this. When Michael started to talk in class, he mentioned that he [had been] a recreation student at George Williams College. "Wait," I said. "Did you say George Williams College? We're George Williams College also!" Michael had no idea that the School of Social Work at Aurora [University] came from George Williams College also. Here we were, thinking the same way of how to use groups and experiential learning to develop cross-racial, cross-cultural dialogue![33]

People who want to remember George Williams College from the past and who want to reexperience what it once was as a college still travel to Williams Bay, where it all began. You cannot be on the site long without stumbling onto something that will recall the past: the rock where the first dedicatory campfire was lit and George Williams College was founded, pictures of students and groups of people from the turn of the century gathered on the shores of the lake. New sights will grab your attention—new buildings, carefully designed to be congruent with history. But for those who lived the past in George Williams College, it's always the people you meet, people who share the history, who bring continuity with the past and enrich the spirit. When you travel to Williams Bay, you will probably meet Bill Duncan. Bill is one of those people who bridges the past with the present and offers a vision of a future for the Williams Bay campus that will reflect the strong roots of the past. Bill is vice president and chief academic officer of George Williams College today at Williams Bay. He has been running the campus throughout the college's tenure in Downers Grove and now at Aurora University.

Williams Bay:
"A sense of place and history that wouldn't let me go"

Bill Duncan, student, ('68) and administrator

I came from California to the college through YMCA connections. I was a student at the Downers Grove campus when the college was making the early transition to the suburbs. I remember two distinctives of George Williams College: experiential learning approaches and quality faculty who effectively used those learning approaches. By that I mean instructors who are humane and people-centered; they cared about students and helped to see them through. Quality instructors were involved in social action in society. Quality instructors engaged students through learning-by-doing. I learned from people who brought their experiences into class, or brought the class into their experiences. It was not typical for a college to use experiential education in this way. I suppose the size of the classes helped. It was a small institution with major players so committed to the teaching style and values of the institution.

Two instructors, for example, were Arthur Steinhaus and Dietrich Reitzes. Steinhaus was a pioneer in neuromuscular relaxation. Reitzes was a community organizer, working with the Woodlawn Organization. He brought into the classroom real-life experiences with community organization. Also, every student had fieldwork. They had internship placements in Ys and social service organizations throughout the city of Chicago. Professors cared about students and their experiences and would process their experiences in class. The city of Chicago was a wonderful laboratory for testing out ideas and experiences. This was more difficult to do when the college moved to the western suburb of Downers Grove.

I also remember high-adventure experiences in travel and the outdoors. As a student who majored in camping and recreation, I went on one of the first travel camps in the United States with professors Nelson Wieters and Don Clayton. The travel camps were called "Man and His Land." Students hiked the Tetons in the Rockies and rafted in Colorado. Their teaching methods were to expose students to an experience and then process that experience. They would use inductive methods to learn. The process of learning was one where the experience came first, and in the reflection and sharing of reflections, certain generalizations would be made and put to further testing in experience. Another experience in the outdoors was September Camp. Students would learn skills and then process them together. Tom Bennett was also an amazing professor in organizational development. He was a major leader in the National Training Laboratory movement. Tom brought his consulting experience into class; he would present case studies. You were getting state of the art when you heard from him. Jeanne Norris and Gladys Robinson were others. They exposed students to direct experiences that they could take back to the classroom. Gladys taught botany, and she would take students into the wetlands on the campus surrounding the college in Downers Grove. . . . Alex Shukin [counseling psychology] used student tapes of interviews . . . for reflection on practice skills. Students used demonstrations and role-playing for learning. Talk about hands-on learning: how about hands-on cadavers? The use of cadavers is a case in point. It was unheard of. Our science lessons came, not from a textbook or simulations, but the real thing. My job as a student was to take care of those cadavers. They were real skeletons!

Another thing that made the college unique was a unity around the mission of human service. It was clear. You are here to serve. You aren't going to make money, because if you stay in this line of service, it ain't going to happen. But the commitment to human service was consistent and unwavering among students and faculty. A spirit of humanism pervaded the place. People truly shared values of service. Everything reflected underlying Judeo-Christian values.

I also learned about other cultures and experiences that were different from my white, middle-class, male experience. My friends were Conrad Worrill ('68) [who was African American] and Lorenzo Barcelo ('68) [who was Puerto Rican]. In the college, friendship across racial and ethnic lines were strong; even in 1968 when Spring Festival was going on.

Now Bill shifts into the present and the future, as he sits in his office at the Williams Bay campus looking out on new buildings built in the last few years by Aurora University, blended in the with old, familiar ones that have come to symbolize College Camp for so many.

Lake Geneva had a sense of place and history that wouldn't let me go. When the college closed in 1985 and other opportunities opened up, I could not leave it behind. The college had a sense of mission, even though it had drifted a bit. Symbolically this place [Williams Bay] is a place of comfort and home. Lake Geneva reflects the tradition of experiential learning. We want to use the experiential method to deliver coursework in those areas where appropriate. We brought the recreation program [that came from George Williams College] here to reconnect those students in outdoor education. [In the Downers Grove days] graduate students started the outdoor ed program [with grade schools in the Chicago area], and now they're coming back. We have students in adventure-based programs, camping programs, Outdoor Leadership [OWL] programs. These all were an outgrowth of the outdoor ed program of the past.

A new program addition is the First Tee program, designed to introduce young people, [particularly youth at risk], to golf for character education and the teaching of life skills. Richard Bowers was instrumental in developing this program sponsored by the USGA [United States Golf Association]. . . . There is a School of Professional Studies here now. We also have a new experiential leadership program. Rita Yerkes is here now on the Lake Geneva campus developing that program. Part of the social work program, [which came to Aurora University from George Williams College], is now operating on the Lake Geneva campus.

I would like to see more short-term educational institutes, as they had in the past at Lake Geneva. I think we can carry it forward now in a way that I never thought possible. Institutes were where it all began in the history of the college, and institutes like camping [ones] have played a significant role in the past with a national audience. We had Spanish immersion language programs held at Lake Geneva, and I hope to see them reintroduced.

We hope to have fifteen degree programs operating here. We hope this will be a national center for outdoor education. We hope to reintegrate "body, mind, and spirit" programs and institutes related to lifestyle and leisure; conferences on wellness; and institutes that will contribute to transformative learning, more interdisciplinary discussions, and programs. We can't lose the spirit component, for fear of imposing a certain spirituality on others. Life-meaning questions are an essential part. I see George Williams College as on the cutting edge of where [holistic] paradigms are going in the professions.

The reason I was hired was to increase the educational use of campus, and all the educational programs that are introduced now will have an experiential base. Experiential learning is transformative. You must have foundational theory. But the real challenge is to make that information come alive, so it means something to the student, not only to the professor. Students and faculty are involved together in the learning process. The professor may be catalyst in the beginning, but students are engaged and responsible for applying the concepts. That's a transformational process. Learning from experience, applying what you're learning, then sharing, reflecting, and doing that together, that's what it's about. The sharing is important because people have different meanings. Different people get different things from an experience. Experiential learning is to be able to understand and appreciate differences, to invite diversity. The outcome of this kind of transformative education is that you're becoming an inclusive community. This fits in quite well with the new mission statement for Aurora University: An inclusive community dedicated to the transformative power of learning.[34]

"Coming full circle, home again"

Rita Yerkes, administrator

In spring of 1987 I came to Aurora University as chair of the LERA program that came from George Williams. I was at State University of New York. I heard about the closing of George Williams College in 1985. Students were calling us to transfer. I thought how sad it was that this wonderful college and program were going under. . . . Then, I got a call from [faculty member] Helen Finch, indicating that the LERA students had made a transition to Aurora University. They got through accreditation but needed a doctoral faculty member, and I was invited to apply. Dr. Alan Stone was president. He told me there was a lot of rebuilding that had to be done, because students and faculty had gone on to other places. They wanted me to take the students and faculty left and rebuild. I knew the tradition of GWC and Helen Finch [chair of the program after Nelson Wieters], I had respect for her work, I had a commitment from the president and the institution to do whatever it takes to rebuild and retain the legacy of George Williams in mission and philosophy. And so I came.

I see the George Williams legacy as service to others. We are here to make the world a better place, lead by example, make an impact on whatever agency and community where we are. I believe in that legacy, and I'm committed to continuing it. Though I had not personally attended George Williams, the programs were respected nationally. Colleagues across the nation grieved when they heard of the closing. For the first couple of years after I came, I traveled the country, holding alumni reunions to inform alumni of the survival of the program, inviting them to be part of process. I felt I had the support of alumni, past faculty, Aurora University, and people of the profession that made the tradition of George Williams College. Through different phases, we rebuilt. First came an affiliation agreement between George Williams College and Aurora University, and eventually a full merger. There were many ways that we tried to keep the spirit of GWC going. We continued the tradition of September Camp. That was crucial. It provided a linkage of alumni to current students. In the beginning we put out newsletters to alumni to retain a connection. We made sure our program stayed accredited. We had receptions at professional conferences. We never asked for donations, but we wanted them to send us students if they felt good about the program. . . . They began to believe Aurora University was a good home for the program from which they graduated. We continued to stay in touch with people on the Lake Geneva campus, though early on, it was not a part of Aurora University.

Continuing to have September Camp in Lake Geneva was helpful in establishing an agreement between both institutions, because we already we had good relations with people up here [in Williams Bay]. The September Camp was required for LERA and recreation administration students and was an elective for physical education students. Quite a few would choose to do it. September Camp was a bonding experience between faculty and students. We continued the tradition of respect for the natural environment. There is one outdoor course that all students take. When we traveled across the country talking to alumni, the first thing they talk about is their experience at September Camp.

Once we had an affiliation agreement to become George Williams College of Aurora University, we did community outreach programs together. The GWC programs at the time were social work, recreation administration, physical education, and education. Since the community outreach programs were supported by the Beasley Foundation, we called them the Beasley Projects. Students and faculty would propose a community outreach program that would be staffed by students. Faculty were mentors and liaisons between students and agencies.

We also did Freshman Year Experience up here for the entire student body. It was a bonding experience. September Camp students put the program on. It was a part of their orientation experience. We had an overnight, group experiences, and problem-solving activities, Students got to know each other. It was used as a final exam for the September Camp course. Students set it up for new students. They were responsible for planning and implementing it, to learn experiential leadership. New students always started out with, "Why do I have to come?" But when they left, they knew each other. It helps to retain students.

What's going on here now is an outcome of the final merger of GWC with AU. President Rebecca Sherrick was working with consultants, looking at the mission of the university, preparing for the North Central Association accreditation self-study. She was asking what we should be doing with the George Williams College campus in Lake Geneva. The new mission statement calls for transformational learning. Bringing academic programs to this campus makes the educational mission of the Lake Geneva campus more pronounced. Educational programs are being transferred to the Lake Geneva campus at a rapid pace. The programs that started up only a year ago are doing well, and they are already getting transfers from other schools.

The First Tee program is an example of experiential leadership development for our students. Sponsors provide the instruction and equipment for that part of the program. Then our students enhance what they're trying to do on the golf course when they come off the golf course. The kids do golf in the morning with their staff, then our staff takes the character-building goals and we reinforce the outcomes. It's not just a recreation program for fun. We have them on climbing towers, or they are on group problem-solving activities. We reinforce those character-building concepts. Our students are involved in delivering the program. They're here a week. We had one group of forty this year, and two groups of eighty. Out of the Experiential Leadership program, the Williams Bay Recreational Center is run by students. The Outdoor Environmental Education program serves eight thousand elementary school children who learn about the outdoors. It's a thirty-year-old program. The Outdoor Leadership program serves leaders using high-challenge programs, athletic teams, and private and corporate groups. Specific goals and objectives are related to team building. Some students and some staff are always involved. For the climbing wall and First Tee program, there are instructor training workshops.

On this campus we developed a curriculum for camp directors on how to run a youth camp. There were summer institutes. It was a national thing. The American Camping Association saw its roots here. Faculty members Judy Myers and Nelson Wieters were involved in a national certification process for camp directors. A whole curriculum was developed for youth camp directors. Hedley Dimock developed group work out of his work to professionalize camping. He developed standards, goals, objectives, and an evaluation process for camping. Teachers and social workers were involved in summer camping programs. The ideas came out of the camping movement. Jane Addams was involved in summer camping. Group work became a combination of social work, recreation, and education. Before Dimock's time, there were no textbooks, no formal training. This campus played a huge part. They were involved in research.

I don't know of too many people in their career who had the opportunity to join a program going down the tubes, to work with so many people who wanted it to succeed—alums, professionals, students, faculty, administrators—all wanted to make this happen. To be on this campus again is very special. The opportunities this campus offers in learning-by-doing are very special. Really, it's where the program began; now it's coming home again. To have it come full circle is a pretty amazing story![35]

Chapter 5

Reaching Around the World

*"A **miniature world** destined to serve the needs of every country and race through its members who come from all ends of the earth and call themselves **deacons of humanity.**"*

(Student Alecos Michaelides from Greece, describing George Williams College, 1922)

From its start, George Williams College had worldwide comings and goings. The YMCA movement, which started in England in 1884, spread quickly as an international movement. A "worldwide brotherhood" was forming, and from 1890, students came from around the world to the "YMCA College" in the Chicago area. Global outreach found expression in many ways. First, the YMCA symbolically publicized that it stood for the social development of people. When the college

was in its infancy in the 1890s, the Y spoke of a "fourfold purpose" to develop body, mind, spirit, *and* the social dimensions of people's lives; it was represented by a cross. This YMCA symbol was later superceded by the "Y triangle" that we recognize today, representing only three dimensions of development. Yet, George Williams College held fast to that missing fourth dimension—the social dimension. The story of George Williams College is all about social development. The college left its imprint on a distinct way of providing human service, wrapping physical education, recreation and camping, and social work into its hallmark group work service. On the local level, the college influenced human services, particularly in Chicago, the Midwest, the West, and Canada. On the global level, service was expressed in the form of social and economic development—doing whatever it took, whether it meant using a soccer ball to build community in Turkey, or piping in clean water and teaching agriculture in a remote Tanzanian village.

Another expression of global outreach was the popular "Student Volunteer Movement." The Lake Geneva Student Conferences played an important role in this movement. Early on, in the 1890s, the thrust of the movement was on evangelical foreign mission work, influenced by Chicago-based evangelist Dwight L. Moody, who urged college students to volunteer for foreign service at his Northfield, Massachusetts, conferences. It was 1889 when the college founders invited Moody to come to Geneva Lake, so that the West could receive "like benefits to the east." When Moody declined their invitation, they moved on, and organized the first of many Lake Geneva Student Conferences in 1890. Its popularity was keen. Up to 700 college students, mostly from the Midwest and who were in YMCA groups on their campuses, came to the Lake Geneva Student Conferences. The conferences developed their own distinction, influenced by the leadership of John R. Mott, who paid regular visits to the Williams Bay campus from 1890 to 1922.

Mott was the national intercollegiate YMCA secretary from 1915 to 1928 and president of the YMCA World Committee from 1926 to 1937. He won a Nobel Peace Prize in 1946 for the role of the YMCA in world service in both World Wars. Under Mott's leadership, the Lake Geneva Student Conferences embraced the Social Gospel movement, with George Williams College being one of the first

room lesson. They regenerated and fueled the spirit of global learning and service for younger generations.

Over time, the global character of this small college extended well beyond the YMCA influence. Distinguished professors like Arthur Steinhaus received world renown for research in exercise physiology, and he attracted many students to the college. Coaches and athletes received world

"[Global connections] were as informative and transforming as any classroom lesson."

places to emphasize the Social Gospel. During the Depression, the focus shifted from foreign mission work to social and economic development both on the homefront and around the globe.

Taking up the cause, the YMCA developed a specialized role, the World Service worker. The mission of these workers was not to proselytize a Protestant Christian faith, but to contribute to the social and economic development of countries. As global connections were made, international students came first to the Chicago campus, and then to the Downers Grove campus of George Williams College. Student friendships developed in this relatively small community. They were as informative and transforming as any class-

recognition for their role in the Olympic Games. Diplomats and children of diplomats came to the college to teach and to learn. Today, we hear stories of recent graduates from George Williams College of Aurora University who may not even be aware of the YMCA influence on the culture of the college. Yet they still catch the spirit of global learning and service, and their lives are transformed.

Photograph, page 199: "Foreign delegates" convene at the George Williams campus in Williams Bay for a student conference. Delegates from Russia, Japan, Africa, China, and Italy are a remarkable world community gathering in 1918.

Early Seeds: YMCA World Service

"The Genius of Lake Geneva"

The *Lake Geneva Chronicler,* 1938

> 1890: This was the period of evangelistic missionary emphasis. . . . A student volunteer representative was invited to be at each of these earlier conferences to keep foremost . . . the missionary emphasis. . . .
>
> 1893: Two hundred students came from one hundred colleges. . . .
>
> 1903: Seven hundred college men came trooping into camp in a heavy rain. . . .
>
> 1910: . . . The beginning interest in social questions. . . . The leaders wanted to influence men to consecrate themselves to social service for Christ. This was a new emphasis. . . .
>
> 1921: . . . It was strange to see the Geneva conferences gradually changing their points of emphasis. They have always seemed adaptable to changing theories and conditions, however. Geneva was one of the first places to emphasize the Social Gospel. . . .
>
> 1924: The conference was called to discuss primarily the relation of college students to a Christian social order. . . .
>
> 1933: Some of the trends of thought we have observed—personal religions, Social Gospel, psychology, social planning—it is a wonder the spirit of Geneva has been so ever changing, yet everlasting. . . . The greatest task of the student Christian movement is to resolve the problems facing the world: . . . unemployment and economic disaster.
>
> 1938: The theme of the conference is "The Essential of Christian Faith and Democracy as a Social Philosophy."[1]

Because of the social development work that was done in countries abroad, by the 1920s students from "all ends of the earth" found their destination point to be Williams Bay, Wisconsin. They came as foreign delegates to the student conferences, celebrating a worldwide brotherhood. They dressed in colorful costumes, displaying flags for photographs, representing their countries.

By the 1920s international students were enrolling in the YMCA College (George Williams College) in Chicago. In 1938 the global outreach included Korea, Japan, China, the Philippines, Hawaii, Scotland, Denmark, England, Czechoslovakia, Switzerland, Turkey, Greece, Palestine, Egypt, India, Ceylon, West Africa, South Africa, Puerto Rico, South America, New Zealand, and Australia.[2]

Both informal student interaction and student clubs tweaked curiosity about other countries and experiences. In some larger universities foreign students had separate housing, which would have obstructed this kind of learning. In the 1920s instead of fraternities, student clubs celebrated the international spirit.

The Ergosandrian Club and Chinese Students Club

Renato Elley de Andrade, Brazilian student, ('24)

It is not a program for foreign students, but an international spirit among all its members. All students are invited and involved.

Yearbook description, 1924

We are justly proud of our foreign group of students from whom we receive that touch of affairs outside our own community. From them we learn of other fields and of their work.

Manuel Bueno, Puerto Rican student, ('25)

To be citizens of the present world, one has to live and adapt himself to all peoples and customs.[3]

Another club was the Chinese Students Club, formed "for devotions and discussion of problems related to the welfare of China."[4]

While students from other countries were coming to the college, students were also going to other parts of the world to do YMCA work. They were called World Service workers. World Service started in 1888 under the leadership of John R. Mott, when he was leading the student conferences at Lake Geneva. Following are stories of World Service workers who were either graduates or friends of the college. Some had children who went to George Williams College, creating a next generation of influence on the college.

When YMCA World Service workers served in other countries, they knew they would be not be as effective if they were proselytizing.

"Proselytizing not allowed"

Bill Glenn, instructor, 1970s and World Service worker, 1950s–1960s

Bill Glenn spent many years as a World Service worker in Turkey. Later in life he taught a not-for-profit management course along with alumnus William Conrad at George

Williams College. Bill Glenn's wife, Mary, full partner with Bill in world service, is the daughter of Paul Anderson, who was a renowned World Service worker in Russia before the Communist revolution. Their daughter Ann ('81) was a graduate of GWC. Bill and Mary Glenn entered World Service work as fraternal secretaries in the mid-1950s. They started working in South America, which included teaching group work and community organization courses in the YMCA training college for South American countries (the Instituto Tecnico). In 1961 Bill went to Turkey to direct the American School of Languages and Commerce. The title would hardly tell that it was a YMCA institute. That's because the "C" in YMCA conjured up a fear of Christian proselytizing in this Muslim country. The board of directors of this YMCA school were mostly Muslim. So were the people in high-ranking staff positions, like Associate Director Esad Kural.

A story that conveys significant personal meaning is told again and again. Bill told me this story, and recently I read the same story in a YMCA publication celebrating World Service workers, "The Human Face of YMCA World Service."

> Dwight Haas, ['60, '61], a recent graduate with a master's degree from George Williams College, accompanied me and worked with me. . . . Esad Kural, a staff member of long tenure, was assigned by the government. His primary charge seemed to be to make sure that an American director in a Turkish institution was not proselytizing. High on my list of priorities was to get to know Esad Bey and to reveal enough of myself that he could trust me [*Bey* is a title of respect given to important people]. . . .
>
> When I arrived at work one morning with a busy schedule ahead of me . . . my secretary alerted me: "Mr. Glenn, I got a call from the police that at precisely four in the afternoon a car will arrive to take you to the central police station. The director of provincial police wants to talk to you." Needless to say, I couldn't imagine what I might have done or what might be on his mind. Until the assigned hour, I spent my time with pangs in my stomach and with Esad Bey, who hadn't a clue as to what might be ahead for me.
>
> I was chauffeured in a 1956 Chevrolet, which was spit and polish, and driven by a driver who was most correct. At the central office, I was led in to wait in a book-lined office with comfortable furniture and pleasant atmosphere. Almost immediately a scholarly gentleman entered with a smile, his hand extended in greeting. He introduced himself as Necdet Ugur, director of provincial police. Picking up a file from his desk, to my amazement and his amusement, he indicated that he probably knew more about me than my wife did. His point was made when he told me how he could help me achieve my goals and objectives if I would use my abilities to help him with a couple of his projects.

With the Menderes political revolution having recently concluded, he was concerned with the unusual number of street kids who were destined to become a greater policing problem. Both of us were aware that I, a foreigner and a Christian, was prohibited by law from influencing children under the age of twelve. . . . I learned that Necdet Bey had studied in Germany and held a PhD in sociology from an American university. This explained to me why we understood one another as well as we did, and we quickly reached an agreement. A key item in his proposal to me was that he assigned five policemen to the Dershane for training in group work and how to work with street kids.[5]

Nicholas Patinos, World Service worker, 1960s

Nick Patinos was another friend of the college whose daughter Margo graduated from George Williams College in 1971. He relates a story as a YMCA World Service worker, also recorded in "The Human Face of YMCA World Service." When he was first assigned to Ecuador, this happened:

The big question . . . arose: How does a Greek Orthodox Christian go into a Roman Catholic country, representing this allegedly Protestant organization? My first mission I felt was to pay my respects to the Catholic cardinal. I arranged an audience, went into the gold-decorated room where the cardinal sat, paid my respects, and began to sit down. The cardinal suddenly said, "You know we are against you Protestant proselytizers!" I replied, "But your Eminence, I myself am not a Protestant." At this, the cardinal said his good-byes, and I was ushered out of the room. Three days later I got a phone call from the cardinal's secretary who said that I was to meet with His Eminence immediately. As I approached the throne room, there was the cardinal standing at the door. "Don Nicholas," he said. "You're of the St. John Rite of Roman Catholicism, welcome to Ecuador. By the way, I hear your wife is an excellent cook. Do you think she would make some American-style hamburgers for me, like the ones I so enjoyed when I visited the U.S.?"[6]

"Truthful to your culture, honest in your beliefs"

Nicholas Goncharoff, World Service worker, 1940s–1980s

Emery Nelson graduated from George Williams College in 1924. He became a World Service worker who worked with war refugees after World War II. One day he came into a Russian refugee camp with Paul Anderson, (Bill Glenn's father-in-law), a renowned World Service worker in Russia who was ousted after the Communist revolution. Emery met Nick Goncharoff, a Soviet soldier, in that camp. Nick tells what happened as the war ended in "The Human Face of YMCA World Service":

> There were thousands of former Soviet soldiers and officers held by the Germans as prisoners of war. Our situation was totally different from those who were American, British, or French. Stalin never recognized the Red Cross or any law, including the Geneva Convention, regarding prisoners of war. His belief was that the men of the Soviet Army should never be prisoners. Prisoners are traitors. The Red Cross, YMCAs, or any other international representatives were not allowed to visit prisoner of war camps that held former Soviet officers and soldiers. The situation was desperate, inhumane, barbaric. . . . Russia suffered more than 30 million dead and about 17 million crippled; a kind of holocaust. . . .
>
> So after liberation by the American troops, we were rounded up, and General George Patton addressed a huge crowd of prisoners by simply saying that he was fighting the war in order to get home. He assumed that the majority of us, if not everyone, wanted to go home as well. . . . We knew that every Soviet soldier would be repatriated home voluntarily, and [if not] they would be returned by force. The situation was rather desperate.
>
> We knew that in big cities in Western Europe, White Russians happened to be located. "White Russians" is a term used from the beginning of the Revolution of 1917. Several millions of Russians emigrated to fight in the White Army against the Red Army, and they represented the first immigration [that] settled primarily through Eastern and Western Europe. The White Russians obviously were able to understand our situation very well, because they had similar experiences following the Bolshevik Revolution.

In 1945, after the American liberation from prisoner of war camps, Nick fled undercover with other Soviet soldiers during night curfew to a refugee camp in Munich, Germany. They became displaced persons.

> One evening . . . we saw a truck entering the gates of the camp. . . . On that truck were the letters YMCA. . . . We knew absolutely nothing about the YMCA. . . . We thought they were engineers because we saw the triangle, which in many countries is the symbol for the engineering profession. . . . Suddenly a truck full of books stopped in the middle of the camp and several people came out . . . many of them speaking Russian. This was the first time I met Paul B. Anderson, Emery Nelson, and Tracy Strong. . . . Anderson greeted every one of us and began to talk in Russian . . . and lo and behold they began to unload thousands of books in the Russian language.

For Nick, this contact was the beginning of a lifelong commitment to YMCA work. The YMCA for Russians resettled in Munich, Germany, because they could not return to Russia, and in time Nick was elected president. Major support came from the United Nations for refugee work. Between 1945 and 155 they created over forty-five programs in the arts, support for higher education, and training in technical trade skills.

Nick immigrated to the United States in 1952. In New York he met Alexandra Tolstoy (daughter of Leo Tolstoy), who encouraged him to develop the Free Russian Youth Club of New York City to meet the transitional needs for immigrant youth settling in the United States. After that, he was hired by the YMCA to develop international programs for the YMCA, but he needed to become certified to be a YMCA worker. He came to George Williams College to take courses to meet his certification requirements.

From 1952 to 1964 he was a well recognized motivational speaker about the importance of world service, particularly for refugees throughout Europe. The work was recognized by the United Nations. As a Danforth scholar, he lectured in colleges and universities on Russian affairs, and served as a consultant on the Hollywood production of *Dr. Zhivago*. In 1979 he was the Welles Visiting Scholar at George Williams College.

Once Nick met Nobel Peace Prize winner John R. Mott, who said, "Well, one of these days there will again be YMCAs in Russia." In 1988 that vision was realized, with the strong support of George Williams College people like Solon Cousins (GWC board member), John Root ('46 and GWC board member), Frank Kiehne ('47 and '51), William Glenn (GWC instructor and son-in-law of Paul Anderson), and Bob Masuda ('65). Nick says:

> World Service is indeed world service to individual human beings—it never tried to save the world, it helped individuals. To me this is the very ecumenical Christian message, to the Christians and to the entire world, with respect for all religions and beliefs without any imposition. I remember Paul Anderson and Emery Nelson said to us, "Be truthful to your religion, to your culture, to your language, and simply be honest in your beliefs, don't be a hypocrite." This is what I have remembered about world service for the last fifty years.[7]

Domestic and global issues come together: "We must know what we are for"

Emery Nelson, student, ('24), World Service worker, 1940s and 1950s, administrator, 1960s–1970s

Emery Nelson is recognized in YMCA circles around the world for his work in the post-World War II era of the '40s and '50s. He provided hands-on service to war refugees like Nick Goncharoff. Emery directed a World Service fund-raising campaign to create "Buildings for Brotherhood." The purpose was to restore YMCA buildings damaged by the war in Europe and to erect new buildings in other parts of the world. He helped raise $26 million for the cause.

In 1961 Emery Nelson returned to George Williams College when it was still in Hyde Park to launch a fund-raising campaign to build the Downers Grove campus. In December 1968, he addressed the student body. It was a time of student unrest and protest at college campuses across the country. Six months after his address there would be major student unrest on the Downers Grove campus in what has been called the Spring Festival of 1969 (a story told in chapter 3, "Building Community Inside and Out").

> Up to a few years ago society protected the [college] campus. Today the campus is being forced to look at the profit-and-loss column in humanity; we still have a large deficit on the humanity side of the ledger. We talk so much about championing justice, but we have really done very little. This college [GWC], because of its role projected by its founders and on through its present leadership, has been close to society and its raw, naked life. Our students, as part of their academic experience, wrestle with these question and problems [of social justice] every day as they leave the campus to work in the YMCA, Boys Clubs, settlement houses, schools, etc. We must know what we are for.
>
> There is much to dissent about, but you should be sure of what you are for before you become against. It is fine to be against war, but that isn't enough. It is hard to find a way to peace. It is fine to be against segregation, but that isn't enough. It is hard to build brotherhood and love. It is fine to be against hunger, but it isn't easy to distribute food and to teach farming across the world to relieve hunger and to bring about land reform. It is fine to be against poverty, but that isn't enough. It is hard to find a job that is lifting and a pay that is adequate. It is difficult to get an adequate education to develop our skills.
>
> Today our campuses aren't safe; they aren't a sanctuary from the hard facts of life. . . . We have no right to retreat behind the walls of our libraries, our studies, our pulpits, and our laboratories. Instead we must seek to use our knowledge to help the world survive.[8]

A wise and experienced Emery Nelson did not see two separate, unconnected worlds when he thought of GWC students leaving the campus to go out into far-reaching corners of the globe to serve people and communities, or leaving the college campus to go down the street or across town to do their fieldwork serving communities. When he spoke of the GWC student living "close to society and its raw, naked life as part of their academic experience," when he acknowledged that they "wrestle with questions and problems of social justice every day as they leave campus to work," he knew this kind of learning experience was good preparation for world service in other countries, whether students realized it at the time or not. He knew they would have to direct their energy not just to protest but to doing something, once they knew "what they are for."

"Looking for someone who fought paternalism at home"

Frank Kiehne, student, ('47, '51), World Service administrator, 1970s–1990s

The individual stories of many of the college students who came to George Williams in this era have common themes. They came from small towns, mostly in the Midwest, South, West, or Canada, to an unfamiliar, dynamically changing urban environment. Their vision of what they wanted to be, no less what they wanted to be for, was small and limited. More often they wanted to be like someone they admired. Often that happened to be a YMCA leader. Maybe they might think of becoming a YMCA director in a small town somewhere. But when they came to the college, everything changed. Their exposure and involvement in the dynamic city of Chicago, with all its problems and strengths was another step, perhaps a giant step. In the mix of things, they would be clarifying and defining by experience, "what they are for." Though most did not know it at the time, they were preparing for world service. This was Frank Kiehne's story.

As a kid, I was active in the Burlington, Iowa YMCA, when we were coming out of the Depression. When the Y could afford a full-time physical director, they hired George D. McBride ['36]. George had just graduated from George Williams. He must have been responsible for sending at least ten students from Burlington to George Williams. After serving in the U.S. Marine Corps, I was released at the end of World War II at the Great Lakes Naval Station. I visited GWC and immediately enrolled to train for the YMCA, as McBride did.

While I was at GWC, I was a product of Harvie Boorman, Hedley Dimock, Harry Edgren ['24, '31], and Arthur Steinhaus ['19, '21, '26], with Dr. Zerfoss being my mentor. But in addition to the learning I got from faculty, I learned from my job and fieldwork in the city of Chicago and my classmates in the college. Levon Melikian ['48] came to the college from the Jerusalem YMCA. As a Palestinian he was the first one to increase my sensitivity to the plight of the Palestinians when he suggested I read an article in the *Atlantic,* "The Arabs Also Live There." Later Levon received his doctorate degree and taught at the American University in Lebanon. He now lives in Ontario, Canada. Another was Juan Pascoe ['46] from the Mexico YMCA. I have lost track of Juan, but I believe his main career was with the United Nations.

I became the first president of the YMCA Club and joined the fraternity Alpha Omicron Alpha (AOA). When I, along with other returning veterans, told the AOA alumni that clearly we were going to integrate the fraternity, this was probably my first social action toward racial equality. One student we urged to join AOA was Quentin Mease ('48). [Quentin went on to become an effective civil rights activist in Texas.]

The integration of my studies with my part-time employment at the Southtown YMCA in Englewood provided me with the best professional education possible. My work at the Southtown Y, which was in a changing neighborhood, was helpfully guided by Matt Thomson, a pacifist during WWII. Together we integrated the Southtown Y with the approval of the youth committee, but the "power boys" who were paying money to keep African Americans out of Englewood demanded that the department executive fire us. This he did. GWC called him in to challenge the action.

This led to job opportunities. I was offered a leadership position in the Illinois Interracial Commission, American Veterans Committee, and also a position on the Mayor's Commission on Human Relations. However, I chose to go to Kansas City, Missouri, to work under another GW graduate, William G. Schmiederer ['31]. Bill said, "This is the kind of person I want to be on my staff." Much to the amazement of my peers on the Chicago YMCA staff, I was promoted after being fired!

I was then recalled by the U.S. Marine Corps to fight in the Korean War. I was in the first racially integrated unit. I finished my master's thesis while in the marines, receiving my M.S. degree in group work administration. When I went to the St. Louis Y, I worked to adopt an integrated membership policy. When I went to the YMCA of Metropolitan Washington, this association was in the mist of racial problems. . . . We wiped out the last vestige of discrimination by taking our Alexandria branch to the Virginia courts.

In 1960 I was selected to be one of four members of the first Youth Workers Exchange with the Soviet Union and arrived there two weeks after they shot down the U-2 spy plane. This experience sparked my international interest and enabled me to later serve the Peace Corps as a full-time consultant for three months in 1961. [In the 1960s] as executive of the Reading, Pennsylvania, branch of the YMCA, joining the "War on Poverty," I worked to develop a comprehensive service program, including a first prime government contract for a Neighborhood Youth Corp, a "detached worker" program, a migrant worker program, and an intercollegiate [initiative] on behavior change in racial attitudes. I was hired as the executive director of the International Committee of the YMCA from 1973 to 1981. They were looking for someone who had fought paternalism at home to serve the YMCA on the world front. I then worked with the World Alliance of YMCAs as secretary for refugees and rehabilitation from 1986 to 1990.

As director of the International Committee, I came across many alumni of George Williams College: I came in contact with Fritz Pawelzik ['67] of Germany who spent his career mainly in Africa as a German YMCA fraternal secretary. Desta Girma ['66] became the general secretary of the YMCAs of Ethiopia and joined me at the International Committee staff in the USA in 1974. Desta headed our Indo-China Emergency Program to care for more than one hundred thousand refugees in five military camps in the United States in 1975. Later he returned to Africa to become the first general secretary of the African Alliance of YMCAs. Returning to the United States, he headed the Africa office for the YMCA of Pittsburgh. Joel Kinagwi ['75] became the general secretary of the National Council of YMCAs of Kenya and was largely responsible for enlarging and consolidating the movement under local leadership. Later he became general. secretary of the African Alliance of YMCAs and then succeeded me at the World Alliance of YMCAs. Cornelius Olaomo ['76] visited my office in New York before returning to Nigeria to take up the position of general secretary of the National Council. Cornelius served with distinction until he retired in the mid-1990s. The Nigerian movement became one of the largest YMCAs in Africa. One of the most colorful leaders I ever had the pleasure of working with was Joe Solomon ['54], general secretary of the National Council of YMCAs of India. His son Ranjan served with me at the World Alliance and, like his father, was a fierce fighter for human rights and the philosophy of self-support and self-governance. There was a period of time when Joe would not accept outside support in funds or fraternal secretaries. I supported his style and had him speak at our international assembly meeting in the 1970s before he died. . . .

I was the first CEO of the Washington-based Private Agencies in International Development (PAID), now called InterAction. InterAction has 160 member agencies involved in overseas development, relief, and refugee work. When we were negotiating a merger with the [New York City-based] American Council on Voluntary Agencies in Foreign Service, we were finding a proper setting to bring the two groups together for joint planning and negotiation. I was able to convince representatives from some one hundred agencies like Save the Children, Church World Service, Oxfam, YMCA, YWCA, and Lutheran World Relief to meet at College Camp [Williams Bay] in late spring of 1984. It is there where the new combined organization called InterAction was born.[9]

From 1990 to 1996 Frank was foreign affairs advisor to U.S. Congressman Donald Payne. In 2005 he was honored by his YMCA peers "for the proliferation of his writing, primarily focused on themes of advocacy, peace and justice."[10] Frank's beginnings in roles of advocacy for peace and justice took shape as a college student on the South Side of Chicago and extended to the world.

"At the time, I had no idea of World Service"

Richard Ortmeyer, student, ('48), World Service worker, 1960s–1980s

Richard Ortmeyer was another student who came to the college without a clue that, when he left, he would spend the defining years of his career in world service.

> While I was a student at GWC, I did not have any close friends who were international students, though several were there. But GWC in the late '40s had a definite international focus. At the time I was a student I had no idea that half of my career years would be in international work with a major focus of activity outside the United States.
>
> After graduation I spent fifteen years in Y work in the [United] States. It wasn't until 1964 that I got involved in world service, when I accepted a position as associate director of the YMCA Institute in Hong Kong, a center for training young persons from different Asian countries in YMCA work as a career. Hong Kong had become headquarters for conferences of the Asian Alliance of the YMCA. I worked there for ten years.
>
> While I was director of the YMCA Institute in Hong Kong, I came back to GWC at least twice while on furloughs. At that time GWC was in Downers Grove, and I felt its international focus had increased—perhaps it was because I was more sensitive to international personnel and issues. I went there on those occasions to talk to students who were there from Asian YMCAs. I had helped send students to GWC from Sabah, Malaysia; Penang, Malaysia; the two YMCAs in Hong Kong; and a few others. I always visited with them on those trips.
>
> My world service focus shifted, when I was asked by Frank Kiehne in 1974 to represent the YMCAs of Asia in "development" work. The United Nations made development their focus, and the United States was distributing grants-in-aid from USAID [United States Agency for International Development].

Dick assisted Asian YMCAs in writing proposals and reporting on progress of projects. In Thailand, there were nutrition and housing projects. In Bangkok, there were agricultural training and school lunch programs. In Fiji, there were rural agriculture clubs, village libraries, and management training programs. In Bangladesh, there were educational and vocational programs, along with relief work for poverty and flooding.

After I left the Institute in Hong Kong and was in Asian development work, Cliff Kessler ['75], a student I met at the college, came to Fiji and Western Samoa where the YMCA had large projects with rural families in various aspects of development. I worked with Cliff for two weeks in these two island countries as Cliff visited villages, families, and sites and learned of their cultures.[11]

Dick is grateful to another friend of the college, John O'Melia, for his support in development work, as John was the head of development work and the director of the International Division of the YMCA. By 1988 Dick was concerned about development funds drying up. Yet he hoped the seeds that were planted among nationals would see fruition, strength, and growth to carry forward the work of development.[12]

Learning to live and work in the hot spots

Norris Lineweaver, student, ('67), World Service worker, 1960s and 2005

I came to the "old shoe factory" all the way from Abilene, Texas. I was headed for Texas Tech [University] to follow my peers. But a few of my friends took alternative routes. Sue Dyrenforth ['65] and Rex Sides ['66] decided to go to George Williams College. Rex sent letters to me about his experiences at this George Williams College. I began to realize I was interested in service leadership, maybe not by that name, but social work was what I was thinking of at the time. I decided to go to George Williams. At that time, it was the Vietnam War. I went into the military reserves for six months, and it took me awhile longer to arrive, but I came to George Williams in the winter quarter of 1964. My friend Rex was drafted into the air force. That changed his career. He never got into Y work.

It [interest in world service] started when I met Desta Girma ['66]. He was one year ahead of me. He came to George Williams from Ethiopia, where he was the general secretary of the Ethiopian Y. When Desta would sit by himself in the cafeteria, I would sit next to him. I was mesmerized by him. I watched him in the pool struggling to learn how to swim. At that time . . . you had to pass a swim test to graduate. I said, "Desta, I'm curious that someone could grow up, and be in your leadership position in the Y, and not know how to swim!" Desta would pull out a picture of Ethiopia. He would say, "The rivers are very dangerous in our country. We don't swim there for recreation." That tickled my imagination. I wanted to learn more about Ethiopia.

Bob Taylor ['66] was a student at the college when I was there. He was a World Service worker for the Y in Uganda. I met Bob at September Camp in Lake Geneva. In my junior year Bob was putting together a group to go to Africa in the summer.

Bob came up to me and said, "Let's go to Africa." The executive director of the Duncan Y raised the money for us to go. My conversations with Desta were good preparation for this experience, because we were headed for Ethiopia. Reuben Davis ['67, '69], Bob Taylor, and I went as students from GWC. Bob Steiger, the graduate dean of the college, went also, along with his daughter Susan. That summer experience in Ethiopia opened new doors in the direction of my life. By the time I was graduating, Cody Moffat ['43] was interviewing me, asking me, "Do you want to go to Ethiopia as a World Service worker for the YMCA?" I jumped at the opportunity and became a World Service worker in Ethiopia from 1967 to 1969, fresh out of college.

The international students had a very strong presence when I was on campus. There was a young man who was an Arab from the Jerusalem Y. Maisie Khoo ['67] and Oon Theam Khoo ['64, '66] were there from Singapore and returned for a long career there. They were very active in college. Of maybe 350 students [that I recall], I'd say twenty-five to forty were international students.

Coming into contact with so many international students was not a new experience for me. . . . My father was in military in the [U.S.] Marine Corps. The international experience was in my blood. As a young child I spent five years overseas when we lived in Tsingtao, China. My first introduction to the Y was using the Armed Services Y.

The setting at GWC was interesting. It was a very small campus. The dormitories and extracurricular activities brought us together. Being a part of the house, we became pretty close. Most of the African American students from Chicago were commuters, but the international students were in residence. The smallness had a strong impact. In other campuses around the country, when international students showed up on campuses . . . they had separate housing. The international students also had to manage living, working, and doing their fieldwork in the Hyde Park community, where it was a time of tremendous tension in the neighborhood.

When I was there, Malcolm X was assassinated in Detroit. We were told to stay off the streets because there was a group from Detroit coming to Chicago to take out Elijah Muhammed. The black students at GWC tried to protect us on the Hyde Park neighborhood streets. I had this accent from Texas. . . . I actually had dialect lessons. They would say, "If one of the Blackstone Rangers asks for a cigarette, don't talk." I took their advice. There were times I wondered if I was naive or they were overacting. I found when I engaged people in the community in conversation, when I said I came here to learn, they were fascinated. . . . But that whole experience was a great laboratory for learning. It gave me confidence to think about careers in communities different from how you grew up. It changed my life.

When I graduated, I went into World Service work in Ethiopia and then returned to my home state of Texas. Ted Beasley invited me to come to Dallas, Texas, to work. I was on a Beasley Scholarship when I was in college, and because of that I felt an obligation to go to Dallas. In 1969 I was in "heavy cotton," working for conflict resolution when riots broke out around racial conflict on the campus of the University of Texas, Arlington. The outbreak centered around the racist symbolism of the university mascot, "Johnny Reb." The mayor of Arlington called the local Y, where I was, and asked for help with conflict resolution. I said, "I'd love to help, but I'm the wrong guy." I called Rad Wilson ['64, '71]. Rad, a colleague at the college, was still in Chicago consulting on conflict resolution. . . . He met with the mayor and the police chief. The police chief said, "We have to do our jobs, but we can't do them with 'Johnny Reb' as mascot. It's just not going to work, when a local institution of higher learning insists on 'Johnny Reb' for a mascot." The mayor called the chancellor. He said, "I got a call from the police chief, who says you . . . have got to change this mascot." And so about Monday noon the chancellor put out the message, "We no longer have a mascot, we no longer have the school song ['Rebels']." They did not have one for two years, until they came to some resolution. That was 1969. The new mascot was the "Maverick," a short-horned steer. All those facilitative skills in group work class were put to use!

And now those experiences and learning from living in communities ridden with intergroup conflict have given Norris confidence and optimism when he faces his new challenge. In 2005 Norris went to Jerusalem to live and work in the Jerusalem Y.

Did you know when His Imperial Majesty of Ethiopia was expatriated by Italy in 1938, he appealed to the League of Nations, and his first home of exile was the Jerusalem Y? I remembered hearing a little about the Jerusalem Y in GWC. I heard that the Y brought together Jewish, Christian, and Muslim children to interact in their programs. What a wonderful concept. Fifty-one percent of the staff were Muslim. Preschool enrollment at the Y is one-third Jewish, one-third Christian, and one-third Muslim! I plan on finishing my YMCA career in Jerusalem. We will be living right in an area of the city where the most tension exists.

But Norris has been in situations like this before: in a place in the city of Chicago many years ago when he went to GWC, and in a place in Texas where he grew up. He has always tried to be a servant-leader and peacemaker in the hard places of the world.[13]

The stories of many other alumni and friends of the college involved in YMCA World Service should be told because their work and its impact has been felt around the world. Their work has been recognized by the United Nations, the U.S. government in the form of grants-in-aid, and by countless advocacy groups for peace and opportunity development in the world.

Other Global Connections

"The Canadians were always with us"

Henry Labatte, student, ('53)

There was a Canadian who was eager to tell his story about his "love affair with George Williams College." It was Henry Labatte, retired director of the Toronto YMCA. He spoke as a member of the group of Canadians who found their way to George Williams. By the time he finished, Henry made a convincing case that neither the college nor the Canadians would be the same, nor could they have done the good things they did without each other. Take Hedley Dimock and Charles "Chick" Hendry, both voices and leaders in group work. Their voices are heard in chapter 1, "Serving Others." Hendry, the voice of the "Community of Living and Learning" (described in chapter 3, "Building Community Inside and Out") at George Williams College, became the director of the social work program at the University of Toronto, Canada. "The Canadians came because the college led the way in group work, and the leaders in group work were Canadians," Labatte says.

> The Canadians came to George Williams for three things: YMCA certification, the opportunity to practice group work in a dynamic urban center, and because they heard about caring faculty who gave individualized attention to students. I came because I was influenced by a generation of Canadians who came to GWC before me. They were Canadians who came out of the Depression years up to World War II. This would be from 1929 to 1939 [World War II started earlier for the Canadians]. For me, they were Don McGregor ['42], George Singleton ['40], Gil Johnson ['42], and Cody Moffat ['43]. There were others there also, who came from the Canadian prairie. What drew them to George Williams was the opportunity to obtain YMCA certification with a college degree, with the courses they offered and the "learning-by-doing" going on in the city of Chicago.
>
> In the late 1920s the YMCA developed certification standards for its workers. The YMCA was professionalizing. You needed a college degree from a higher education institution and several courses, including community organization, group work, religion, Y administration, and a course in counseling. Then if you worked satisfactorily in the YMCA for two years, you became a YMCA secretary. Up to that time, you started as teens in the YMCA, then moved up to staff. Then certification

came along. You had to have a college degree. George Williams College had the reputation of being the YMCA school.

The second reason they came was the influence of John Dewey and his philosophy of learning-by-doing. The Y was no longer driven by evangelism but by the Social Gospel. The Social Gospel was not just the gospel, but the values that came through its expression in social action. These guys had a great belief in the Social Gospel. The Depression really affected the Canadian West. Out of the West came Don McGregor ['42] from Regina. Then the war came. Many served in the YMCA Canadian War Services. George Singleton ['40] was one. McGregor only had one eye and didn't have to go to war. Bill Naylor ['38] was another. He worked for a short period in the Y and then went into war services. The next generation of Canadians came to the college from 1939 to 1945. The 1930s were a time when group work was taking hold as a helping profession, and George Williams became a center for development of group work, often expressed in community development, and the city of Chicago was the perfect urban center for practice. After the war these men came back to Toronto, got their degree from George Williams College, and influenced a whole generation of people like myself. They were influenced by the Social Gospel. The Canadian Y movement was more secular than the American Y movement. We were much more humanistic for decades. We were not touched by religious conservatism at all. The Canadians were to the left, Americans in the center, and Europeans were to the right. The YMCA was influenced by the United States, particularly the larger cities like Chicago, Cleveland, and New York. Before this time, the [YMCA] movement was concentrated on the East Coast. Now whole generations of Canadians came to Chicago and to George Williams College. In Chicago there was a confluence of the Y movement with the settlement house movement. Even to the time when I was there, Chicago was the sociological center. Chicago had come up from evangelism to Social Gospel.

The next generation came to the college from 1945 to 1953. This was the period of my personal involvement. I came out of a working-class area in the city of Toronto. I didn't have any aspirations for higher education. I wanted to be in the Y, but then I learned I would need a college education. At that time George Williams College was a revolutionary educational environment. Three things made the educational environment revolutionary: a learning-by-doing approach, a dynamically changing urban center to practice the learning-by-doing approach, and the faculty-student relationship. John Dewey affected the whole educational environment at the college. All courses were geared toward learning-by-doing. For example, I had a course with Arthur Steinhaus in health education. We always had projects we had to carry out in the community. Mine was to go to Holman School and try to convince the school to have physical exams for all students. Then some students from

Northwestern [Medical] School were hired to staff the clinic. It was real social action for the betterment of community.

George Williams College practiced what it was preaching in terms of its reputation and record in group work, personal involvement, and opportunities to develop yourself personally. In our community organization course, the learning would be some kind of community project. We were working with kids in small groups. You always had an opportunity to get out in the community and practice. The whole environment of Chicago was a learning laboratory. People worked not only in YMCAs, but in Boys Clubs, settlement houses, the whole area of social work. Chicago had all kinds of part-time jobs for students. How vital that was, to learn by doing! Karl Zerfoss and Sylvanus Duvall were fine teachers who really cared about you. Channing Briggs ['48] was a student of Hedley Dimock. What we learned in the 1940s and 1950s was going on right there in the Chicago community. We learned about Saul Alinsky, moving the stockyards, and all that. He would bring it into the classroom, when he would teach "community org." Harry Edgren ['24, '31] was a recreation specialist, a short Scandanavian who went on to teach at Purdue. He would teach us games and how to use them employing certain principles. I'll always remember him saying, "When you're playing a game, stop at the point of highest enjoyment." They will remember it at the highest moment. "Stop at the top," he would say. I remember I was honored to be chosen to be part of a group of students that traveled to Rockford, [Illinois], and Wisconsin. We planned and carried out a community recreational event. Learning-by-doing. They put us out there to conduct the event.

The theories developed in sociological studies about Chicago—like concentric zone theory in ethnic neighborhoods—you would go out and see it every day. Japanese Americans moved into the Hyde Park area after internment on the West Coast during the war. There was a large Jewish community that migrated into the area after the war. There were many African Americans coming to Chicago in the postwar migration from the South. African Americans lived within a restricted covenant, where they couldn't live outside [certain neighborhood boundaries]. As a Canadian, that blew my mind. Yet there was no racial tension in the college. As an educational environment, that was absolutely unique.

The labor movement was felt on campus. For years after the war, the American labor movement brought people from Europe. Labor unions would have labor institutes that the college would host. On Sunday night they would have folk songs coming out of the labor movement. The whole environment was liberal. There was no attempt to influence people in an evangelical way. But there were very strong values, and they influenced the YMCA. A whole generation of Y people at the college ended as leaders in the Y movement—John Root ['46] and John Kessler ['49] are examples. George Williams was at that time an urban institution. You can't take an urban institution and put it in a suburb and have it maintain its viability. The environment is not conducive to what it was.

Also, many students from the international YMCAs came there. I had my first international experience there. People from outside the United States were there as students. I remember Joe Solomon ['54] attended the college from India.

The third reason Canadians came was because they heard of a caring faculty. Faculty not only taught courses, they influenced character. Students could be critical of what they were learning, but they weren't critical of faculty. This is difficult to make work. Faculty were not threatened. That was the nature of relationship. [Now he utters three words emphatically] Every student mattered! You could talk with each other anytime by formal appointments or informally. You could be eating with a faculty member and bring up a concern. Faculty knew everything about you—where you came from, your financial situation   the whole environment was one of their concern for the students.

After graduation many of us returned to Canada to become leaders in the Canadian [YMCA] movement. John Smythe ['54] was of my generation. Rich Bailey ['62 and an Aurora University Board of Trustees member in 1999] was my successor as CEO of the Toronto Y. In the 1950s and 1960s, the effect of GWC on programs of Canada was enormous. We developed the "Toronto model" for Ys in Canada. It was based on what we learned from GWC. It was a model of comprehensive programs in child care, physical education, camping, and immigration support. Programs were designed to meet the needs of the community.[14]

Henry's wife, Marie Krakora Labatte ('53), who recently passed away, is another Canadian who made her mark with what she learned from GWC. Marie was from Chicago, but she met Henry at George Williams, and when they married they settled in Canada, where Marie entered politics. She was elected councilor for the municipality of metropolitan Toronto. Marie worked for ten years to officially change the term from the gender-limited term *alderman* to *councilor*. She was an advocate for women's rights, child care, employment opportunities, and a clean environment including non-smoking laws. "She was great at mobilizing volunteers to action and community organization," Henry commented in the *Toronto Star*. "She was not concerned about her political role and influence, but the needs of her constituents." The *Toronto Star* called Marie Labatte a "pioneer who didn't flinch from a fight."[15]

Years ago Marie recorded her appreciation of the "many strengths" of George Williams College. For her, it was "student-faculty relationships, concern for the individual, personal growth, the practical application of course content, and the spinoff of one course on another." Harry Edgren ('24, '31) was her favorite professor.

Faculty reach around the world

Harry Edgren, student, ('24, '31) and professor; Del Kinney, professor; and Arthur Steinhaus, student, ('19, '21, '26) and professor

While students were coming and going to places around globe, so were faculty. Sometimes they were exporting research and ideas, mostly in areas of group work and physical education. Sometimes it was to nurture student connections, as they were spread out globally.

Marie Labatte spoke of Harry Edgren ('24, '31) as her favorite professor. In 1954 Dr. Harry Edgren went to India as a Fulbright professor in group work and recreation. He spoke of camping and recreation, physical education, and social work as if they were one in purpose; the way Henry Labatte saw it being taught at George Williams College in his era.[16]

In 1971 social work Professor Del Kinney took a world tour, lecturing, consulting on group work and social work, and nurturing connections with college alumni. At the Jerusalem Y, Del found Rizek Abusharr ('61), Shafik Saikaly ('58), and Nicola Ghawi ('69). In New Delhi, India, he visited Monie George ('64) and George Thomas ('64). In Tehran, Iran, he visited with Mohssen Ghandi ('65). In Singapore he saw Oon Theam Khoo ('64, '66) and Maisie Khoo ('67). In Hong Kong he saw Richard Ortmeyer ('48) at the Hong Kong Institute. There, Kinney assisted in classes taught by two other GW graduates, Bick Chu ('69) and Lee Choi ('61). In Hawaii he saw Robert ('65) and Judy Masuda ('69), Jane Holt ('69), and Vincent Lee ('70).[17]

Professor Arthur Steinhaus spent his entire career exporting his ideas and research in physiology, sports medicine, health, and fitness. His international work spanned over four decades. In 1931 he was a Guggenheim Foundation fellow for study in Europe. In 1936, before the opening games of the XI Olympiad in Berlin, he lectured at the Student International Congress of Physical Education. In 1952 he received the Italian Federation of Sports Award. In 1952 he did research for the United States Navy in Germany and lectured in England, Egypt, Italy, and Finland. In 1953 he lectured at the International Congress of Physical Education at Istanbul, Turkey. He was the guest of the Ministry of Education in Israel in that same year. In the summer of 1955 he was a Fulbright lecturer in Germany. In 1960 he addressed the World Forum on Health and Fitness and the YMCA's World Consultation on Physical Education in Rome. He represented the United States in the International Federation of Physical Education and Sports Medicine. In June 1961 he lectured at the first Olympic Academy in Olympia, Greece.

Steinhaus's research reputation brought students to George Williams College from all points on the globe.

Michio Ikai, MD, professor of physiology and physical education, University of Tokyo, Japan

I must confess why I came to George Williams College. When I was in Japan in 1957, I found the name of Dr. Arthur H. Steinhaus in *Who's Who* at the library of my school of education. I had been interested in an article, "The Chronic Effects of Exercise" by Dr. Steinhaus, which appeared in *Physiologial Review* in 1933. Really, I was thrilled to find the name of Steinhaus at George Williams College in this library. I decided to ask the Fulbright Committee to help me to go to the United States. In September of 1958 I arrived in Chicago with a big hope. The Green Room became my working place with Dr. Steinhaus. He was interested in physiological and psychological limits of human performance. . . . The name of Dr. Steinhaus is familiar along with the name of George Williams College in my country.

A. D. Munrow, professor of physical education, University of Birmingham, England

It was through a colleague of mine that I first wrote to him. He sent me a great deal of his published material . . . and arranged a tour of significant institutions in the United States, which I visited in the spring of 1949. . . . Arthur made no attempt to impress me with his own work but simply turned me loose among colleagues and students and was happy that I gained an impression of him through others rather than through himself. . . . His publication, "The Chronic Effects of Exercise," was a landmark in the development of clear thinking about physical education in this country.

Carl Diem, *Sporthochschule,* University of Cologne, Germany

When the committee for the 1936 Berlin Olympic Games decided to inaugurate the event with an international scientific congress, it assured itself of the participation of Arthur H. Steinhaus. He gave the outstanding lecture on "The Science of Educating the Body." He spoke for physiology but thought and constructed his remarks as a philosopher. When I reflect on the many reprints reporting his works, I marvel over the many gains we have made through his research. Among Americans, he ranks among the top men who seek to improve the poor physical status of American youth brought on by the ease of living, overeating, and the craving for stimulants. His works encompass fitness, relaxation, and recreation. He himself is both physically and mentally symbolic of striving youth.[18]

The German student exchange

Don Glaze, student, ('60, '66) and Bob Bratton, student, ('59)

Steinhaus was not content to be leaving the college to travel abroad to lecture and develop international collegial relationships. Always a teacher first, he wanted his students to have an international experience. So he set in place a German student exchange program, based on his connections with Carl Diem from Germany.

Don Glaze:

> I grew up involved in the YMCA program operating in a tiny facility in McCook, Nebraska, a little town, almost Colorado, almost Kansas, with [fewer] than five thousand people. When Herman Hertog ['52] came to Nebraska from George Williams to recruit students, he said, "It's going to be a complete change of environment for you." I said, "Hey, I'm ready." When I came to Chicago, the tall building that got my attention was the Lawson Y. Fifty stories high! I had seen this calendar picture of it, and I thought it was beautiful! . . . I got a job at the Lawson Y while going to school, majoring in physical education. Val Keller ['53] worked at Lawson Y. He came through GW, coached the GWC championship volleyball team, and went on to write books on volleyball. . . . I joined the volleyball team and made some friends on the team. One was Bob Bratton. Bob was a Canadian, a few years ahead of me in school.

Bob Bratton:

> My roommate suggested that I come out and play with the team. I had not encountered "power volleyball" prior to the first practice, and when I was "six packed" with a spiked ball, I was motivated to get even. Val Keller was the coach, and since there were not that many players around, he kept me around for comic relief. I recall playing in the U.S. collegiate championships in Memphis, and Val allowed me to play against a very weak local team. My first set was over the net, and the big player on the other team jumped up and hit the ball into the net, so we scored. I looked over at our coach, with a big smile on my face, and he had his head in his hands.

Subsequently Bob Bratton made a significant contribution to volleyball in Canada. He was inducted into both the Alberta and Canada Volleyball Halls of Fame. He has written several books, one of which was translated into Chinese.

Don Glaze:

> One day, in my freshman year, Dr. Steinhaus said, "Would you guys be interested in being exchange students at the University of Cologne in Germany?" The University of Cologne had a sports school (*Sporthochschule*) there. There was this guy

named Carl Diem; he and his wife were teachers in physical education. They were involved with Dr. Steinhaus in the Olympics, and Steinhaus had taught courses for them in Germany. I had to have enough money to get there, but once there they would provide a scholarship, room, and board. I thought I could put together enough money to do this. So four of us from GWC went. Based on that experience, we've stayed in contact all these years. The four of us were Bob Bratton ['59, who became a professor at the University of Calgary], Bob Hansen ['60, '62, who became professor and associate dean of the School of Veterinary Medicine, University of California-Davis], Bob Steinhaus ['61, Professor Steinhaus's son], and myself.

One year later we convinced our roommates in Germany to come back to George Williams College to get their master's [degrees]. One was Hermann Gall ['61]. Hermann became the dean of sports sciences at Peddagogische Hosdchschule in Ludwigsburg, Germany. Though Hermann is retired, he is still teaching in Kenya, Argentina, Columbia, and South America. The other was Horst Schroeder ['61].

Bob Bratton:

While in Germany we became rather close with these two. . . . I also have several close friends from among the fellow students at the *Sporthochschule*. From his university position in Germany, Hermann Gall embarked on a two-year trip with his wife, from Alaska to the southern tip of Chile. He purchased a motorhome in Vancouver and drove to Calgary where we spent a few days equipping his vehicle for the trip. He did make it to Alaska and then down through Mexico to Panama. Within the next two weeks he should continue his trip to Columbia and then through South America. He does return to Germany two or three times a year to break up the trip!

Horst phoned today and he was on his way to Spain for two weeks. He retired from teaching several years ago and is still quite active with a thirteen-year-old daughter. . . . It is interesting that of the six amigos three ended up as professors.

I am extremely grateful for the efforts of Dr. Steinhaus to make that opportunity available to all of us. While my degree from GWC was a B.S., I felt that that one year in Germany was the equivalent of a B.A. degree. I learned a language, learned a great deal of history and geography, as well as the cultural experience. I am also confident that the year in Germany on my resume opened the doors to my initial position at the University of Calgary.

Don Glaze:

The Germany exchange program continued. Roger Seehafer ['63] was on his way when we came back. Roger Seehafer went on to teach at Purdue. Others were Mel Elliott ['64] and Mickey [Michal] McCord ['65], who are now teachers in Chicago Public Schools.

Before they graduated, volleyball and the German exchange program came together in a memorable way. Don Glaze:

> When the GWC volleyball team won the nationals, for their award ceremony the head of the Olympic committee handed them out to us! . . . [In my work now] I still encourage my employees to hook up with my network in Germany for an eye-opening experience. . . . It's a good experience, whatever you end up doing with your life.[19]

"The World Is Our Textbook": Programs and People, the Downers Grove Years

A few years later the college moved to the suburbs of Downers Grove, Illinois, where the international spirit continued to thrive. Dr. Charles Rhee joined the faculty in 1965 as professor of political science. Before coming to George Williams College, Rhee served as chief of American and European affairs for the Republic of Korea. He was chief negotiator for South Korea in the Korean-Japanese peace talks. He was also on the Korean delegation to the United Nations. As soon as Charles Rhee came, he introduced a Model United Nations program on campus. It took hold in 1967. The idea of the Model United Nations program was that students would represent a certain country; study the economic, social, health, and political issues from the perspective of the country; and then represent that country in a simulated UN session with other colleges across the United States who were representing different countries. Students were judged on how well they did, using the United Nation's rules of motion. The Model United Nations program was a winner from the start, both for student involvement and achievement. By 1975 the Model United Nations team of students brought home its eighth top delegation in the country award in eight years of participation with about 120 colleges.[20]

From Model United Nations to the real thing

Jawan Empaling, student, ('72), UN representative to Malaysia

Jawan was one of the GWC students who participated in the Model United Nations program. He came from the state of Sarawak, Malayasia. He returned to his native state to become only the second person to have received a degree from an American college. His father was "a long-house chief, a respected community leader," the founder of a political party at a time when Malaysia was gaining independence from Great Britain. After graduating from GWC, Jawan received his master's degree in Asian politics from New York University. In 1973 he returned to Malaysia and was elected to Parliament in both 1974 and 1978. In 1976 he was appointed by the prime minister to serve as parliament secretary, equivalent in rank to U.S. secretary of state. He was responsible for the supervision of programs in various Malaysian states, with a special emphasis on social and human service programs. He was at the same time, appointed to the Malaysian mission to the United Nations.

In a visit to the George Williams College campus in 1981, Jawan commented, "The similarities between the Model United Nations program and the real United Nations, in which I now represent Malaysia, are amazing. The enormous amount of research, the hard work, and the excitement are almost the same."[21]

The Intenational/Intercultural Studies Program (IISP), 1970s–1980s

Mary Beech, professor

In 1976 the college introduced the International/Intercultural Studies Program (IISP). The IISP was a certificate study program that students could integrate with their academic major. Many traveled internationally for fieldwork study. "More than fifty students studied on every continent except Antarctica and in such diverse places as Nepal and Colombia, Kenya and Japan, Mexico and Italy." On the home front, some engaged in language immersion programs. Professor Luz Berd creatively used the Williams Bay campus for language immersion weekends. The weekend language experience began with a vow to speak only the language featured that weekend. There were also individualized language programs including Swahili, Greek, and Mandarin Chinese. Students used what they learned from a bicultural, bilingual experience in human service fields after graduation, as professor and coordinator Mary Beech reported in 1985:

> For example, both Ana Wiener King ['81] and Karen Stanbary ['81] are on the staff at the National College of Education, Chicago, where seven hundred of the one thousand students are newly arrived political and economic refugees. Karen is the coordinator of student activities, and Ana is the coordinator of the language laboratories. Anita Zibton ['81] uses her knowledge of Hispanic cultures in administering a multicultural preschool curriculum for Head Start at the Bensenville Home Society. Octavio Mateo ['79] established the Midwest Hispanic Professionals, an executive search and management consulting firm. . . . Sue Larimer ['80] and Jim Harding ['78] completed a two-year stint with the Peace Corps in Fiji. Among their community development activities, Sue invented a stove for rural use, which the Peace Corps is patenting.[22]

The International Student Association

Helping with the special needs of foreign students was the principal function of the International Student Association: things like what to do during the Christmas break, where to get a small, short-term loan, or how to get a ride to the airport. The president was a foreign student (in 1985 it was Ronald Serrant ['86] from Trinidad), although membership and activities were open to all, and American students loved to join in on the group and activities. Faculty advisors were internationals, like Professor Africanus Okokon, a native of Nigeria. Students put on two major activities: the international dinner dance, featuring foreign dishes, and an international variety show, performed by both international and national students. The events were fund-raisers for the Emery M. Nelson International Scholarship Fund and the Powell Fund, designed to supply interest-free loans to foreign students in emergency situations.

Local Downers Grove neighbors supported their global neighbors. Harry and Peg Haberman created a local, support team for the international students. They assisted in providing temporary housing, helped with certain student functions, and helped the students and community become better acquainted. They sponsored receptions, progressive dinners, and picnics throughout the year.[23]

Many of the international students at Downers Grove were a new generation from YMCA families.

The second-generation World Service international student

Clelia Guastavino Giles, student, ('78, '79)

When my dad was a young boy, about ten or twelve years old, his family was strained economically. My dad had a delivery job after school, and every day when he walked doing his deliveries, he would stop outside the Associacion Cristiana de Jovenes (YMCA), and he would look longingly through the fence at the boys on the other side who seemed to be having so much fun. One time a tall American gentleman came out and spoke to him for awhile. He asked him if he wanted to come in. My dad told him he had to work. The gentleman asked him how much he got paid. My dad told him. The American, "Don Augustin" as he was known, then asked him if he wanted to work there instead, every afternoon, and he would pay him the same amount.

With that simple act of kindness, Mr. Austin Turner [a historical YMCA figure who spent years establishing YMCAs in Latin America] changed my dad's life and future. From that moment he became a part of the Y family. As he grew, he was given more responsibilities until a few years later, after he graduated from high school, the YMCA sent him to study at the Instituto Tecnico de la Association Cristiana de Jovenes [the YMCA training school for Y directors in South America]. It was in Montevideo, Uruguay. He met my mother at a summer camp in Uruguay where he was working. After they were married, they lived in Chile where my dad continued to work for the YMCA. Then my parents returned to Uruguay to work as house parents at the Institute Tecnico and supervise the home where the young men lived while they took their classes. I was born there, and when I was still a baby they went back to Chile, where my dad became secretario general [executive director]. When I was eleven, my dad accepted a position in the YMCA of Aruba. We were supposed to be there for only five years, but my parents are still there after thirty-seven years!

When I finished high school, the Rotary Club of Aruba gave me a scholarship to go to George Williams College, in turn for my working in the YMCA four years after I graduated from college. That was not a problem for me at all, because I wanted to work for the YMCA just as my dad had. His love for the Y had been passed on to me. At that time I already had a friend from the Aruba Y, Phyllis Gilhuys ['76], who had also decided to prepare herself for YMCA work and was already attending George Williams College.

So when I arrived at George Williams, I already had a friend I could go to with things I might not understand. Phyllis Gilhuys married David Stowe ['76], son of Ned Stowe who directed the financial aid office at GWC. Phyllis and Dave moved to Aruba, and she worked for the Y for many years and eventually became its executive director after my dad retired from that position. One wonderful discovery when I came was meeting Marcel Neumann ['78], a Peruvian student who was the son of good friends of my parents. It was nice to have Marcel there.

The International Students Association was the organization that gave us an initial sense of belonging and an opportunity for cultural expression. I met a couple from Hong Kong, Shiu-Wing Fung ['76] and his wife, Esther, who often gave me rides to church on Sundays and ate lunch with me after church. Shiu-Wing was also a Y director. Then I met Armando Smith ['75, '82] from Panama. Another student, Joel Kinagwi ['75], was a YMCA director from Kenya. Then there was Cornelius Olaomo ['76] from Nigeria and Martin Msseemmaa ['75, AU '98] from Tanzania. Through my years at GW, many more foreign students came and went, most of them because they had a YMCA connection. Though we were from vastly different countries and cultures, we all shared a sense of being perplexed at times by the culture we found ourselves in.

I was a part of the Model United Nations program, which was another wonderful program. Manjula Shyam was the faculty member who worked with us. She was a Rhodes scholar and had a law degree; she had done much research on her native country of India. She became a good friend. Once the Model United Nations met in New York City in the UN building. We were actually allowed to meet in the same room where the real UN representatives have their sessions! George Williams always did well.

There were also service opportunities for students in developing countries. My friend Celeste Gambino Peña ['79] spent one quarter in a study-abroad program to Bogota, Colombia, with three other students: Octavio "Chico" Mateo ['79], Ana Wiener ['81], and Celmira Bolanos ['80]. The four of them went to work with gamines, homeless boys who tried to survive living in the streets. The YMCA of Bogota had a program for gamines directed by another GWC alum, Myrl Weaver ['72, '77], who spent many years working in Colombia.[24]

In 1984 there were thirty-one foreign students on campus. Ten were from Nigeria; five from Hong Kong; two each from India, Malaysia, and Trinidad; and one each from Aruba, Chile, Japan, Kenya, Korea, Panama, the Philippines, South Africa, Taiwan, and Uganda. Twelve were graduate students, and nineteen were undergraduate students. The international spirit was thriving.[25]

"Exchange of people and ideas"
Kwok Lee, professor, 1985

At the close of the Downers Grove years, professor Kwok Lee, who came from Canton, China, had this to say:

> Foreign students serve as windows to different parts of the world. This interaction broadens the views and enriches the minds of both the foreign and domestic students. In many cases, such intercultural interaction also increases awareness of the fact that other cultures are not superior or inferior to one's own, but simply different. GWC strongly believes in the value of this contribution of foreign students. We believe that the exchange of people and ideas promotes international understanding. And isn't that one practical thing that colleges can do to bring us closer to a world of peace and global cooperation?[26]

"World outlook is vital to college mission"
John Kessler, student, ('49) and GWC president, 1985

The new college president celebrated the "world concern" necessary for leadership in human service as he observed the state of the college in 1985.

> The college's mission demands that humanity everywhere on the globe be considered. It is simply incongruous to talk about humanitarian services in an institution

engaged in educating people to creatively provide these services, without a world outlook and without international concern. Like it or not, the United States and the communities within it are a part of a world community.

Nowhere is this fact more forcibly demonstrated than in the economy. As developed nations shift their emphasis on what to manufacture and the degree to which their economies will be service-oriented, their relationships with other nations are profoundly affected. Then there are a host of undeveloped countries struggling to get any small part of the "action" so their people will be able to work and avoid starvation.

This country has experienced some of the problems of the millions of people displaced by the forces of war, changing economies, or ideological struggles. Yet our experiences are but a drop in a very large bucket compared to those of other countries whose political and social processes have been completely distorted by these forces. As economies continue to shift and political strife continues, these distortions will continue and the suffering will go on—as will the need for skilled, intelligent, and sympathetic persons to provide the human services so necessary throughout the world today.

George Williams College has a long history of world concern and as a leader in providing well educated women and men to the fields of human service. The college will continue to be sensitive to total world needs and will continue to educate its students to be leaders in building equitable and positive relationships around the world.[27]

This declaration from George Williams College's new president came eleven months before the college closed in 1985.

Carrying On the Tradition: Aurora, Illinois

"The African Alliance": A story of Martin Msseemmaa ('75, AU '98)

Pat Hammond Msseemmaa, student, ('75, '77) and Neseriani Msseemmaa, daughter

Several years later, in the mid-1990s, a new academic year was starting up for George Williams College of Aurora University. For the social work program, the beginning of a new year meant going through the fall ritual of traveling up to Williams Bay for the Orientation Practicum. When each new class of strangers gathered for the first time together in community at Williams Bay, I told them "the story." The story was about students like themselves, to whom they owe something for their work to keep the GWC spirit alive, as they found their new home in Aurora University.

I brought with me two telegrams of congratulations from Africa I received when we celebrated our safe arrival at Aurora University. One was from Samuel Nyame ('79), saying, "Glad that GWC is still alive!" The other was from Joel Kinagwi ('75), saying, "I was very depressed with the news of GWC closing. But now I am delighted with this new development of the GWC/AU program!" Samuel was from Ghana and Joel was from Kenya; both worked for the African Alliance, "a federation of twenty-one national YMCAs in Africa," Joel explained. I was about to drive home the point to this new group of students, that the decision to continue on together after the college closed had a ripple effect felt around the world. Suddenly one new student jumped up from his seat and exclaimed to everyone in the room, "That was me! I mean those are my friends! I am the African Alliance!" It was Martin Msseemmaa ('75, AU '98).

Martin was not new to George Williams College. He had received his undergraduate degree in applied behavioral science at George Williams College in 1975; Joel and Samuel were there at the same time. Martin was from Tanzania and started the YMCA there before he came to George Williams. When he graduated he was going to return to Tanzania to do community development, but since a replacement had already been found, Martin went on to the University of Oklahoma to get his master's degree in public administration, sponsored by John Peters. He returned to Illinois, married a fellow George Williams student, Pat Hammond ('75, '77), and settled in LaSalle, Illinois. Martin's career in human service was almost entirely with the Illinois Department of Children and Family Services in Ottawa, Illinois. His wife, Pat, was a school social worker, having received both her undergraduate and her MSW degree from George Williams. By a strange full circle of events, Martin was able to come back to his old "George Williams" and attend the same social work program to get his MSW degree. In the early 1990s, the Department of Children and Family Services had a contract with Aurora University to pay tuition for their supervisors to go back to school for a MSW degree (an initiative steered by his colleague in undergraduate school, Celeste Gambino Peña). So Martin could come home for his degree.

Hardly a week went by that Martin did not urge me to work on a new global connection between George Williams College of Aurora University and the African Alliance. He even arranged a formal invitation for me to come to Nairobi. Attempts were made, but it was not to be at that time. Martin's energy and enthusiasm about making a global connection has stayed with me all these years, like some unfinished business that lurks in the back of the mind. It came up again for me when students of other generations told me their story about George Williams College. So often I would hear about the learning influence of their friends from other countries. I thought it was time to call Martin. Sadly, his wife, Pat, told me Martin had succumbed to a rough battle with cancer only a few months ago. But Pat wanted me to come to Ottawa anyway to put together, as best we could, Martin's story, which is also her story. Their daughter Neseriani, who is graduating from high school, wanted to be present with us to hear more about her dad. Nesi is studying to be a social worker (she entered the GWC social work program in 2007) and would like to go to Tanzania some day to do community development work.

Pat greeted me at their home dressed in comfortable African attire. Hanging on a prominent wall was a huge painting of a group of Maasai people, a wedding gift from their African friends. I picked up a framed picture of Martin that looked like it might have been taken when Martin was a student at George Williams. Pat began their story:

> I got acquainted with Martin some time between 1973 and 1975. He lived on campus. We would meet at the library, and he would tell me all these cool stories about the Maasai, his traditions, whenever we needed a break. I found him to be smart, articulate, with a great sense of humor. When bad things happened to him, he never held a grudge. He was logical in his thinking; he always thought about the motivation of people, particularly when it came to racial prejudice. He tried to understand.
>
> I heard this amazing story of how he started the YMCA in Tanzania. He was given a Land Rover and he literally built a road up this mountain. He ended up building a medical clinic and a building where he taught animal husbandry and agriculture. The Maasai people were nomadic. The government was worried that foreign people were coming in and claiming the land, registering it with the courts. The Maasai felt that land could not be owned, because they were nomads. So his job was to teach them agriculture, to grow food [and] get attached to the land. He even constructed a pipe hooked into a reservoir so they could have water.
>
> The YMCA he built was in a town called Monduli Juu. When he came back to Tanzania, he always visited Monduli Juu. His heart was always there because he started that YMCA. When he came back for visits, the doctor was still there. Martin was well respected because he brought medical care and literacy. When we went back in 1991, word of mouth spread that Martin was coming. Their name for him was *Marti,* which is "mountain" in Maasai. We were greeted there by a group of Maasai warriors holding their spears. They threw the spears into a crowd in celebration. Then they sat down in a huge circle. They presented us with a live goat, symbolic of their finest treasure. Martin was able to converse fluently with everyone. Some didn't understand Maasai, they only knew Swahili, but Martin knew both so he could interpret for everyone.
>
> Martin was, by birth, not a Maasai, but a Choga. The Choga are a tribe near Moshi. His mother died, and his father would take him to villages and leave him there to fend for himself. He remembered working the potato fields, doing a lot of hard work. People started to give him money to work the fields for them. He

had no idea how old he was, maybe six, maybe ten years of age. He ended up in Kingarooka, where there was another boy writing his name in the dust. He thought, "That's unbelievable. How could you make these marks and they would mean anything?" He asked if he could go with this boy to school. The headmaster there took an interest and said, "Where are your parents?" Martin told them. The headmaster asked if he'd like to continue school; he said yes. So the headmaster offered to let him live with them. Eventually he became an adopted son, a favorite of the family, a "first son," according to his adoptive sister, Lillian. In Africa there are no courts to tell everyone, "This is my first son." It is a deeper bond than a blood brother; you are bonded in heart. His adoptive family was Maasai. Maasai people believe all children are gifts from God. It doesn't really matter who your parents are. They are accepting of all children. There is no word in Maasai for *bastard*.

Pat got up from her chair to head for some of the pieces of art in their home.

All of their culture, all their art reveals that no one exists by themselves. You are always in relation to one another. You don't survive alone. Martin completed high school in the boarding school and went two years to college. He was going to be a junior high teacher. He and his friends would walk to villages to teach. Once, an entire village went to hide, because the Maasai were known to be warriors, not teachers. The Maasai were a proud and revered people. I remember when I was engaged to Martin, he shared an apartment at the University of Chicago with another African student. The African women, while fixing dinner, would come to me and say, "You must be so proud to be marrying Maasai."

In Tanzania education was so close to survival and basic human needs, and teachers were stretched to do whatever it takes to meet those needs. As a school social worker, when I went to visit the school where Martin attended, I was amazed. The TMH classes had long waiting lists. Kids never had breakfast, never had lunch. They walked to school. They had no textbook—maybe one for sixty kids. The same teachers gave six-week courses on speech pathology, a highly specialized area here.

I'm not clear how Martin came to the decision not to become a teacher in Tanzania, how he got connected with the YMCA and chose to come to America for training. Perhaps he heard of the YMCA through his boarding school, which was well respected. A schoolmate became the prime minister of Tanzania. Perhaps it was Bishop Ryan who was influential. Perhaps it was John Peters from the World Neighbors program who mentored him. Perhaps the connection was from the Lutheran seminary, which Martin attended after high school. Nevertheless, it was through the African Alliance of YMCAs that he came to George Williams College on a scholarship. The African Alliance was composed of mostly Swahili-speaking countries like Kenya, Uganda, and Tanzania—what was considered East Africa. . . .

The YMCA is very different over there. Here it has more of a recreational base. There it was basic life-and-death community development issues—food, water. The church was focused that way also. They were into creating fisheries, engaged in animal husbandry projects, finding solutions to the need for electricity to replace wood so they wouldn't destroy the rain forests.

When Martin arrived in Downers Grove, Illinois, to be a student at George Williams College, it was his first time in this country. His first impression was that it was very cold here; he had never experienced cold. He quickly connected with African friends at the college. It was somewhat disconcerting to be viewed as only black by white people around him. When he and his African friends went to a bar, they were told by some other patrons, "You need to leave." He asked the barkeeper, "Is there a law against our being here?" When he was told, reluctantly, that by law they could stay, he and his friends did just that. Others in the neighborhood received him openly. Always a hard worker, thinking nothing was beneath him, he would clean houses and mow lawns, and he was paid well. Sometimes neighbors would open their homes to international students from GWC for holiday dinners. Martin joined the International Student Association on campus. They would host parties, celebrating the culture of the countries students represented.

Martin did get his chance to be a teacher, as well as a student, at GWC. Through the International/Intercultural Studies Program (IISP), he taught a course on Swahili for a group of about twelve students. He was paid as a part-time instructor.

It was during this time that I met Martin. He was in applied behavioral science, and I was in psychology, but because the college was small, we mixed quite easily on campus. At first when Martin asked me on a date, he was very formal about it. We had to have another person to chaperone our dates. We asked a classmate, Corinne Samyn ['75, '79] to chaperone. For three dates, Corinne was with us. Then she said, "Look, I have five boys to raise. I just don't have the time to chaperone your dates. You'll have to be on your own!" We didn't marry right away. When he graduated, Martin went to the University of Oklahoma to get his master's in public administration, and I went on to get my master's in social work at George Williams College. We were reunited at a retirement dinner for Dr. Don Lathrope, the director of the social work department, around 1977 or 1978. Shortly after Martin asked my father for my hand in marriage. Martin always revered my parents, and they loved him.

When Martin settled down in Illinois, he went to work for the Illinois Department of Child and Family Services and stayed with them for twenty-five years. He started out as an investigator for cases of abuse and neglect. We also became foster parents for seven years, until it became a conflict of interest with his work. With his experience and a professional master's of social work degree, Martin moved into a leadership role as a case reviewer, a person who monitors decisions made by case-workers to assure the best interests of the child.

As we were talking about her dad's long commitment to child welfare services, Nesi said, "I wonder if he felt like he owed something. He was so grateful to have an adoptive home." Martin still had unfinished business about being adopted. He put off talking openly about it, even with those closest to him in his own family, until he was diagnosed with cancer. It was only then that he disclosed he was adopted. He wanted to return to Tanzania to find his blood relatives. Two years ago he did that, bringing his daughter Nesi with him.

Nesi Msseemmaa:

> Dad remembered an address that was in his head. He went there. Each time people would say something, like a cousin was there, but he died, but they know someone down the road. Dad learned that his older blood brother Wensislo was looking for him. He tried the school and different places, but they kept missing each other. Finally they connected. We went to Moshi. It was very rural. I remember seeing this big group, so many people, maybe twenty or thirty. Dad started crying, saying, "My sister, my brother." I couldn't understand Swahili, so I couldn't understand what they were saying, but it was very emotional. I kept thinking, "These are my blood relatives."

Pat Msseemmaa:

> Two things Martin loved about the college: He learned what it was to be American, and people cared about him. He loved America for its freedom of speech. The ability to speak your mind; that's American. In the classroom, ideas presented could be challenged and respected. It's not like "Don't speak up if you want a good grade." He also liked the closer, smaller college, where people really got to know you, and they cared.[28]

Faculty interest in global social development continued in George Williams College of Aurora University, kindling student interest.

"The group-work approach is a social development approach"

John Morrison, professor, 2004

> The group-work approach is a social development approach [for international work]. The George Williams College approach is not built on a view of deficits and pathology of people; it's the other side of social work, a view of people's strengths, an in-

terest in their holistic development. It is about hope, possibility, and development that come through the use of normal activities, rather than through therapy. The group approach that the college is known for is grounded in the view that people have strengths to be called upon through their ties of affiliation with others. That's a "social development approach," the building of social capital. It's a collective way of solving problems.[29]

Faith, spirit, and social development

Don Phelps, professor, 2004

I got into this through John Morrison. He has been a key mentor for me. When I first came into the social work program as a student, John would have dinner or lunch with me. We would talk about international stuff, community organization, and macro-level skills. He has played that role for me for fifteen years. After I graduated, we stayed in touch, and he continued to mentor me. He encouraged me to get my PhD as soon as possible. I probably would not have it now, without his encouragement. Now that I am on the faculty here, he continues to encourage me. . . . John passed on to me his interest in international social work. He took a sabbatical in South Africa and has been instrumental in developing connections between social workers there and here, through the National Association of Social Work international group. He said, "Don, you would be interested in this." He was right about that. My wife and I travel internationally. We are both social workers, so even when traveling for leisure we would stop at YMCAs (Don was formerly employed as a YMCA director) and other social service agencies to see how they were run and how social work was defined and operationalized in other countries.

And so I went to South Africa with a delegation from the National Association of Social Workers [Illinois chapter]. There were eighteen of us. We were hosted by the University of Durbin, where John taught when on sabbatical. Durbin is on the east coast of South Africa in the state of Kwazula Natal. We visited social service agencies, heard from scholars at the University of Natal, had dinner invitations with social workers, and the mayor had a reception for us with community leaders. We saw social work in the city of Durbin and traveled one hundred miles north to rural Zulu villages to see how social work was done there.

The thing that impressed me the most from my experience there was the faith and positive spirit of the people. People are struggling against all odds, dying by thousands every day, and they still have incredible spirit. I started to reflect on this. When I came back home I presented at several conferences on faith and social development in South Africa. I focused on how communities use their beliefs—

Christian, Buddhist, Hindu; it's very diverse over there—how they use their faith to instill hope. I saw expression of spirituality every place I went. Upon entering and exiting agencies, you will hear a spiritual song. Imagine walking in to the office of the Department of Children and Family Services and being greeted with a spiritual song! They are songs of overcoming. You would expect, when the tables turned and they were in power, people would say, "Execute them, imprison them, get them out of this country now." But their leaders came together to say, "No, we need to forgive them." Now you can see Afrikaans, Indians, and native black South Africans side by side. Of course, all the tensions are not worked out, but this is now a ten-year old democracy.

I also learned that the only way to practice social work is through community organization, using a social development model. In child welfare, social workers have caseloads of five hundred. You can't do intensive clinical work with a caseload like that. The schools of social work there view their work as preparation for social development. Social work is lodged within the same organizational structure as policy planning, urban housing, architecture, and public administration. The social work dean there had visited George Williams College in Aurora before we came there. She advocated for social workers to play a stronger role in urban planning and social development. When I came home, I immediately had a course on social welfare policy to teach. I devoted a full session talking about my experience and what social welfare policy was like there.[30]

Finding self and a passion for service

Brad Burger, student, (AU '04) and Chris Blackburn, student, (AU '04)

Brad Burger:

It all started for me, when Don Phelps shared an experience in his social welfare policy class. Don had just completed a three-week trip to South Africa through the National Association of Social Workers' international social work program. He was showing us pictures of his trip to South Africa. Sitting there, I was blown away by his emotion that came through as he showed those pictures. He said [that], having kids of his own, it really hits home to see the social issues families face living in South Africa. You could tell how much of an impact this experience had on his life. And he was just there for three weeks. Professors here are so passionate about what they teach. I was struggling. I thought, "I just don't feel anything. I don't know what I want to do with my life . . . still." It was frustrating to see these professors with passion and knowledge about world views. I didn't have that. You know how it goes. You give these assigned class presentations, and they mean nothing to you. I went up to him after class, and said, "I want that experience. I want to be able to feel and see and hear some of those things you are describing." I never made international travel a priority in my undergraduate years. I was busy playing sports. I never envisioned going to South Africa.

Chris Blackburn:

I regard the relationships I've made with professors as the most significant thing at George Williams College. John Morrison cared about my own growth and how I learn. He has incredible experiences to share. Listening to his stories about South Africa, I thought about international travel. I thought I could learn about other countries, and [if] I could have more knowledge of myself, it could help me reflect more on how we live here, what's important and what's not.

Brad and Chris did not know each other before they began to plan together for a trip to South Africa that summer. Other students were interested but backed off because the Iraq War was pending. Though the faculty were not able to join them on this visit, they built a travel plan based on the connections their mentors John Morrison and Don Phelps had made in South Africa. They signed up for a service learning course at the University of Natal. Brad Burger:

On my second week there, as part of our service learning project, we were assigned to a particular community township to learn and provide some kind of service outreach. Three of us students were taken to this warehouse building that appeared to be a community center. A woman there escorted us to a meeting room, with chairs set up in a circle. The set-up was great, so we would not be looking at each other's back but to each other. Gradually thirty-four people arrived. As students, we joined the circle but wondered what role we had to play there. As the group got started, the woman leader said, "Brad, we have a lot of problems here. We have economic problems. We have an AIDS crisis. How can you help us?" I looked at the pastor who was sitting next to me and said, "Is this question for you?" I had been there for two weeks, thinking I would just observe and learn. Was this a joke? I wondered, I'm an American, and they think I'm coming here with answers to help them out. I started out just mumbling. Then I started asking them more questions. As I got to hear a little more about the problems they were facing, some of the things I learned from class about community started kicking in. So many things seemed tied to money. I asked them about what resources and skills they thought they did have? Are there young people who could unite together to face these things and problem solve together? Could those who had certain knowledge and skills educate others? Did they have a name for their group? Would naming the group help them to have recognition and identity as a group that wants to help solve community problems together?

They then broke into small groups to talk more intensively about what they thought were problems and resources they had. We were there for about two hours and it seemed they accomplished something.

Chris Blackburn:

We were assigned to field experiences in particular agencies. I was assigned to Sinecatempa. I attended a support group held every Tuesday. The group of about fifty people, ranging from their teens to about sixty in age, all had been diagnosed with HIV/AIDS. Since there were not many support groups, people would take buses for a two-hour trip to come to Sinecatempa. When they came, they received a big bag of groceries. They were always stuffed with an abundant supply of garlic, because they thought garlic would stimulate the immune system. The group would start out with prayer and singing. The leader there was diagnosed with HIV for nine years. Her name was Puni. She took me on a visit to her home. From there we went to a very small apartment across the street. A woman there was in the final stages of AIDS. They call it "bones disease." I asked if I could come in. Unfortunately people seeing a white male walking into their house, and he's an American, they expect good news . . . that Americans can do something for their condition. Her husband contracted AIDS from a woman there at the ports. He has it, but not like her, weak and shunned from others. I could see a three-year-old around the corner, crying. This mother was living with her father and had a few months to live. She was not able to make it to the support groups any longer, and so Puni came to visit her. In the evening, Brad and I would reflect on how precious life is.

Brad Burger:

Here [in the United States], community is not viewed as being important. In South Africa, it's health, family, and community that gives them hope. In fact, they seemed happier than I was. I have everything I want, and if I don't have it, I can get it. How is it, then, that they are happier? Here, it's how much money you make, what kind of car do you drive, where do you live? I thought, "What's important in my life?"

Chris Blackburn:

I learned about a hospitality that I did not expect or understand in the impoverished informal settlements built into the hillsides that did not have access to city services. An American from a social service agency arranged for me to spend the evening and stay overnight in the home of a family. The small, cinderblock house had about fifteen children, and they had three beds. As I understood it, some of the children were orphans from AIDS and some had parents who were away, working in the mines. And yet I was welcomed, and they gave up their bed for me to sleep. I played with the children, and I was served a meal. All night in the background I could hear dancing and music, celebrating Nelson Mandela's birthday. When I said I was from Chicago, they laughed. "Chicago" was another informal settlement down the road.

Brad Burger:

I was impressed, not only with how people drew on each other for support within their community, but how their sense of community extended to the stranger. I was the first white person invited into their home, let alone to stay there overnight. They were so open in their hospitality. And they were not looking for anything from you. In our country, if you meet somebody, invite them to your home, give them dinner, and invite them to stay overnight, I would wonder what you want.

Chris Blackburn:

One day the university arranged a trip to the YMCA in Durbin. I found it odd to be going to a YMCA. We were looking for social service experiences. On this particular night they were having a song and dance contest. Different groups were dressed in colorful sport coats and suits. They were singing their songs, redemption songs. The dance was slow in step. They were telling stories of suffering through music and dance; songs about their history, their oppression. The audience would respond, singing songs for fifteen minutes, then the group would quietly walk off stage. It lasted all night. While this was going on, there was a church service going on downstairs. When I think of the YMCA, I'm thinking swimming, lifting weights, and so on. However, this was different.

Brad Burger:

They don't have health, they don't have economic security. Still there is happiness. They were joyful, always singing. We regularly visited Open Door Crisis Center, [a multiservice center serving all of South Africa for HIV/AIDS victims and their families]. When we went to their support group, the first thing we would do is hold hands and pray. Then everyone who could, got up and started singing and dancing. Some AIDS victims were too weak, lying on the floor. But, as one woman said, "Singing makes me happy." Some drove up to three hours to attend the center each week, for information and support. I'm not a very religious person, but I found this to be a spiritual experience for me. I found myself thinking about what is important in life. It changed my life. I couldn't look myself in the mirror now if I didn't try to do something about the HIV/AIDS crisis. I took an AIDS course. I thought the course was interesting. But after going to South Africa, I think AIDS is the most significant health issue in our times. I walked around with some of those kids who do not have parents because of AIDS. Now I want to be that voice for those fourteen million children orphaned from AIDS. I feel an obligation, whether to go there and learn some more or stay here and be a voice in the Rockford community for people in Africa and throughout the world.

When I came back to school I attempted to communicate my experience, and concern about the AIDS crisis with my fellow social work students. It did not go well. I felt I could not step out of what I thought was a boring, ritualistic class presentation format. I learned a lot from that experience. I said, "Brad if you're going to help somebody, you need to stand up before groups. And you have an obligation to be an articulate voice."

Brad then created a video called "Living with Hope." The video blends his personal experiences in South Africa; sights and sounds of AIDS orphans; children's voices on what they think and feel about AIDS; adults dealing with news of their own diagnosis; people coping and educating others through dance, drama, song, and drumming.

Brad Burger:

I've given numerous presentations at my field agency, my former college class, to churches and grade-school children. I never speak without giving people an opportunity to do something. When speaking to grade-school children, I use what could be called a workable Band-Aid approach. Instead of talking about condoms, I talk about other issues, like Africans not having access to Band-Aids. Students can collect Band-Aids and Neosporin. They can write letters to children at the Open Door [Crisis Center] in South Africa. They can send a picture, anything to make it personal for these kids.

After graduation Brad returned to South Africa with two hundred pounds of medical supplies for the Open Door clinic. His goals are to educate Americans about the AIDS crisis, to connect social agencies between the United States and South Africa, and to enlist a volunteer program for doctors visiting from the United States. He hopes to raise financial support to develop his work; Rotary International is sponsoring him. He acknowledges he is starting out small, but "it's about providing the crisis center in South Africa with hope." He hopes the social work program will be able to start a formal international program in South Africa and elsewhere, so other students can have transformative experiences as he had.

Brad Burger:

This experience changed my life . . . to experience a different culture, different views, different values in life, to have a sense of global community, not just a Rockford or Aurora or Chicago community.

After graduation Chris Blackburn headed for one of the most remote areas of Alaska. Trained as a school social worker, he will be working with communities and schools. His South African experience led him to this place.

Chris Blackburn:

I enjoyed working within a different culture. It was a brand new experience for me. I'm going to work with Yup'ik people. I'll be four hundred miles southwest of Anchorage, by the Bering Sea. I'll fly into a village hub for neighboring outposts. I'll travel from station to station during the week to work with the community elders, students, and teachers. I expect to see alcoholism and poverty, as I have seen in South Africa. I've seen African AIDS-infected teens who self-medicated through alcohol to avoid facing their diagnosis and their fate. They found community support groups essential for coping. . . .

I expect it might be difficult to motivate them to learn. I expect they may be more interested in where the caribou tracks are going over the hill than in school. They rely on fishing and hunting; they're not so concerned with education, I'm told. I expect them to say, "Chris, white guy from Chicago with brand new boots and coat, who will be telling us, 'No, no you've got to do it this way.'" That's not my game plan. I won't be pushy.

Being in South Africa, I got to think about myself. Who am I? To become a good social worker and be effective with others, you have to know who you are. You learn that when you are in a completely different environment. My cross-cultural class with Glenda Blakemore helped. We talked a lot about what it means to be black and what it means to be white. I became aware that as a white male, I have major privileges. We tend to look for our own in social groups, and in doing so, we tend to shut other people out. In South Africa I felt accepted regardless of our difference. I'm sure I will see my self differently, and I will see them differently in time.[31]

Conclusion

"The college campus as we remember it may be gone . . . but the spirit that helped make George Williams a great institution **continues to live** *in every one of us. No one can separate us from our education, from our memories, . . . from our friendships."*

(The Alumni Committee: Armin Luehrs, Joe Nasvik, Helen Scoggins, 1986)

This is the big story from hundreds of little stories told by people whose generations spanned over one hundred years. They happened to have spent some of their years in the same George Williams College; some for a few years, some for the good part of their lifetime. Some were drawn to the college because its purpose matched their life's purpose; it was about human service. Some came because they admired what they saw in their mentors who modeled those values, and their mentors had spent years at the college. Some drifted in to the college; they were not clear about these values when they came, but they discovered and incorporated them while they were there, tested them out, and found them to work in real life. They went out into communities to live them out for themselves and for others. Those same values show themselves in every person's story, no matter what generation. We can call them strong roots. They are about service, building community, about learning-by-doing, about developing the whole person in body as well as mind and spirit, and about reaching around the world in human connection and service.

The seeds were planted by the YMCA, which has called itself a "movement" for generations. The movement caught on because it struck a chord of social need. The visionary was Robert Weidensall, who planted the seeds, creating a place as early as 1884 for training YMCA workers at Williams Bay in the Lake Geneva area in Wisconsin.

If you were to call this college merely buildings and grounds with a name and classrooms of teachers and students, it may appear that the college did not survive, many times over. The name of the college has changed several times. The locations have changed. Students and teachers came and went. It started on the remote shores of Geneva Lake in Wisconsin, moved into the dynamic urban environment of Chicago, then into a newly developing suburb of Chicago, then into a regenerating industrial town that has grown into a city, then back to Geneva Lake. From these stories we see that values connect every era. In that sense, the college survived and thrived through each era. These values were revealed and exercised in times of crisis, be it doing urban youth work when hope and possibility declined in the college's surrounding neighborhoods of Chicago, regenerating an internal community fragmented by racial tension, or mobilizing a student community to "keep George Williams College alive" when the college at Downers Grove declared itself closed. The roots just seemed to get stronger when tested in hard places of adversity.

Working from these values, the college made contributions to society. In the 1930s George Williams College was a national center for the development of group work as a profession; the values and methods of group work have been incor-

"We can call them strong roots."

porated into many academic disciplines, including recreation, camping, social work, organizational development, youth development, sports, and physical education. From its YMCA heritage, the college was a forerunner of the idea of holistic health, with the integration of body, mind, and spirit. Dr. Arthur Steinhaus broke ground in physiological research and the practice of health and wellness, moving it from the laboratory and doctor's office to the general public for use in their everyday lives; others from George Williams College followed his footsteps. The college never relinquished the progressive education idea of John Dewey that learning happens by doing. While professional human service societies moved in the direction of the "medical model," focusing on pathology, labeling, medication, and "treatment" of specific problems, the college held firmly to a practice model focused on human strengths, possibility, and relationships for

holistic development. The college continued to teach the value of community, being part of a whole, in times when it appeared that society had lost sight of its value. These days we rarely hear of "giving back for what you have been given" and how that notion builds communities. The college always maintained a global perspective. At first, students from foreign lands came to the college because they were touched by the YMCA movement. The world came to them, and they went out into the world to serve. They formed personal relationships and learned from each other, gaining a bigger picture of the world, our differences, and our commonalities.

The stories told here, remind us that the college also had an influence on the YMCA. People who came out of the college influenced the national YMCA to confront prejudice and injustice, take action, and get involved in social policy

Photograph, page 243: Author and research fellow, Sandy Alcorn, with her "Minnesota Archive Diggers" who assisted her at the Kautz Family YMCA Archives, University of Minnesota. From left to right: Clelia Guastavino Giles ('78, '79), faculty member Lyle Johnson ('79), Corky Johnson ('73), the late Jim Gilbert ('56), Sandy Alcorn, Kautz reference archivist Dagmar Getz, and Whitey Luehrs ('46, '48).

issues that affect the well-being of people served. Though the YMCA moved in the direction of a threefold purpose, recognized as the YMCA triangle of "body, mind, and spirit," the college always held on to the "fourfold purpose" that preceded the triangle. That fourth purpose was the social dimension; individuals and groups are not whole or fully developed without relationships, and they must always be interconnected to grow.

The roots are strong. It is hoped that as George Williams College continues on in relation to Aurora University, it will endure, not only in name but in spirit. The location is changing again, back to Williams Bay. The students and faculty have come and gone. Names, buildings, programs, and organizational structures have come and gone. Through it all, it is hoped, there will always be a George Williams College, and people will know what that means. From the stories told here, we know there is a George Williams College within the hearts of people who have been touched by it along the way.

Notes

Chapter 1: Serving Others

1. Robert Weidensall to I. E. Brown, 1885, Kautz Family YMCA Archives, University of Minnesota Libraries. This personal letter from Weidensall to I. E. Brown, sent from Yutan, Nebraska, responding to "the topic assigned to me." I. E. Brown asked Weidensall what he envisioned the "Institutes" to be.

2. Sir George Williams was involved in the Early Closing Movement in London to advocate for no more than an eight-hour workday for men who worked as apprentices; he thought "there was no class more degraded and dissolute than the shopmen in London." See Galen Merriam Fisher, *Public Affairs and the Y.M.C.A.: 1844–1944* (New York: Association Press, 1948), 23.

3. Comments on the "foursquare man" or "fourfold purpose" are cited in the annual yearbook, *The Crucible,* from 1914 to at least 1917, Aurora University Archives, Aurora, IL. The original Articles of Incorporation By-laws of the Secretarial Institute and Training School of the YMCA, George Williams College Archives, Aurora University, Williams Bay, WI.

4. Fisher, *Public Affairs,* 61.

5. Ibid.

6. *The Crucible,* vol. 4 (Chicago/Lake Geneva: The Institute and Training School of the YMCA, 1912), 26.

7. *The Crucible,* vol. 7 (Chicago/Lake Geneva: YMCA College, 1914–1915), 28.

8. *The Crucible,* vol. 8 (Chicago/Lake Geneva: YMCA College, 1916), 32.

9. Ibid., 42.

10. Henry Kallenberg, "The Profession of Physical Education" [1913], public relations box. 1896–1913, Kautz Family YMCA Archives, University of Minnesota Libraries.

11. *The Crucible,* vol. 7 (Chicago/Lake Geneva: YMCA College, 1914–1915), 52.

12. F. H. Burt, "The Men's Student Conferences" and "The Women's Conferences," George Williams College Early Historical Essays, 1887–1947, George Williams College Archives, Aurora University, Williams Bay, WI.

13. Andrea Hinding, *Proud Heritage: A History in Pictures of the YMCA in the United States* (Norfolk, VA: Donning, 1988), 146–47. Hinding reports from Gordon Poteat, ed., *Students and the Future of Christian Missions* (New York: Student Volunteer Movement for Foreign Missions, 1928), 75–93.

14. *The Crucible* (Chicago/Lake Geneva: YMCA College, 1917), 98.

15. *The Crucible* (Chicago/Lake Geneva: YMCA College, 1920), 73.

16. Gisela Konopka, *Eduard C. Lindeman and Social Work Philosophy* (Minneapolis: Univ. of Minnesota Press, 1958), 27.

17. Memorandum, "George Williams College—A Recreational Link with the Past and Future," n.d., George Williams College Archives, Aurora University, Williams Bay, WI, p. 4.

18. Jane Addams, *Twenty Years at Hull-House: With Autobiographical Notes* (New York: Macmillan, 1945), 124, 126, 115, 443, and 444–445.

19. Wallace Kirkland and Mary Ann Johnson, ed., *The Many Faces of Hull-House: The Photographs of Wallace Kirkland* (Urbana, IL: Univ. of Illinois Press, 1989). The introduction reports a history of Wallace Kirkland.

20. Mary Stowe, "In Memoriam," *George Williams College Bulletin* 766280 (Downers Grove, IL: George Williams College, December 1979). Mary Stowe submitted this column to the *Bulletin* on the event of Kirkland's death on September 14, 1979.

21. A family member was interviewed on the event of the death of Kirkland's son in the fall of 2003.

22. Clifford Putney, *Muscular Christianity: Manhood and Sports in Protestant America, 1880–1920* (Cambridge: Harvard Univ. Press), 186. Putney also quotes President Taft saying the work of the YMCA in World War I was "one of the greatest achievements of peace in all the history of human warfare," 190.

23. "Historical Chronology of GWC," in *Alumni Directory: Aurora University; Sir George Williams College* (White Plains, NY: B.C. Harris, 1994), viii. See also "The College in War Time," in *The Crucible* (Chicago/Lake Geneva: YMCA College, 1920), 75–76; History of College Camp, a Collection of Historical Manuscripts, George Williams College Archives, Aurora University, Williams Bay, WI.

24. Hedley Seldon Dimock, Charles E. Hendry, and Karl P. Zerfoss, *A Professional Outlook on Group Education* (New York: Association Press), 5–6.

25. Charles E. Hendry, in Hedley Seldon Dimock, Charles E. Hendry, and Karl P. Zerfoss, "The Emergence of Group Education" (1947), 8.

26. Hedley Seldon Dimock in Hedley Seldon Dimock, Charles E. Hendry, and Karl P. Zerfoss, "The Marks of a Profession" (1947), 23–26. See further reading from these authors and also Harleigh Trecker a GWC graduate and prolific writer on group work. (The social work library at the University of Connecticut is named the Harleigh B. Trecker Library in his honor, where he was dean and professor.) See, for instance, Hedley Seldon Dimock and Charles E. Hendry, *Camping and Character: A Camp Experiment in Character Education* (New York: Association Press, 1929); Hedley Seldon

Dimock, "Leadership in Group Work: The Executive as Educator," in *New Trends in Group Work,* ed. Joshua Lieberman, 182–89 (New York: Association Press, 1938); Hedley Seldon Dimock, *Rediscovering the Adolescent: A Study of Personality Development in Adolescent Boys* (New York: Association Press, 1941); Hedley Seldon Dimock and Harleigh Bradley Trecker, *The Supervision of Group Work and Recreation* (New York: Association Press, 1951); Harleigh Bradley Trecker, "A Methodology for Research in Group Work," in *New Trends in Group Work,* ed. Joshua Lieberman, 215–18 (New York: Association Press, 1938); Harleigh Bradley Trecker, *Group Process in Administration* (New York: Women's Press, 1950); Harleigh Bradley Trecker, *Social Group Work: Principles and Practices* (New York: Whiteside, 1955); Charles E. Hendry, "A Review of Group Work Affirmations," in *Proceedings of the National Conference of Social Work: Selected Papers, 65th Annual Conference, Grand Rapids, Michigan, May 26–June 1, 1940* (New York: Columbia Univ. Press, 1940), 539ff.

27. Helen Cody Baker, "The Age of 'Informal Recreation,'" *Chicago Daily News,* March 16, 1940.

28. Jane Addams, "Social Settlements," in *Proceedings of the National Conference of Charities and Correction, 24th Annual Session, Toronto, Canada 1897, July 7–14,* ed. Elizabeth Barrows, 338–51, 473–74 (Boston: George Ellis, 1898).

29. "George Williams College Graduate? So What!" in the "Grins 'n' Gripes" section of a 1952 issue of the student newspaper of George Williams College, Downers Grove, IL, private collection of Ned Stowe ('52).

30. "College Gets Free Ad Time. What Ever Happened to Altruism," *George Williams College Bulletin* (Downers Grove, IL: George Williams College, Fall 1967).

31. Duane "Dewey" Cedarblade, in discussion with the author, October 8, 2005.

32. United Way of America, "Statement Honoring John O. Root," (February 27, 1978). John's wife Betty Root contributed this pamphlet, adding her comments from John in February 2004.

33. Self-study Report Submitted to North Central Association (NCA) for College Accreditation, 1979, George Williams College Archives, Aurora University, Aurora, IL, p. 15.

34. Mary Ryba, "The Arts and the Mission," *George Williams College Bulletin* (Downers Grove, IL: May 1985), 1.

35. John Kessler, "Steadfastness in Our College Mission Requires Transformation," *George Williams College Bulletin* (Downers Grove, IL: May 1985), 8–9.

36. On May 17, 1991, GWC board member and president Philip Harper sent a letter and report addressed to alumni Del Arsenault, Fred Lickerman, and John Pruehs regarding the status of group work in the city of Chicago, and the interests of Chicago Community Trust to contribute over $30 million dollars to support "primary services" in the city. Harper said Harold Richman, former dean of the School of Social Service Administration at the University of Chicago, and head of Chapin Hall Center for Children at the University of Chicago, along with others from Chapin Hall "are convinced that the reduced emphasis on the teaching of Group Work in human service and Social Work education over the past twenty years has had a significant negative impact on the availability of qualified youth services staff. . . . Because of the historic role of GWC in the teaching of Group Work from 1934 to 1972, . . . what can be done to revive the teaching of Group Work in the Chicago area? . . . This may be an opportunity to put GWC back in the business of teaching Group Work." Harper commissioned a scholar from the University of Chicago to research the status of group work in social work educational programs throughout the United States.

37. Mary Nelums, in discussion with the author, October 13, 2005.

38. Dovetta McKee, in discussion with the author, November 3, 2005.

39. Chris Ahlman, in discussion with the author, fall 2003.

40. Robert D. Putnam, *Bowling Alone: The Collapse and Revival of American Community* (New York: Simon & Schuster, 2000).

41. Michael Fabricant and Robert Fisher, *Settlement Houses Under Siege: The Struggle to Sustain Community Organizations in New York City* (New York: Columbia Univ. Press, 2002).

42. John D. Morrison, Sandra Alcorn, and Mary Nelums, "Empowering Community-Based Programs for Youth Development: Is Social Work Education Interested?," *Journal of Social Work Education* 33, no. 2 (1997): 321–334. The blind reviewer's comments were made on a prepublication draft.

Chapter 2: Developing Body with Mind and Spirit

1. Arthur H. Steinhaus, "Whither Bound—YMCAs Physical Education" (paper read before the Indiana Employed Officers' Conference and the Illinois State Physical Directors Society Meeting, September, 1928). George Williams College Archives, Aurora University, Aurora, IL.

2. Arthur H. Steinhaus, "Your Heritage, Opportunity and Challenge" (lecture presented to GWC students on November 14, 1967).

3. Gen. 3:19 (New Revised Standard Version).

4. Theodore Roosevelt, "Machine Politics in New York City" *Century* (November 1886), quoted in Clifford Putney, *Muscular Christianity: Manhood and Sports in Protestant America, 1880–1920* (Cambridge, MA: Harvard University Press, 2003), 26.

5. Clifford Putney, *Muscular Christianity: Manhood and Sports in Protestant America, 1880–1920* (Cambridge, MA: Harvard University Press, 2003).

6. J. Wilbur Chapman, *The Life and Work of Dwight Lyman Moody* (London: James Nesbit, 1900). Originally published in 1900 as a 555-page book; available on http://www.biblebelievers.com.

7. Minutes of Trustees, Years of 1888, 1889; The Geneva Students Summer School: Seventh Annual Report, College Camp Historical Manuscripts, pp. 23, 30, 60, George Williams College Archives, Aurora University, Williams Bay, WI.

8. Billy Graham Center Archives, "Guide to the Papers of William Ashley 'Billy' Sunday and Helen Amelia (Thompson) Sunday—Collection 61," http://www.wheaton.edu/bgc/archives/GUIDES/061.htm.

9. The Young Men's Christian Association Training School—Chicago 1890–1891, public relations box 11 B, Kautz Family YMCA Archives, University of Minnesota Libraries.

10. Billy Graham Center Archives, "William Ashley 'Billy' Sunday."

11. The Geneva Students Summer School. Seventh Annual Report. College Camp Historical Manuscripts, p. 30, George Williams College Archives, Aurora University, Williams Bay, WI.

12. Basketball Hall of Fame, "Amos 'Alonzo' Stagg," *Hall of Famers,* http://www.hoophall.com/halloffamers/Stagg.htm.

13. Memorandum, "George Williams College—A Recreational Link with the Past and Future," n.d., George Williams College Archives, Aurora University, Williams Bay, WI, pp. 4–5. This anony-

mous ten-page paper was apparently written by the LERA (Leisure and Environmental Resources Administration) program of George Williams College.

14. *The Crucible,* (1909).

15. "A Recreational Link," pp. 4–5. See also "Summer Training School," College Camp Historical Manuscripts, George Williams College Archives, Aurora University, Williams Bay, WI, p. 29.

16. Basketball Hall of Fame, "James Naismith," *Hall of Famers,* http://www.hoophall.com/halloffamers/Naismith.htm.

17. Newsclipping, "Obituary of Henry Kallenberg," box 11 H public relations 1886–1933, Kautz Family YMCA Archives, University of Minnesota Libraries.

18. The Basketball Attic, "History," http://www.basketballattic.addr.com/history.htm.

19. David Hudson, "The Origins of Basketball at the University of Iowa," The Brockway Family Website, http://www.brockwayfamily.com/origins_of_basketball_at_the_uni.htm.

20. C. J. Kurtz, "Reflections on GWC on the occasion of the celebration of his 90th birthday," April 4, 1962, George Williams College Archives, Aurora University, Williams Bay, WI.

21. John William Fuhrer, "Steinhaus" (pamphlet, 1962). This was published on the occasion of the retirement of Dr. Arthur Steinhaus, June 2, 1962.

22. Arthur H. Steinhaus, "Your Heritage, Opportunity and Challenge" (lecture presented to GWC students on November 14, 1967), pp. 8–9.

23. Kurtz, "Reflections," p. 5.

24. Ibid., p. 4.

25. "A Recreational Link," pp. 4–5.

26. Jane Addams and Eva Warner Case, *Twenty Years at Hull House, with Autobiographical Notes* (New York: Macmillan, 1945), 66.

27. "A Recreational Link," pp. 4–5.

28. Ibid.

29. Ibid.

30. Ibid.

31. *The Crucible* (1906), p. 23.

32. David I. Macleod, *Building Character in the American Boy, 1870–1920: The Boy Scouts, the YMCA and Their Forerunners* (Madison: University of Wisconsin Press, 1983).

33. Eva and Arthur Steinhaus, "The Romance of Service: A Pageant for the 50th Anniversary of the Founding of GWC in Chicago," box 11 B public relations, Kautz Family YMCA Archives, University of Minnesota Libraries.

34. Fuhrer, "Steinhaus" p. 3.

35. Steinhaus, "Whither Bound."

36. Arthur Steinhaus, "A Biologist Looks at Group Work," *George Williams College Bulletin* 44, no. 1 (October 1949).

37. Steinhaus, "Your Heritage," pp. 13–15.

38. Ibid., p. 10.

39. Ibid.

40. Fuhrer, "Steinhaus," p. 4.

41. Fuhrer, "Steinhaus," pp. 4–5.

42. Steinhaus, "Your Heritage," p. 15.

43. Steinhaus, "Your Heritage," pp. 18–20.

44. *The Collegian* 2, no. 1 (October 14, 1966), George Williams College Archives, Aurora University, Aurora, IL.

45. Fuhrer, "Steinhaus," p. 8.

46. Ibid.

47. Ibid., p. 11.

48. Ibid., p. 10.

49. Emery Nelson, "Tribute to Arthur Steinhaus," *George Williams College Bulletin* (March 1970).

50. Fuhrer, "Steinhaus," p. 11.

51. Ibid., p. 12.

52. Steinhaus, "Your Heritage," p. 12.

53. John D. Fair, *Muscletown USA: Bob Hoffman and the Manly Culture of York Barbell* (University Park, PA.: Pennsylvania State University Press, 1999), 4.

54. Bruce Lee and John R. Little, *The Art of Expressing the Human Body* (Boston: C. E. Tuttle Co., 1998), 56–57.

55. John Hoellen, "Forest Park's Gajda Doesn't Feel Like a Freak Anymore," *Suburban Tribune,* March 29, 1978, sec. 3.

56. Fair, *Muscletown,* 236.

57. Bob Gajda, in discussion with the author, February 3, 2005.

58. Henry Labatte, in discussion with the author, June 16, 2005.

59. James Brown, *George Williams College Bulletin* (1970).

60. James Gleason, *George Williams College Bulletin* (1970).

61. "We Can't Let Them Get Away: The Urban Youth Development Project," *George Williams College Bulletin* (October 1968). George Williams College Archives, Aurora University, Aurora, IL, p. 1, 2.

62. Good Neighbors, *University of Chicago Magazine,* Spring, 1984, 24.

63. Michael Kraus, "Sport as Education," *University of Chicago Magazine,* Summer, 1977, 4.

64. Larry Hawkins, "Sports Can Play Key Educational Role," High School Sports Extra, *Chicago Sun-Times,* January 26, 1966.

65. Larry Hawkins, in discussion with the author, March 30, 2005.

66. Monice Mitchell, "Program Moves Education from Classroom to Gym," *Hyde Park Herald,* June 5, 1996.

67. Larry Hawkins, personal note responding to request for alumni feedback, 1972.

68. "Spanning the Abyss: Meet the Pied Pier for Urban Gateways," *George Williams College Bulletin* (October 1968). George Williams College Archives, Aurora University, Aurora, IL, pp. 3–4.

69. "You Can Go Home Again," *George Williams College Bulletin* (May 1971). George Williams College Archives, Aurora University, Aurora, IL.

70. USA Volleyball, "USA Volleyball Saddened by the Death of Jim Coleman," (August 3, 2001), http://www.bvbinfo.com/news.asp?ID=270.

71. Natalie Moore, "Go for the Gold," *Aurora University Magazine* (Summer 2000), pp. 19–22.

72. USA Volleyball, "Saddened."

73. Ibid.

74. Ibid.

75. "Coleman Coaches Olympic Volleyball," *George Williams College Bulletin* (October 1968). George Williams College Archives, Aurora University, Aurora, IL.

76. Jerry Angle, in discussion with the author, September 2003.

77. "Teacher Gives Up His Job for Olympic Volleyball," Sports/Business, *Chicago Tribune*, sec. 2, January 27, 1979.

78. Moore, "Gold," p. 20.

79. Moore, "Gold," p. 22.

80. Jerry Angle, in discussion with the author, September 2003.

81. Moore, "Gold," p. 22.

82. Ibid.

83. Nora Campbell, in discussion with the author, September 2005.

84. Moore, "Gold," p. 22.

85. "Women's Athletics Spells Success," *George Williams College Bulletin* (Spring 1975).

86. Mary and Ed Langbein, in discussion with the author, October 2005.

87. Jerry Angle, in discussion with the author, September 2003.

88. Cindy Schendel, in discussion with the author, September 2005.

Chapter 3: Building Community Inside and Out

1. Galen Merriam Fisher, *Public Affairs and the Y.M.C.A.: 1844–1944* (New York: Association Press,1948), 23.

2. Robert D. Putnam, *Bowling Alone: The Collapse and Revival of American Community* (New York: Simon & Schuster, 2000).

3. James Robert Austin, "A History of the YMCA, Chicago-Lake Geneva, 25th Annual Commencement at Lake Geneva, July 25, 1915, Thesis, History of College Camp," George Williams College Archives, Aurora University, Williams Bay, WI, p. 9.

4. "Our Obligation to the Brotherhood," *The Crucible* (The YMCA College, 1916), private collection of Jean Bilstrom, daughter of Walter Steffen, who last attended GWC in 1917, p. 77.

5. "Weidensall (The Weidensall Club)," *The Crucible* (The YMCA College, 1916), "'Each for all' is the unuttered motto of the membership, and with the example of 'Uncle Robert,' before us, we cannot help but progress toward the objective of the great brotherhood of which we are a part," p. 142; See also *The Crucible* (1917), private collection of Jean Bilstrom, daughter of Walter Steffen, p. 104; The YMCA Hotel is "an attempt to keep the young man at home, . . . the thing that makes it 'homelike' is the fact that it has a heart and an atmosphere of fellowship . . . help in getting a job; a vocational talk; just a friendly chat, a vital thing for the lonesome fellow who is homesick" pp. 76–77.

6. Paul Aravathan, "Bits of History" in "College Camper" (1930), p. 10; J. S. Hotton (1939); *College Camp on Lake Geneva: The Golden Jubilee, 1933* (Chicago: George Williams College, 1933).

7. I. E. Brown, "A Historical Sketch of the Western Secretarial Institute, GWC Early Historical Essays" (1887), George Williams College Archives, Aurora University, Williams Bay, WI.

8. Frank H. Burt, "The Women's Conferences, GWC Early Historical Essays" (1937), George Williams College Archives, Aurora University, Williams Bay, WI.

9. Ray Johns, "How Association College Strikes a Freshman," *The Crucible* (The YMCA College, 1921), Aurora University Archives, Aurora, IL, p. 32.

10. Hedley Dimock, "Last Lap Ceremony" (1932), *George Williams College Bulletin* (George Williams College, 1934), Aurora University Archives, Aurora, IL.

11. Charles Hendry, "A Community of Learning," *Progressive Education* (January 1939), Public Relations, 1933–1965, Box 12 H, Kautz Family YMCA Archives, University of Minnesota Libraries. Hendry quotes Eduard Lindeman, *Social Education: An Interpretation of the Principles and Methods Developed by the Inquiry During the Years 1923–1933* (New York: New Republic, 1933).

12. Esther Lloyd-Jones, "The College Becomes a Laboratory for Democratic Living" (paper presented at annual meeting of American College of Personnel Association, press release). Public Relations Box, Kautz Family YMCA Archives. University of Minnesota Libraries.

13. Karl Zerfoss, *George Williams College Bulletin* 17, no. 8 (April 1938). Kautz Family YMCA Archives, University of Minnesota Libraries.

14. Henry Louis Gates, *America Behind the Color Line: Dialogues with African Americans* (New York: Warner Books, 2004), 338, 359, 360–361; 365; 367–368.

15. Verneta Hill, videocassette of interview on the occasion of honoring Verneta with a lifetime achievement award, October 12, 2000, George Williams College Archives, Aurora University, Aurora, IL.

16. Howard and Roberta Winebrenner, in discussion with the author, October 2003.

17. *George Williams College Bulletin* (October 1949).

18. "The Embers" (George Williams College, 1952), Aurora University Archives, Aurora, IL.

19. Ned and Mary Stowe, in discussion with the author, summer 2004.

20. Sam and Mary Chollar, in discussion with the author, October 8, 2005.

21. Fred Lickerman, in discussion with the author, 2004.

22. Paul Staudenmaier, in discussion with the author, 2003.

23. Timuel D. Black, "Looking Back, Looking Up," in Henry Louis Gates, *America Behind the Color Line: Dialogues with African Americans* (New York: Warner Books, 2004), 365.

24. Chicago is still protesting the injustice of the Emmett Till murder: Keith A. Beauchamp, *The Untold Story of Emmett Louis Till* (New York: Thinkfilm, 2005); Mike Conklin, "Courtroom sketches of Emmett Till Trial Bring History to Life," Tempo, *Chicago Tribune,* sec. 5, August 11, 2004; Clarence Page, "Freedom Summer of '64: I Was 16 Years Old, Angry at America's Homegrown Apartheid and Delighted to Rub Up Against a Small Part of History," Commentary, *Chicago Tribune,* June 23, 2004.

25. "College Association of George Williams College to Attorney General of the United States, November 30, 1955," *George Williams College Bulletin* (December 7, 1955) 2, Kautz Family YMCA Archives, University of Minnesota Libraries.

26. Tom Scott, in discussion with the author, January 2004.

27. Mary Wiseman Walter, in discussion with the author, March 18, 2004.

28. Judy Sutherland Dawson, in discussion with the author, March 18, 2004.

29. LaVerne Siemsen Duncan, in discussion with the author, May 10, 2005.

30. "Intellectualism Suffers: GWC Student Satisfied," *The Collegian* (January 28, 1966), George Williams College Archives, Aurora University, Aurora, IL, p. 2.

31. Ellen Goldberg, in discussion with the author, October 2004.

32. Reuben Davis, in discussion with the author, November 16 and 18, 2004.

33. Daniel A. Logan, "Confrontation and Progress: The Response of a College to Black Students" (Downers Grove, IL: George Williams College, 1969), public relations box, Kautz Family YMCA Archives, University of Minnesota Libraries. All excerpts in conversation format, interspersed with the author's narrative, are based on this document. As a graduate student, Logan was appointed by a presidential steering committee to record on the spot, all events taking place in Spring Festival. Before publication, the document was approved by all constituents who were represented in the document, for accuracy.

34. Harry Walter, in discussion with the author, March 18, 2004.

35. Yevette Newton, in discussion with the author, 2004.

36. Richard Hamlin, in discussion with the author, August, 24, 2005.

37. Richard Hamlin to George Williams College students, alumni board members and constituents, August, 1969.

38. Peter Sorensen, in discussion with the author, 2004.

39. Gregg Robinson, e-mail correspondence with the author, 2004.

40. Richard Wyman, in discussion with the author, March 18, 2004.

41. Richard Hamlin, in discussion with the author, August 24, 2005.

42. Ibid.

43. "She's No Token Activist," *George Williams College Bulletin* (March 1971), George Williams College Archives, Aurora University, Aurora, IL, p. 4.

44. Richard Hamlin, in discussion with the author, August 24, 2005.

45. "No Token Activist," p. 4.

46. "George Williams College Faculty Staff Reunion," (commentary booklet, 2002), Aurora University Archives, Aurora, IL.

47. Richard and Dee Wyman, in discussion with the author, March 18, 2004.

48. Ibid.

49. Clelia Guastavino Giles and Calvin Giles, in discussion with the author, April 2004.

50. Ibid.

51. Ibid.

52. Helen Scoggins (George Williams College commencement address, 1986). Personal copy contributed by Helen Scoggins.

53. Ben Granger, "Accreditation Site Team Visit Report," (Council on Social Work Education, 1986), Aurora University Archives, Aurora, IL.

54. Sara Bonkowski, in discussion with the author, 2005.

55. Janet Yanos, in discussion with the author, October 26, 2005.

56. John Morrison, in discussion with the author, September 27, 2005.

57. Joy Howard, in discussion with the author, October 12, 2004. Joy was the recipient of a Manny Jackson Scholarship, a fund initiated by alumni in his honor for African American students.

58. Beth Plachetka, in discussion with the author, January 13, 2005. See also "Beth Plachetka: Motivating Spirit to Work with Youth," *Aurora Beacon News,* February 18, 1996.

59. John D. Morrison, Joy Howard, Casey Johnson, Francisco J. Navarro, Beth Plachetka, and Tony Bell, "Strengthening Neighborhoods by Developing Community Networks," *Social Work* 42, no. 5 (September 1997): 409–536. This article was subsequently reprinted in Patricia L. Ewalt, Edith M. Freeman, and Dennis L. Poole, eds. *Community Building: Renewal, Well-Being, and Shared Responsibility* (Washington DC: NASW Press, 1998), 107–116.

60. John Morrison, in discussion with the author, September 27, 2004.

Chapter 4: Learning-by-Doing

1. Clyde Binfield, *George Williams and the Y.M.C.A.: A Study in Victorian Social Attitudes* (London: Heinemann, 1973), 121. The first small prayer group that became the origin of the YMCA was so democratic that it appeared difficult to trace exclusive leadership to Sir George Williams. Surviving group members affirmed "Williams was the man" but "Williams was simply one among a band of brothers in the enterprise" (121).

2. J. E. Hodder-Williams, *The Life of Sir George Williams: Founder of the Young Men's Christian Association* (New York: International Committee of Young Men's Christian Associations, 1906), 135.

3. Binfield, *George Williams,* 273.

4. Gisela Konopka, *Eduard C. Lindeman and Social Work Philosophy* (Minneapolis: University of Minnesota Press, 1958), 27–34.

5. "The Chicago School of Pragmatism," The Pragmatism Cybrary, http://www.pragmatism.org/genealogy/chicago.htm.

6. Mary Jo Deegan, *Jane Addams and the Men of the Chicago School, 1892–1918* (New Brunswick, NJ: Transaction Books, 1986), 15–17; "Robert E. Park, Sociology," The University of Chicago Centennial Catalogues, The University of Chicago Faculty, A Centennial View. http://www.lib.uchicago.edu/projects/centcat/centcats/fac/facch17_01.html.

7. "The Practical Side," public relations paper, Public Relations: 1896–1913, Box 10–12, Kautz Family YMCA Archives, University of Minnesota Libraries.

8. Arthur Steinhaus, George Williams College, Public Relations 1933–1965, Box 12 H, Kautz Family YMCA Archives, University of Minnesota Libraries.

9. Charles E. Hendry, ed. *Appraising the Summer Camp* (New York: Association Press, 1937) 3, 22–23.

10. Alexander J. Stoddard, "The Propositions of Democracy" and R. E. Davis, "Deepening Our Understanding of Democracy," in *Toward Christian Democracy: A Profession Takes in Bearings, Summary Proceedings of the Forty-seventh Conference of the Association of Secretaries of the Young Men's Christian Associations of North America, May 29 to June 3, 1939, Toronto, Ontario Canada,* ed. Spurgeon Milton Keeny, 45 and 64–65 (New York: Association Press, 1939).

11. Charles Hendry, "A Community of Learning," *Progressive Education* (January 1939), Public Relations, 1933–1965, Box 12 H, Kautz Family YMCA Archives, University of Minnesota Libraries.

12. Everett W. Du Vall, *Personality and Social Group Work: An Individual Approach* (New York: Association Press, 1943) 69, 6, ix, 11–13, ix; and 70.

13. Armin Luehrs, in discussion with the author, October 12, 2005.

14. Frank H. Burt, "Guiding Youth in the Modern World: Summer School for Professional Workers in Leisure Time Agencies," promotional pamphlet, Public Relations 1933–1965, Box 12 H, Kautz Family YMCA Archives, University of Minnesota Libraries.

15. Janet Peck, "Play Is Work at this South Side College: It's No Breeze Getting Recreation Degree," *Chicago Daily Tribune,* March 26, 1950.

16. Richard Bowers, in discussion with the author, February 8, 2005.

17. Juanita Copeland, in discussion with the author, October 11, 2003.

18. Jim Collins, in discussion with the author, October 2003.

19. "The Teacher," *George Williams College Bulletin,* 7, no. 2 (Winter 1974).

20. Lyle Johnson, in discussion with the author, Spring 2004.

21. Alfred North Whitehead, *The Aims of Education and Other Essays* (New York: Macmillan, 1929) as quoted in Sandra Blumenshine, John Lewandowski, and Barbara Schuppe, "Practicum: A Unique Approach to Professional Social Work Orientation" (master's thesis, George Williams College, 1979), 6.

22. Ray Lestina, in discussion with the author, September 21, 2005.

23. Jack Lewandowski, in discussion with the author, August 1, 2005.

24. Jim Sheffer, in discussion with the author, 2003.

25. Lee Bay, in discussion with the author, October 8, 2005.

26. "Commencement Remarks," *George Williams College Bulletin* (March/Spring 1980) #766–280.

27. Sally McCarthy, in discussion with the author, October 27, 2005.

28. Carol Donegan, unpublished data. This paper was submitted for an MSW course on community organization during the winter term of 1986, one month after the college closed.

29. Pat Connelley, unpublished data. This paper was submitted for an MSW course on community organization during the winter term of 1986, one month after the college closed.

30. Laurie Munson, unpublished data. This paper was submitted for an MSW course on community organization during the winter term of 1986, one month after the college closed.

31. Glenda Blakemore, in discussion with the author, September 21, 2005.

32. Melissa Sofia, in discussion with the author, January 13, 2005.

33. Ann Bergart, in discussion with the author, September 20, 2005.

34. Bill Duncan, in discussion with the author, May 10, 2005.

35. Rita Yerkes, in discussion with the author, May 10, 2005.

Chapter 5: Reaching Around the World

1. "The Genius of Geneva" (1939) compiled by a group called "The Geneva Chronicler" presented by Ned Linegar, summer 1947 in "GWC: Early Historical Essays," George Williams College Archives, Williams Bay, WI.

2. *The Crucible* (1938).

3. "The Ergosandrian Club," *The Crucible* (1924), George Williams College Archives, Aurora University, Aurora, IL, p. 11.

4. "Chinese Students Club," *The Crucible* (1920), p. 99.

5. William Glenn, in discussion with the author, fall 2003.

6. Murray Faulkner, Jerry Prado Shaw, and Guanthar Chan, eds. "Human Face of YMCA World Service" (draft of booklet, YMCA World Service, 2005), p. 68.

7. Ibid., pp. 50–54.

8. Emery Nelson, student address on the occasion of receiving the Doctor of Humane Letters Award (1968), George Williams College informational file, Emery Nelson, Aurora University, Aurora, IL.

9. Frank Kiehne, in discussion with the author, October 2005.

10. Statement on Frank Kiehne on the occasion of receiving the William Stahl Award, NAFYR, October 2005.

11. Richard Ortmeyer, e-mail messages to the author, December 11, 2003; January 30, 2004; March 6 and 15, 2004; and April 4, 2004; Richard Ortmeyer, "My Work in Asia with the YMCA Training Institute in Hong Kong, My Years with the International Division, YMCA of the USA, My Years as Liaison Representative/Program Support Services in Asia" (personal memoirs); Also Richard Ortmeyer, "Growth Spurts Rekindle the YMCAs of China and Taiwan" *Perspective* (March 1989).

12. Richard Ortmeyer, "A Century of World Service: from Evangelism to Development" *Perspective* (1988).

13. Norris Lineweaver, in discussion with the author, June 14, 2005. See also "Rebel Theme Controversy," *UTA Magazine* (Fall 2003).

14. Henry Labatte, in discussion with the author, June 16, 2004.

15. Steve Kravitz, "'Pioneer' Didn't Flinch From a Fight: Battled Over Using Title of 'Alderman' Marie Labatte Was Small but Steadfast," *Toronto Star,* February 16, 2004.

16. Harry Edgren, "Fulbright lectures on group work and recreation. YMCA College of Physical Education, Madras, India" [1955], informational files, Aurora University, Aurora, IL.

17. Del Kinney, "Working Tour Gives World View," *George Williams College Bulletin* (March, 1971).

18. John William Fuhrer, *Steinhaus: The Story of Arthur Steinhaus, Eminent Physiologist, Teacher, and Dean* (Chicago: George Williams College, 1962), pp. 8–11.

19. Don Glaze, in discussion with the author, September 27, 2005. Robert Bratton, e-mail correspondence with the author, October 23, 2005.

20. John Kessler, "World Outlook Is Vital to College Mission," *George Williams College Bulletin* (1985), George Williams College Archives, Aurora University, Aurora, IL.

21. Larry Levinson, "GWC Students Practice World Diplomacy at Model U.N.," *George Williams College Bulletin* (1985). See also "Summer Model U.N. Program," *Alumni Notes* (1985), Aurora University, Aurora, IL. See also "United Nations Representative for Malaysia a GWC Alum," *George Williams College Bulletin* (Winter 1982).

22. Mary Beech, "Dreams of Travel and Study Abroad Come True at George Williams College," *George Williams College Bulletin* (1985).

23. "International Students Help Themselves . . . And Are Helped by Local Residents," *George Williams College Bulletin* (January 1985).

24. Clelia Guastavino, in discussion with the author and e-mail correspondence with the author, January 2004; March 15–17, 2004; April 23, 2004; May 28, 2004; June 3, 2004.

25. "Special Issue: The World at GWC," *George Williams College Bulletin* (January 1985).

26. Kwok Lee, "Foreign Students Provide Windows to the World," *George Williams College Bulletin* (January 1985), p. 3.

27. Kessler, "World Outlook."

28. Pat Hammond and Nesi Msseemmaa, in discussion with the author, October 23, 2005.

29. John Morrison, in discussion with the author, fall 2004.

30. Donald Phelps, in discussion with the author, fall 2003.

31. Brad Burger and Chris Blackburn, in discussion with the author, fall 2003 and winter 2004, and "International/Intercultural Program," *George Williams College Bulletin* (1977).

Personal Name Index

Gallery refers to the section of photographs that follow page 112.

Fabricant, Michael, 34
Fair, John D., 252n53, 252n56
Falussy, George, 53
Faulkner, Murray, 258nn6–7
Fencik, Gary, 56
Fenstemacher, William, 62
Finch, Helen, 196
Fisher, Galen Merriam, 247n2, 247nn4–5,
    253n1
Fisher, Robert, 34
Forbes, Robert, 8
Foreman, Jim, 58
Foster, E. H., 43
France, Erwin, 161
Frank, Elliot, 128–29
Freeman, Edith M., 256n59
Fritz, Jean, 138
Fuhrer, John, 42, 49, 52, 58, 100, 102, 159
Fung, Esther, 227
Fung, Shiu-Wing, 227

Gajda, Bob, 54–57
Gall, Hermann, 223
Gambardella, Bob, 75
Gambino, Celeste. See Peña, Celeste Gambino
Gandhi, Mohandas Karamchand, 15–16
Gant, Harvey, 162
Gates, Henry Louis, 93, 103
George, Monie, 220
Getz, Dagmar, 243, 245
Ghandi, Mohssen, 220
Ghawi, Nicola, 220
Gilbert, Jim, 243, 245
Giles, Calvin, 131, 133–35
Giles, Clelia Guastavino, 131–36, 226–28, 243,
    245
Gilhuys, Phyllis, 132, 227
Girma, Desta, 112, 211, 213–14
Glaze, Don, 222–24
Gleason, Gloria Williams, 58
Gleason, James, 58–59
Glenn, Ann. See Schmidt, Ann Glenn
Glenn, Bill, 203–05, 207
Glenn, Mary, 204
Goldberg, Ellen, 111, 113–19, 121
Goncharoff, Nicholas, 205–08
Graham, George, 109
Granger, Ben, 256n53
Grant, McNair, 58
Guastavino, Clelia. See Giles, Clelia Guastavino

Guastavino, Jorge, 131, 226–227
Gulick, Luther, 1, 40–42, *gallery*

Haas, Dwight, 204
Haberman, Harry, 226
Haberman, Peg, 226
Hall, Barb. See Merritt, Barbara Hall
Hall, G. Stanley, 44
Hall, Winfield Scott, 43–44
Hamlin, Joan, 120
Hamlin, Richard "Dick," 100, 115–20, 122–24,
    126–28, 131, 159
Hammond, Pat. See Msseemmaa, Pat Hammond
Hampton, Fred, 114
Hansel, John, 42–43, *gallery*
Hansen, Bob, 223
Harding, Jim, 225
Harper, Edward, 40
Harper, Philip, 249n36
Hawk, G. C., 47
Hawkins, Larry, 30, 58–67, 69, 115, 188
Hayworth, Denise, 147
Healey, Pete, 167–68
Helms, Jesse, 162
Hendry, Charles "Chick," 17, 91–92, 151, 157,
    216
Hertog, Herman, 222
Hetherington, Clark, 45
Hill, Verneta, 94–96
Hilloway, Wardell, 22–23
Hinding, Andrea, 248n13
Hodder-Williams, J. E., 256n2
Hoellen, John, 252n55
Hoffman, Bob, 54–56
Hogrefe, Russell, 25, 53, 101
Holmes, Cliff, 116, 120
Holt, Jane, 220
Hoover, Keith, 120
Hotton, J. S., 254n6
Hotton, Sidney, 42
Howard, Joy, 145–50, 256n57
Hudson, David, 251n19
Hughes, Bill, 69
Hughes, David, 109
Hupp, Sandra, 32
Hussein, Robert, 28
Huxley, Aldous, 51
Hyman, Ann, 24